"We've been hearing a lot about how the food we eat can make us sick. But [Lisanna's] story and magical recipes are a triumph in showing how food has the power to heal. The recipes in this book are not only good for you, but thoughtful and appealing, too. If food is our medicine, then let's make it delicious!"
—**RICH LANDAU,** James Beard Award finalist and coauthor of *Vedge* and *The Vedge Bar Book*

"In *Plant-Based Magic*, Lisanna draws on her experience of nourishing herself through chronic illness and beautifully blends the wisdom of herbalism with science. She shows how plants can support health through flavorful, approachable recipes made with mostly everyday ingredients."
—**RHYAN GEIGER, RD,** author of *Vegan Slow Cooking for Two*

"Lisanna Wallace imbues the world of vegan cooking with much-needed spark. The herbalist's knowledge she brings to these recipes ensures you'll have a functional and enjoyable time at the table."
—**ALICIA KENNEDY,** author of *No Meat Required*

"A feast for the senses—vibrant, inspiring, and deeply informative. Blending the wisdom of herbal traditions with the artistry of plant-based cuisine, this book invites readers to experience food as a source of nourishment, beauty, and joy. The recipes are not only stunning but also practical, making this an invaluable resource for anyone seeking to elevate their plant-powered lifestyle."
—**BRENDA DAVIS, RD,** author of *Becoming Vegan*

Plant-Based Magic

ALSO BY LISANNA WALLANCE

The Natural Witch's Cookbook:
100 Magical, Healing Recipes & Herbal Remedies
to Nourish Body, Mind & Spirit

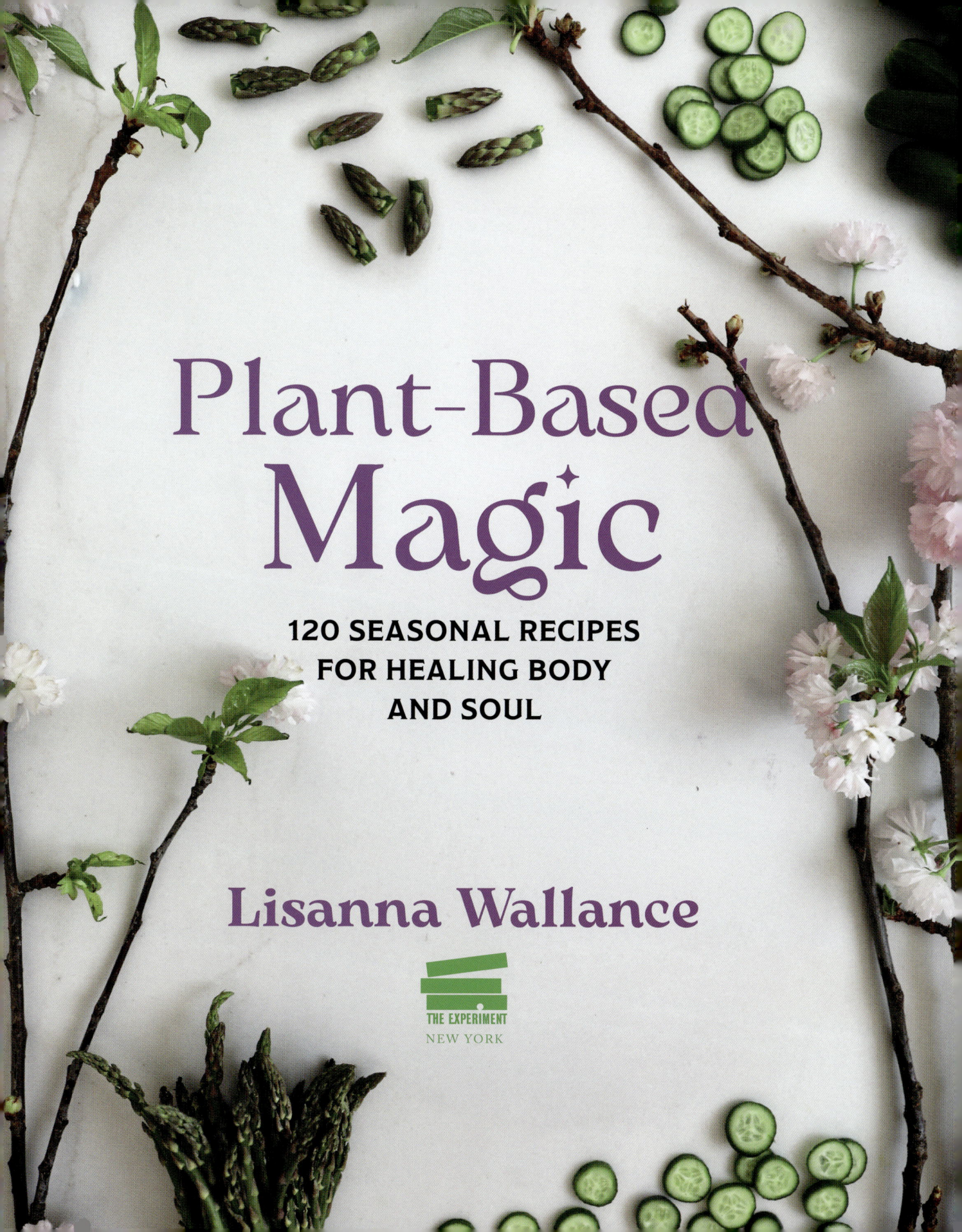

PLANT-BASED MAGIC: *120 Seasonal Recipes for Healing Body and Soul*
Text and photographs, including cover photograph, copyright © 2026 by
Lisanna Wallance

All rights reserved. Except for brief passages quoted in newspaper, magazine,
radio, television, or online reviews, no portion of this book may be reproduced,
distributed, or transmitted in any form or by any means, electronic or
mechanical, including photocopying, recording, or information storage or
retrieval system, without the prior written permission of the publisher.

The Experiment, LLC | 220 East 23rd Street, Suite 600
New York, NY 10010-4658
theexperimentpublishing.com

This book contains the opinions and ideas of its author. It is intended to
provide helpful and informative material on the subjects addressed in the book.
It is sold with the understanding that the author and the publisher are not
engaged in rendering medical, health, or any other kind of personal professional
services in the book. The reader should consult a medical professional before
adopting any of the suggestions in this book. The author and publisher disclaim
all liability in connection with the use of this book.

THE EXPERIMENT and its colophon are registered trademarks of The
Experiment, LLC. Many of the designations used by manufacturers and
sellers to distinguish their products are claimed as trademarks. Where those
designations appear in this book and The Experiment was aware of a trademark
claim, the designations have been capitalized.

The Experiment's books are available at special discounts when purchased
in bulk for premiums and sales promotions as well as for fundraising or
educational use. For details, contact us at
info@theexperimentpublishing.com.

Library of Congress Cataloging-in-Publication Data available upon request

ISBN 979-8-89303-041-9
Ebook ISBN 979-8-89303-042-6

Cover and text design by Beth Bugler
Author photograph by Lies van Veen

Manufactured in China

First printing March 2026
10 9 8 7 6 5 4 3 2 1

To the farmers who grow the plants that nourish us

CONTENTS

- 1   Magic: An Essential Nutrient
- 3   The Magical Pantry
- 7   Plant-Based Diet Tips
- 9   Herbalism 101
- 13   Potion Extraction Methods

SPRING

MAINS & SIDES

- 19   Lentil-Chard Plant Parcels FOR ENERGY
- 20   Endive and Leek Quiche FOR FERTILITY
- 23   White Bean Soup FOR DIGESTION
- 24   Lemon-Artichoke Pasta FOR DETOX
- 27   Caramelized Zucchini and Peas with Citrus-Dill Sauce FOR VISION
- 28   Mushrooms with Artichoke-Potato Purée FOR DETOX
- 31   Asparagus and Pea Quiche FOR DIGESTION
- 32   Creamy Mushroom Pasta FOR METABOLISM
- 35   Adaptogenic Stuffed Zucchini FOR STRESS RELIEF
- 36   Mushroom Pizza FOR PASSION
- 39   Baked Asparagus with Almonds FOR FERTILITY
- 40   Citrus, Sugar Snap Pea, and Endive Salad FOR GLOWING SKIN
- 43   Cucumber and Asparagus Salad FOR INFLAMMATION RELIEF
- 44   Balsamic Mushrooms and Radishes FOR MOOD BALANCE
- 47   Lemony Lettuce Wedges FOR HYDRATION
- 48   Asparagus and Artichoke Salad FOR HEART SUPPORT
- 51   Mustard-Caper Potatoes and Radishes FOR DETOX
- 52   Raw Zucchini and Sprouted Pea Salad FOR STRENGTH
- 55   Radish, Cucumber, and Hibiscus Salad FOR DETOX
- 56   Squash and Asparagus Sauté FOR ENERGY

SUMMER

MAINS & SIDES

81	Zucchini Quiche FOR HORMONE BALANCE
82	Lion's Mane Cakes FOR COGNITION
85	Blueberry Pizza FOR HEART SUPPORT
86	Rainbow Antioxidant Roots FOR IMMUNITY
89	Corn Chowder FOR SATIETY
90	Savory Fruit Sauté FOR RESTFUL SLEEP
93	Sunny Summer Pasta FOR EUPHORIA
94	Roasted Eggplant FOR COGNITION
97	Pesto Avocado Salad FOR HORMONE BALANCE
98	Shielding Succotash FOR PROTECTION
101	Honeydew-Basil Salad FOR HYDRATION
102	Blueberry-Beet Salad FOR COGNITION
105	Cucumber-Fennel Salad FOR DIGESTION
106	Lemony Okra and Squash FOR DIGESTION
109	Raw Corn and Squash Salad FOR GLOWING SKIN
110	Baby Greens and Radish Salad FOR DIGESTION
113	Peach and Flower Salad FOR SUN PROTECTION
114	Chilled Melon-Cucumber Soup FOR INFLAMMATION RELIEF
117	Potato-Beet Salad FOR HEART SUPPORT
118	Tomato and Beet Soup FOR STRENGTH

DESSERTS

59	Strawberry Cream Cupcakes FOR FERTILITY
60	Lilac Panna Cotta FOR PASSION
63	Strawberry-Lemon Squares FOR EUPHORIA
64	Adaptogenic Chocolate Mousse FOR ENERGY
67	Chocolate Cake FOR LUCID DREAMS

POTIONS

68	Anti-Allergy Vinegar FOR IMMUNITY
71	Flower Syrup FOR LIBIDO
72	Herbal Vinegar FOR FERTILITY
75	Lotus-Elderflower Liqueur FOR EUPHORIA
76	Citrus-Scallion Sauce FOR SATIETY

DESSERTS

121 Lychee-Cherry Soup FOR CALM
122 Nectarine and Berry Galette FOR ENERGY
125 Almond-Cherry Clafoutis FOR RECOVERY
126 Ginger-Lychee Slushy FOR DIGESTION
129 Rose and Peach Cupcakes FOR GLOWING SKIN
130 Balancing Chia Lemonade FOR SATIETY
133 Simple Dressing FOR IMMUNITY

POTIONS

134 Iced Rose Latte FOR EUPHORIA
137 Magic Pesto FOR RECOVERY
138 Turmeric Ginger Ale FOR INFLAMMATION RELIEF

AUTUMN

MAINS & SIDES

143 Whole Roasted Pumpkin FOR IMMUNITY
144 Golden Cauliflower with Scallion-Ginger Cream FOR INFLAMMATION RELIEF
147 Comforting Potato and Corn Soup FOR DIGESTION
148 Greens with Coconut Cream FOR EUPHORIA
151 Buckwheat and Fungi Risotto FOR SATIETY
152 Creamy Mushrooms and Beets FOR STRONG BONES
155 Beet-Leek Quiche FOR DEFENSE
156 Stewed Cabbage with Apple-Mustard Cream FOR DETOX
159 Broccolini with Puréed Eggplant FOR COGNITION
160 Sweet Potato Kale Salad with Magic Pesto FOR CIRCULATION
163 Maple-Roasted Roots FOR IMMUNITY
164 Squash and Parsnip Soup FOR DETOX
167 Smoky-Sweet Brussels Sprouts FOR DEFENSE
168 Illumination Squash Soup FOR GLOWING SKIN
171 Kale and Cabbage Coleslaw FOR DETOX
172 Balsamic-Roasted Onions FOR IMMUNITY
175 Mixed Greens Salad with Candied Pecans FOR FERTILITY
176 Ghostly Stuffed Squash FOR DEFENSE
179 Seaweed and Beet Salad FOR OXYGENATION
180 Breaded Brussels Sprouts FOR RECOVERY

DESSERTS

183 Eve's Apple Torte FOR COGNITION
184 Spiced Sweet Potato-Hibiscus Pie FOR IMMUNITY
187 Fire-Cooling Cinnamon Rolls FOR INFLAMMATION RELIEF
188 Marzipan Muffins FOR MOOD BALANCE
191 Ginger-Spiced Hibiscus Pears FOR DIGESTION

POTIONS

192 Adaptogenic Vinegar FOR STRESS RELIEF
195 Forest Tincture FOR IMMUNITY
196 Floral Tea FOR VIVID DREAMS
199 Flower Vinaigrette FOR RADIANT SKIN
200 Guarana Latte FOR ENERGY

MAINS & SIDES

205 Field and Forest Soup FOR ENERGY

206 Caramelized Onion, Potato, and Bean Gratin FOR STRENGTH

209 Balsamic Parsnips with Citrus Cream FOR EUPHORIA

210 Cabbage and Potato Gratin FOR COMFORT

213 Celery Root Steaks with Red Wine–Prune Sauce FOR DIGESTION

214 Baked Purple Cauliflower and Potatoes with Rosemary Vinaigrette FOR HEART SUPPORT

217 Whole Roasted Cauliflower FOR DETOX

218 Leek and Potato Dauphinoise FOR SATIETY

221 Sadness-Smashing Potatoes and Brussels Sprouts FOR MOOD BALANCE

222 Crispy Kohlrabi Steaks FOR DETOX

225 Creamy Baked Portobellos FOR MOOD BALANCE

226 Slimming Seaweed and Mushroom Soup FOR METABOLISM

229 Persimmon and Spiced Walnut Salad FOR GLOWING SKIN

230 Parsnip, Leek, and Orange Soup FOR SERENITY

233 Balsamic-Caramelized Endives FOR METABOLISM

234 Smoky-Sweet Glazed Mushrooms FOR IMMUNITY

237 Blood Orange–Endive Salad FOR ENERGY

238 Citrusy Kale and Apple Salad FOR IMMUNITY

241 Pear, Fennel, and Grape Salad FOR DETOX

242 Radicchio and Grapefruit Salad FOR METABOLISM

245 Adaptogenic Apple Crumble FOR STRESS RELIEF

246 Candied Citrus Cream Pie FOR IMMUNITY

249 Spiced Speculoos Cookies FOR PAIN RELIEF

250 Spiced Pavlovas with Ginger-Coconut Cream FOR DEFENSE

253 Rosemary-Clementine Cake FOR COGNITION

254 Antiviral Syrup FOR IMMUNITY

257 Hawthorn-Hibiscus Tonic FOR HEART SUPPORT

258 Creamy Citrus Vinaigrette FOR IMMUNITY

261 Probiotic White Hot Chocolate FOR COGNITION AND DIGESTION

262 TranquiliTea FOR DEEP SLEEP

264 Glossary of Essential Vitamins and Minerals

269 Acknowledgments

270 Index

278 About the Author

Magic: An Essential Nutrient

Magic has always been my happy place. When I was a child, it was a place of wonder. I grew up playing in forests, building fairy houses from sticks and bark, and dreaming of witches and magic.

As a child, I also dreamt of being a doctor. Many days from my childhood were spent in and out of medical offices and hospitals, searching for the cause of my diverse health problems. As a teenager, I was diagnosed with celiac disease followed by Ehlers-Danlos Syndrome, a genetic disorder that causes mutated collagen and fragile connective tissues. Connective tissue is found throughout the body, from your skin, tendons, ligaments, and fascia—connective tissue that surrounds all the body's organs, muscles, and nerve endings—to your bones, brain, and hair. It is the structural glue that holds the body together. When connective tissue becomes fragile, it triggers widespread symptoms, including chronic pain, allergy and autoimmune issues, organ and digestive dysfunction, renal complications, neurological manifestations, and more. I've also been diagnosed with POTS (Postural Orthostatic Tachycardia Syndrome—a condition where dysfunction of the autonomic nervous system causes spikes in heart rate) and a co-morbid immunological condition known as Mast Cell Activation Syndrome (in which this type of white blood cell becomes overactive, triggering allergic reactions).

With the help of my doctors, I have spent much of my life since my diagnoses figuring out how to adjust to the barrage of evolving symptoms. After graduating from college and moving to Paris, my Ehlers-Danlos symptoms became debilitating. Pharmaceutical medications helped to an extent, but they could not address all of my symptoms, and they came with side effects. My health worsened and my doctors didn't know what else to do for me.

So I turned to the healer archetype of the witch to help me transform this burden into something lighter and more manageable. Magic became a tool for taking control of my life. The knowledge and recipes in this cookbook are the culmination of years of using magic to navigate chronic illness.

There was a specific moment when I realized I could use my childhood love for magic to help myself feel better. Treating my symptoms meant having to open a dozen pill packets and bottles throughout the day. My boyfriend, seeing the weight this put on me, wanted to make the daily act of taking pills feel more like a potion-making ritual, so he gifted me a one-hundred-year-old apothecary kit filled with little glass pill vials with silver tops. Transferring my pills into those vials replaced my medical reality with magic. I no longer thought of myself as "sick" or "a patient." I was a witch.

I now know that magic really does exist, and that it is everywhere. It is the kind of magic we see in nature, science, and plants.

In addition to my doctors' prescriptions, I found healing solutions in herbalism, medicinal mushrooms, and by using food as a form of nutritive medicine. I aligned the necessity to soothe my pain and digestive issues with my passion for cooking, so I began experimenting with my diet. I noticed how consuming certain foods, specifically plant-based foods and herbs, impacted my symptoms. I spent the next decade immersing myself in the world of medicinal plant and mushroom healing. I rebuilt my gut microbiome with vegetables, used detox-supporting teas to soothe my inflamed liver and tired kidneys, extracted immune-regulating and anti-allergy herbs into oil-based tinctures that I infused into vegetable-based dishes, and drank hormone-regulating teas every morning to help my body find balance and manage the side effects from my medical treatments.

I wanted a deeper understanding of plant healing, so I enrolled in a clinical herbalism graduate school program at l'École des Plantes de Paris. I wanted to sublimate my medical battles into knowledge that could help ease the suffering of others.

I learned to extract plant blends and brew my own medicinal tinctures, teas, and syrups. I discovered that I was better able to take powdered herbs and plant potions when I integrated them into everyday recipes like lattes, soups, purées, sauces, and salad dressings.

I realized more and more that nature was filled with magic that could be harnessed for healing.

I write cookbooks because I want to share my healing knowledge and bring joy to others. I needed to make something good come from all my pain. I dreamed up my first book, *The Natural Witch's Cookbook*, after my health first worsened. As I delved deeper into my studies, I began to increasingly embrace the potent healing properties of in-season plant-based foods. *Plant-Based Magic* reflects my new appreciation for the healing power of a plant-based diet when combined with the principles of herbalism.

These recipes are also a reflection of my health battles and years of experimenting with food. The produce, herbs, and mushrooms featured here are the ones that have brought me the most relief and joy. All the recipes in this book are gluten-free—a reflection of how I've had to eat for years due to celiac disease, but also a way to make the recipes more accessible to anyone navigating sensitivities or doing an elimination diet or reset. You'll also find many recipes labeled No Sugar Added and Nut-Free. These labels aren't about fear or restriction, but about helping you tune into what supports your body best. Additionally, some of the tips that accompany each recipe feature substitutions to make a dish lower in histamines (compounds that can cause allergy symptoms) or FODMAPs (certain kinds of carbohydrates that can cause digestive issues for some people). Some of the most nourishing foods out there are high in histamine or FODMAPs, just as nuts and natural sugars can be perfectly healthful for many people. But for those of us working with sensitivities, allergies, or trying to pinpoint triggers, these notes can be a helpful way to navigate what might bring relief—or discomfort—on any given day.

But of course, just as important as a recipe's medicinal potential is how it tastes! This cookbook is a celebration of the magic of plant-based foods, and these recipes show you not only how to potentialize their nutritive benefits, but how to make them taste incredible.

When you cook one of these seasonal recipes, I hope it makes your day feel just a little more magical.

—Lisanna

The Magical Pantry

You'll find the ingredients here popping up again and again in my recipes due to their versatility, flavor, and nutritional magic. Keeping your pantry stocked with them is a great way to ensure you're able to brew up some plant magic whenever inspiration hits.

PANTRY STAPLES

Gluten-Free Grains

Whole grains are nutrient-dense staples that provide lasting energy, essential minerals, and a satisfying base for both sweet and savory dishes. My favorites include **amaranth**, a tiny, complete-protein pseudo cereal; **buckwheat**, robust and nutty in flavor; **millet**, mild and fluffy when cooked; **quinoa**, versatile and slightly earthy; and **rice**, neutral and endlessly adaptable.

Legumes

Legumes, plants that produce seeds inside pods, are essential sources of plant-based protein, fiber, and minerals. I use dried **red** and **green lentils**, various **beans**, including **chickpeas**, and **green peas** all the time in soups, stews, sautés, sauces, dips, and sides.

Nuts and Seeds

Nuts and seeds are dense with nutrients and rich in healthy fats. They add texture and flavor to both sweet and savory dishes. I like to keep a few kinds on hand, including **cashews**, unmatched for their ability to blend into silky sauces and dairy-free fillings; **chia seeds**, which absorb liquid and add body to desserts and drinks; **pumpkin** and **sunflower seeds**, which bring crunch to everything from salads to soups, and **walnuts**, which can be used whole in stuffings, roasted and mixed into salads, or chopped and baked into tarts or baked goods. **Nut and seed milks** are another everyday staple, used in smoothies, soups, baking, and any dish where a little creaminess is needed.

Binding and Thickening Agents

I rely on **arrowroot flour**, a neutral-tasting starch, to thicken sauces, fillings, and puddings and to add elasticity to gluten-free baked goods. **Agar-agar** is a seaweed-based gelling agent used in place of gelatin. **Flaxseeds** are packed with fiber and omega-3s and are often used as a binding agent in place of eggs when ground into flaxseed meal (sometimes labeled as flaxseed flour).

> ### Where to Find These Ingredients
>
> Many of these ingredients can be found in well-stocked supermarkets, natural food stores, health shops, and some specialty food stores. For harder-to-find items—especially certain herbs and mushrooms with adaptogenic properties (which help the body adapt to stress by balancing the nervous and hormonal systems)—try local herbal apothecaries and co-ops or online retailers such as Mountain Rose Herbs, Pacific Botanicals, Oshala Farm, Sawmill Herb Farm, Starwest Botanicals, Frontier Co-op, Organic Herb Trading Co., Herbathek, or Richters Herbs.

Gluten-Free Flours

Gluten-free all-purpose flour is a one-to-one stand-in for regular flour. Look for blends that contain a mix of rice, tapioca, and/or potato flours with a binder such as xanthan gum. My go-to brands are King Arthur, Bob's Red Mill, and Schär. If you don't follow a gluten-free diet, you can substitute the same amount of regular flour. I also use **almond flour** in baking recipes for richness and moisture and in savory gluten-free breadings; **buckwheat flour** for its nutty flavor and nutrient density; and **oat flour** for a soft, mild option.

Canned Goods

I usually prefer to use fresh produce rather than canned, but there are a few canned products I turn to all the time. **Coconut cream** and **coconut milk** offer richness and creaminess in both sweet and savory dishes. Coconut milk (10 to 15 percent fat) enriches soups, sauces, and dressings, while coconut cream (20 to 25 percent fat) adds body and indulgence to mousses, frostings, and fillings. Other plant-based creams such as **almond**, **cashew**, and **soy** can make good substitutes. **Aquafaba**, the liquid reserved from canned or boiled chickpeas, is my go-to egg alternative—3 tablespoons equal one whole egg, 2 equal one egg white. It works wonderfully in baked goods, batters, and meringues.

Sweeteners

When eating plant-based, it's helpful to understand alternative sweeteners, since ingredients like honey and conventional white sugar (which is often processed with bone char) may not be suitable. Organic, unbleached **cane sugar** is made without bone char. **Agave syrup** is a low-glycemic sweetener with a neutral flavor that blends easily into other liquids. **Maple syrup** brings an earthy, subtly woody depth along with its sweetness.

Oils

Plant-based fats carry flavor, add richness, and support the absorption of key nutrients. **Extra virgin olive oil** is my go-to oil for cooking; it deepens the flavor of sautés, dressings, and roasted vegetables. For frying or extra-high-heat searing, I use **avocado oil** for its neutral taste and high smoke point, or virgin, cold-pressed **coconut oil**, which is also stable at high temperatures and lends a subtly sweet note to baked and fried foods. Although not a pure oil, **plant-based mayonnaise** such as Sir Kensington's Vegan Mayonnaise or Chosen Foods Vegan Mayo is primarily oil-based and enriches sauces and dressings.

Vinegars

Thanks to their fermentation, vinegars bring acidity, balance, and tang to everything from salad dressings and sauces to braises and reductions—and they also serve as powerful solvents in herbal extractions and infusions. The kinds I use most often are raw, unfiltered **apple cider vinegar**, which is full of natural probiotics; **balsamic vinegar** for sweet, fruity intensity; and **white balsamic vinegar** for a more delicate touch.

Whole Spices

Whole spices offer deeper aroma and longer shelf life than ground, and a kind of slow magic is released in its most potent form when steeped, crushed, or toasted. Here are a few I like to keep in my pantry: **black peppercorns**, sharp and warming, draw out flavor and enhance absorption of other plant compounds; **cardamom pods**, citrusy and lightly floral, brighten teas, lattes, and sweets; and **cinnamon sticks** and **cloves**, with their sweet heat, bring comfort to everything from elixirs to desserts. **Nutmeg**, most potent when freshly grated, adds subtly sweet depth to roots and sauces, and **star anise**, bold and aromatic, infuses lattes and desserts with its licorice-like warmth.

Flavor Powerhouses

A few deeply savory or aromatic ingredients can instantly elevate the flavors of plant-based cooking. **Miso paste** brings salty, umami depth that enhances broths, glazes, marinades, and dressings. **Nutritional yeast**, with its nutty, cheese-like flavor, is a pantry essential for dairy-free sauces and as a garnish for sautéed vegetables and pastas. **Rose extract**, distilled from fragrant rose petals, brings a soft perfume to baked goods and desserts.

The Magical Pantry

HERBAL APOTHECARY STAPLES

Roots

Root-based extractions are foundational to herbal traditions. There are many medicinal roots to explore, but I recommend starting with versatile, strengthening ones such as **ashwagandha**, a powerful adaptogen known for reducing cortisol and supporting the nervous system. **Astragalus**, an immune tonic with a licorice-like flavor, strengthens white blood cell production, eleuthero (Siberian ginseng) is used for stamina and resilience, and mineral-rich maca supports libido and energy.

Berries and Seeds

These small but potent herbal allies are filled with concentrated phytochemicals—natural compounds that support plant growth, reproduction, and defense—and can benefit human health when consumed. There are many to choose from, but I like to keep a few of the following on hand: **amla berries** have a citrusy flavor and are known for their ability to combat oxidative stress, **chasteberry** (vitex) helps support hormonal balance, **elderberry** enhances immunity, and antioxidant-packed **hawthorn berries** support heart function.

Flowers

Flowers offer more than just aroma. Out of the numerous calming flowers to choose from, I like **blue lotus** water lilies, which promote vivid dreaming and relaxation, and **passionflower**, which helps regulate mood, sleep, and nervous tension. **Echinacea**, with its peppery-sweet bite, is used short-term to stimulate immune response at the onset of illness. Other flowers like **goldenrod** and **hibiscus** stimulate detox mechanisms.

Delicate Herbs

Nutrient and chlorophyll-rich leafy herbs offer vital support to our health. **Stinging nettle** has anti-inflammatory and anti-histamine properties. **Tulsi**, also known as holy basil, is a fragrant adaptogen that helps soothe nerves.

Mushrooms

Mushrooms are rich in medicinal compounds known to support immunity, cognition, and energy. Antioxidant-rich **chaga** is traditionally used to support gut and immune health and reduce inflammation. **Cordyceps** enhance stamina, oxygen absorption, and energy production; **lion's mane** supports memory, focus, and nerve health; and **reishi** contains calming, adaptogenic, and immune-modulating triterpenes (phytochemicals with anti-inflammatory properties).

Plant-Based Diet Tips

Plant-based eating is all about balance. Too often, vegan diets are associated with restriction, focusing on what we cannot eat rather than on the immense variety and nutritional benefits of plant-based foods. These tips can help you optimize the healing—and flavor!—potential of a plant-based diet.

Eat enough calories!
One of the biggest mistakes some people on plant-based diets make is not consuming enough calories to meet their energy needs, especially if they are physically active. Consuming calorie and nutrient-dense foods such as legumes, healthy fats, and high-fiber complex carbohydrates is essential.

Eat the rainbow
The pigments in fruits and vegetables reflect different antioxidant-rich phytochemicals, including flavonoids—plant compounds that help reduce inflammation and protect cells from damage. Consuming produce with a variety of colors will ensure you get a wide range of nutrients and antioxidants.

Get enough protein
To meet your protein needs and ensure you get a complete profile of essential amino acids, incorporate a variety of plant-based protein sources into your meals, such as beans, lentils, chickpeas, soy, nuts, and seeds, as well as plenty of whole grains, including complete-protein sources such as amaranth, buckwheat, and quinoa. (But note that there's no need to pair a grain and a legume at every meal; eating both on a regular basis is enough!)

Include healthy fats
You should regularly consume sources of healthy fats such as avocados, nuts, seeds, and cold-pressed plant-based oils such as extra virgin olive oil, coconut oil, and flaxseed oil. Such healthy fats are essential for brain function, hormone production, and absorbing fat-soluble vitamins A, D, E, and K.

Don't forget fiber
Prioritize fiber-rich foods like vegetables, fruits, legumes, nuts, seeds, and whole grains. Fiber helps keep digestion moving, feeds your gut microbiome, and supports hormone balance and blood sugar regulation, in addition to increasing satiety and keeping you energized throughout the day.

Keep an eye on certain micronutrients
For most people, a balanced plant-based diet shouldn't require much supplementation; however, it's a good idea to keep an eye on your nutrient levels and increase your dietary intake or supplement if necessary.

- **Vitamin B12** is primarily found in animal products. It is essential for vegans to obtain it through supplements or fortified foods like plant milks or nutritional yeast to prevent deficiency.
- Ensure adequate **calcium** intake by consuming fortified plant milks, fortified orange juice,

legumes, tofu, almonds, tahini, and leafy green vegetables such as kale and collard greens. Lightly cooking greens that are high in oxalates (compounds that can block calcium absorption, irritate sensitive guts, and contribute to kidney stones), like spinach and chard, helps reduce their effects.

- Depending on your sun exposure and where you live, consider incorporating sources of **vitamin D** such as fortified plant milks, fortified orange juice, UV-exposed mushrooms, algae-based supplements, or other vitamin D supplements.

- **Iron**-rich plant-based foods such as lentils, chickpeas, soy, spinach, kale, quinoa, fortified cereals, and pumpkin seeds support healthy blood cell formation and oxygen transportation. Since iron from plant sources is less bioavailable than that from animal sources, it's important to be intentional about consuming enough and pairing iron sources with vitamin C–rich foods, which enhance absorption.

- Plant sources of alpha-linolenic acid (ALA), a type of **omega-3** fatty acid, include flaxseeds, chia seeds, walnuts, and hemp seeds. However, the body's ability to convert ALA into the active forms of omega-3s, EPA and DHA, primarily found in fatty fish, is very limited. This makes it challenging to meet EPA and DHA needs through ALA alone. For plant-based diets, algae-based supplements or fortified foods offer direct sources of EPA and DHA, bypassing the conversion process.

- **Zinc** is an essential mineral crucial for immune function, wound healing, DNA synthesis, protein synthesis, and cell division. The zinc found in legumes, nuts, seeds, and whole grains is less bioavailable compared to that found in animal sources, so conscious consumption is important. Consider consuming zinc-fortified foods or supplements.

> ### Optional Tips
>
> **Sprout to reduce anti-nutrients**
> Sprouting grains, legumes, and seeds not only reduces the concentration of nutrient-blocking compounds like phytates but also makes their protein easier to digest and improves the bioavailability of iron, zinc, magnesium, and calcium.
>
> **Ferment to enhance nutrient absorption**
> Fermented foods such as vinegar, miso, and kimchi show improved bioavailability of B vitamins, zinc, magnesium, and iron. They also support gut health for better overall digestion and nutrient uptake.

Herbalism 101

Herbalism is one of the most ancient crafts of the witch. Healers have extracted medicine from plants since the earliest civilizations, laying the foundation for modern medicine. Herbalism involves harnessing the power of certain plants that contain particularly high concentrations of medicinal compounds. When concentrated in extractions, these plant compounds can have "actions" (effects on the body) that closely resemble those of pharmaceutical medications. Many common modern medications are based on medicinal plant compounds, such as the drug diazepam (commonly sold under the brand name Valium), which was originally extracted from the root of the valerian plant, and aspirin, which was derived from the bark of willow trees. That's not to mention antibiotics like penicillin, which originally derived from the *Penicillium* genus of fungi. While all plant-based foods contain medicinal compounds in the form of nutrients, certain plants like blue lotus flowers, maca root, or St. John's wort flowers, and mushrooms like reishi, chaga, and cordyceps are especially potent. These are just some of my favorites thanks to their specific medicinal actions, and I call for them often in this book, but there are many other medicinal plants and mushrooms to choose from.

Herbalism certification and practices vary by country and knowledge is constantly evolving. If you're interested in learning more about herbalism, I encourage you to do further reading or take a course. However, these foundational principles are widely agreed upon by herbalists around the world.

SAFETY AND INTERACTIONS

First, consult with a medical professional

Before starting any herbal or medicinal mushroom regimen, it's essential to consult with a qualified clinical herbalist or health care provider. They can provide personalized guidance based on your health history, current medications, and individual needs. Be extra cautious using certain medicinal plants and mushrooms if you have preexisting health conditions, never use if pregnant or breastfeeding, and never give to children without first speaking with a medical or naturopathic doctor.

Understand herb-drug interactions

Some medicinal herbs can interact with medications or medical conditions, potentially affecting their effectiveness or the safety of your health. It's crucial to disclose all your medications, including herbal and nutritional supplements, and health conditions to your health care provider to avoid potentially dangerous interactions.

Stay grounded in science

While herbalism draws on traditional knowledge and wisdom, it is essential to be informed about the latest scientific studies and clinical trials on herbal medicine. Rely on information from reputable sources, such as the American Botanical Council.

Start slowly and mindfully

When incorporating herbs into your diet, start with small doses and observe how your body responds. Pay attention to any changes in your symptoms, energy levels, or side effects. It's essential to listen to your body and adjust your herbal regimen accordingly.

Quality is key

Choose high-quality herbs to ensure potency and safety. Look for organically grown or wildcrafted (foraged) herbs whenever possible, and avoid products with additives, fillers, or contaminants.

PREPARATIONS AND EXTRACTIONS

Combine medicinal plants

When extracting plant medicine, always try to make blends of at least three and ideally five different plants to balance and optimize their interactions. This approach helps ensure you get a wider range of beneficial compounds while avoiding excessive amounts of any single one, ultimately enhancing outcomes and reducing potential side effects.

Use medicinal plants in various forms

Medicinal plants can be used in varied ways, including teas, tinctures (see pages 13–15 for more), capsules, powders, and topical creams. Each form has its own advantages and may be suitable for different situations or preferences, so experiment to find what works for you.

Store properly

Properly storing herbs preserves their freshness and potency. Store dried herbs in airtight containers away from heat, light, and moisture to prevent degradation. Label the containers with the herb's name and the date of preparation or harvest for easy identification.

Rotate herbs and formulations

To prevent developing a tolerance (desensitization) to specific medicinal compounds, rotate your herbal formulations (the specific combinations used in your tinctures or infusions) periodically. Alternate between different herbs with similar actions or rotate between different formulations to keep your body responsive to their effects. For longer-term wellness goals like supporting the liver's natural detoxification processes or promoting hormonal balance, rotate every 4 to 6 weeks to prevent adaptation and ensure a range of

support. For acute conditions like colds or infections, rotate herbs every 3 to 7 days as symptoms change. For preventive or wellness use, rotate every 6 to 8 weeks or seasonally. Take 1- to 2-week breaks between treatments to allow the body to reset, to monitor how your body responds and adjust treatments as needed. Always tailor the approach to your individual needs and consult a qualified herbalist if uncertain.

SUSTAINABILITY AND ETHICS

Practice ethical and sustainable harvesting

When gathering herbs in the wild, use sustainable techniques to protect plant populations and ecosystems. Harvest responsibly by taking only what you need and focusing on parts of plants, like leaves or stems, that allow them to regrow. Use baskets for mushroom foraging to help spread spores and support their natural reproduction. Avoid foraging rare or endangered species to help preserve biodiversity.

Respect cultural traditions and plant origins

Many herbs have been used for centuries in traditional healing systems around the world. Research the origins of the medicinal plants you use and respect the cultural traditions of the communities that depend on them.

Take an active role in your well-being

By learning about medicinal plants and mushrooms and incorporating them into a plant-based routine, especially when paired with nutritional knowledge, you can cultivate a deeper connection with nature and its healing potential.

TREATMENT AND DOSAGE

Emphasize prevention

Herbalism places a strong emphasis on preventive health care and maintaining wellness. Incorporate herbs and holistic practices into your daily routine to support your overall health and prevent illness before it occurs.

Live by "less is more" when it comes to dosage

Dosage is the difference between medicine and poison. Plant medicine can be powerful medicine, but overdosage can bring out the "shadow side" of plants, meaning the negative effects of certain compounds.

Be mindful of the length of treatment

Medicinal plant infusions and tinctures can often be consumed as a preventative measure for weeks at a time. When treating ailments such as the flu, adrenal fatigue, detox support, or hormonal imbalances, the ideal length of treatment varies and should be determined by a medical practitioner or clinical herbalist.

Address underlying imbalances

Clinical herbalists focus not only on treating illness but also on identifying and addressing underlying imbalances in the body. They take a holistic approach, considering how lifestyle factors, diet, and stress may contribute to health issues, and working to develop personalized treatment plans to restore foundational balance.

Keep detailed records

Keep a journal or log of your herbal usage, including the medicinal plants and mushrooms you use, their dosages and effects, and any notable observations. This information is valuable for tracking your progress, identifying patterns, adjusting your regimen over time, and sharing with medical professionals as needed.

Develop herbal first-aid skills

Plants can be used as part of a first-aid toolkit for addressing acute health issues and injuries. Learn basic herbal first-aid skills, such as how to make herbal poultices, compresses, and tinctures, to address common health concerns effectively (see Potion Extraction Methods on pages 13–15 for more).

Support the kidneys and liver

When preparing medicinal plant blends, always include plants that support the kidneys and liver, such as dandelion root, milk thistle flowers, stinging nettle leaves, or turmeric root. Supporting your body's natural detox mechanisms is essential regardless of the organ system or issue you are targeting.

Support digestive health

Balanced digestion is key to overall health, as it affects nutrient absorption, immune function, and mental well-being. Incorporate plants that support digestion, such as ginger, cardamom pods, peppermint, fennel seeds, and chamomile flowers, into your daily routine.

Nourish the nervous system

Stress and emotional well-being play a significant role in health and vitality. Use plants and mushrooms with nervine and nootropic effects, such as ashwagandha root, holy basil leaves, chamomile flowers, St. John's wort flowers, and lion's mane mushroom to support the nervous system by promoting relaxation, relieving tension, and improving cognitive function.

Customize your herbal formulations

Herbalists often create herbal formulations tailored to their individual needs and constitution. Experiment with creating personalized formulas that address your specific health needs and goals.

Cultivate herbal connections

Herbalists all have their favorite plants to work with. Develop a deeper relationship with medicinal plants by learning how to identify, harvest, and use them, or try growing your favorite plants.

Potion Extraction Methods

INFUSIONS

Infusion, the practice of soaking dried or fresh medicinal plants in near-boiling water (essentially making a tea), is the chosen method for the extraction of delicate plant parts, such as flower petals and leaves, that contain compounds that risk getting destroyed by hard-boiling.

Classic Infusion Method

Heat water until just short of boiling; when small bubbles begin to form, remove it from the heat and pour over the prepared dried or fresh plants. Cover and let infuse for about 5 minutes (for delicate plant parts such as petals and leaves) to 15 minutes (for hardy plant parts such as roots, bark, seeds, and berries) to extract their water-soluble medicinal compounds.

Slow Infusion Method

Place the plants directly in a pot with cold water and gently heat the water until just short of boiling; when small bubbles begin to form, turn off the heat, cover, and let infuse for 30 to 60 minutes. This method allows for the medicinal compounds to be slowly and gently extracted, preventing the potential breakdown of certain compounds.

INFUSION TIPS

- Use filtered water.
- Note that the infusion will take longer if using fresh plants than if using dried plants.
- Cover your infusion while it steeps to prevent the volatile medicinal compounds from escaping.
- Drink your infusions ideally within 1 hour, and not more than 24 hours after preparing them, as the organic and volatile plant compounds will break down over time.

COLD WATER INFUSIONS

This slow, cold water method involves adding plant material to cold water and steeping for 4 to 12 hours to gently extract their beneficial compounds. Although this method takes more time than hot water infusions, it can be beneficial for preserving heat-sensitive compounds, such as mucilages (gel-like fibers that draw moisture to tissues and support digestion), catechins (bioactive, antioxidant-rich plant compounds that have cell-protective effects), anthocyanins (natural pigments that give red, purple, and blue plants their color and offer antioxidant, anti-inflammatory, and cell-protective benefits), certain aromatic compounds, and vitamins like vitamin C. This method also reduces the presence of tannins, which some people have difficulty tolerating. Try to consume cold water infusions ideally within 1 hour and not after 24 hours, as the risk of oxidation, fermentation, and mold and bacteria growth increases with time. The medicinal compounds in the infusion are most potent and effective when fresh, and their stability can degrade if stored for too long.

OIL EXTRACTIONS

Also known as oil maceration, oil extraction involves infusing dried or fresh medicinal plants directly into an oil solvent such as extra virgin olive oil and either leaving them to extract slowly at room temperature or heating the oil in a double boiler for faster extraction. Dried plants are best used for oil extraction, as the high water content of fresh plants can interfere with the extraction of their medicinal compounds.

DECOCTIONS

In a decoction, dried or fresh medicinal plants are boiled directly in water. This is often the chosen method for extracting medicinal compounds from hardy plant parts.

Decoction Method

Place medicinal plants directly in cold water, bring to a rolling boil, and continue boiling for 5 to 15 minutes (depending on the plant part being extracted). Then turn off the heat, cover, and continue to let the decoction infuse for another 15 minutes.

DECOCTION TIPS

- Use filtered water. **Hard Parts:** Boil plant parts such as berries, seeds, hard leaves (such as bay and artichoke), medium-hard bark and branches (such as slippery elm and elder), and medium-hard dried mushrooms (such as shiitake and cordyceps) for around 5 minutes.
- **Very Hard Parts:** Boil roots such as ginger and turmeric, very hard bark (such as cinnamon and astragalus), and hard dried mushrooms (such as reishi and chaga) for at least 5 to 15 minutes.

TINCTURES

A tincture is a maceration of dried or fresh plants in vinegar, alcohol, glycerine, or other solvent. Alcohol tinctures are common because they are potent, shelf-stable, and instantly processed by the body. However, other solvents work well if you're avoiding alcohol.

Alcohol Tincture Method

Use a strong alcohol, ideally 40- to 90-proof. Chop the plants as finely as possible or grind them into a powder. Fully cover the plants with the alcohol to prevent oxidation and mold growth. Label the jar with the date and plants used and let the tincture macerate for 2 to 4 weeks, storing in a cool, dark place and agitating it every few days to ensure even extraction.

TINCTURE RATIOS

- **Dried Plants:** Use a 1:5 ratio (1 part dried plants to 5 parts alcohol by volume).
- **Fresh Plants:** Use a 1:2 ratio (1 part fresh plants to 2 parts alcohol by volume).

POWDER EXTRACTIONS

Dried and powdered plant parts can be taken as pills, in tinctures, or integrated directly into recipes like soups, broths, sautés, smoothies, teas, coffee, or baked goods. Although plant powders allow for more efficient extractions, the downside is that the medicinal compounds deteriorate more quickly as more plant matter is exposed to oxygen, so use shortly after making them. Pulverize dried medicinal plant parts to a fine powder using a mortar and pestle, spice or coffee grinder, or blender.

POWDER EXTRACTION TIPS

- Grind powders as finely as possible. The finer the powder, the more smoothly it will blend into recipes, be digested if made into pills, or be extracted into a solvent.
- To prevent breakdown and oxidation of medicinal compounds, store powders in an airtight container in a cool, dry location, away from sunlight.
- Label and date powders, and use within 2 to 4 months for optimal potency.

Lentil-Chard Plant Parcels
FOR ENERGY

Gluten-Free ✦ No Sugar Added ✦ Nut-Free

To wake us up after the sleepy winter months, early springtime calls for energizing plant-based foods. Invigorating plant magic is tucked inside these chard-leaf bundles. Stuffed with lentils and leeks and served with a savory caramelized-onion-and-soy-cream sauce, this dish pairs well with a protein-rich grain such as amaranth, buckwheat, or quinoa.

Serves 4 as a main

PLANT PARCELS

2 cups (480 ml) vegetable broth or water

½ cup (100 g) green lentils, rinsed

3 tablespoons extra virgin olive oil

6 chard leaves, stems separated and chopped

1 leek, thoroughly rinsed, chopped

2 fresh rosemary sprigs, leaves removed and minced (about 1 tablespoon)

3 tablespoons white wine or lemon juice

CARAMELIZED ONION CREAM

3 tablespoons extra virgin olive oil

2 large onions, chopped

1 cup (240 ml) soy cream

Grated zest of 1 lemon plus juice of ½ lemon

1 **To make the plant parcels,** preheat the oven to 350°F (180°C).

2 Combine the lentils with the vegetable broth in a medium saucepan over high heat. Bring to a boil, then reduce the heat to low, cover the pan, and simmer for 20 to 25 minutes, until the lentils are tender but still hold their shape. Turn off the heat, drain any excess liquid, and set the lentils aside.

3 Heat the oil in a large pan and sauté the chard stems, leek, and rosemary over high heat for about 20 minutes, or until tender and browned, stirring frequently. Deglaze with the wine whenever the vegetables begin to stick and scrape the bottom of the pan to reincorporate any browned bits.

4 Add the lentils, mix well, and season with salt and pepper. Scoop a few tablespoons of the lentil mixture into the center of each chard leaf. Fold the sides of the leaf around the filling as if wrapping a package, then flip the parcel over to ensure that it does not unfold.

5 Place the parcels in a 9-by-13-inch (23 by 33 cm) baking dish or large oven-safe pan and set aside while you prepare the onion cream.

6 **To make the caramelized onion cream,** heat the oil in a medium pan and sauté the onions over high heat for about 20 minutes, or until tender and caramelized, stirring frequently. Deglaze with a few tablespoons of water whenever the onions begin to stick and scrape the bottom of the pan to reincorporate any browned bits.

7 Add the soy cream and let the mixture gently simmer for about 10 minutes, or until the cream thickens and reduces by about half.

8 Add the lemon zest and juice and season with salt and pepper. Carefully pour the caramelized onion cream into the baking dish, using a spoon to spread the sauce around each of the parcels.

9 Bake for 15 to 20 minutes, until the chard leaves are lightly browned and crisp, then remove from the oven and let cool for a few minutes before serving.

TIP: To give your parcels extra revitalizing magic, consider adding 1 to 2 teaspoons of energy-boosting herbs such as ginseng root powder, ground guarana bean, or eleuthero root powder, or stimulating mushrooms such as cordyceps or lion's mane to the lentil filling or the caramelized onion cream before baking.

MAGICAL BENEFITS

Iron ✦ Chard, lentils, and leeks are rich in iron, which helps red blood cells bind to oxygen and transport it throughout the body.

Complete Protein ✦ Lentils are nearly a complete protein, meaning they contain considerable amounts of nearly all the essential amino acids that are the building blocks for energy production, but they are low in methionine and cysteine. Although soy isn't especially rich in these amino acids, it provides enough to help round out this dish's protein profile.

Endive and Leek Quiche
FOR FERTILITY

Gluten-Free ◆ Nut-Free

Endives and leeks are suffused with fertility-boosting nutrients, and they manage to grow both in the cold of winter and the early months of spring. This egg-free quiche gets its lightness and volume from whipped aquafaba. The creamy leek filling, scalloped potato crust, and caramelized endive topping is the perfect celebration of the early spring season. To make this a heartier main, serve with a protein-rich grain such as amaranth, buckwheat, or quinoa.

Serves 4 to 6 as a main

POTATO CRUST

3 tablespoons extra virgin olive oil

1 pound (450 g) waxy potatoes (such as red or Yukon Gold), peeled and cut into ⅛-inch (3 mm) slices

FILLING

3 tablespoons extra virgin olive oil

2 leeks, thoroughly rinsed, finely chopped

Grated zest and juice from 1½ lemons

¼ teaspoon agave

2½ cups (600 ml) soy cream

3 tablespoons all-purpose gluten-free flour blend (see page 5)

1 tablespoon ground flaxseed

½ cup (120 ml) aquafaba (see page 5), chilled

4 endives, halved lengthwise

MAGICAL BENEFITS

Isoflavones ◆ Soy and flaxseeds contain isoflavones, a type of plant estrogen (phytoestrogen) that may have hormone-balancing effects when consumed in moderation.

Vitamin B9 ◆ Endives, soy, and leeks contain vitamin B9 (folate), which supports healthy hormone levels and ovulation and is essential for preventing birth defects during pregnancy.

Iron ◆ Getting enough iron by eating plant-based foods such as soy and endives is crucial for regular menstrual cycles, ovulation, and energy.

1 Preheat the oven to 350°F (180°C).

2 To make the potato crust, grease the bottom and sides of a 9-inch (23 cm) springform pan with 2 tablespoons of the oil and arrange the potato slices in concentric, slightly overlapping circles over the bottom of the pan. Add a second layer, staggering the slices to cover the gaps in the first layer.

3 To form the edges of the crust, press a layer of potato slices (edges touching but not overlapping) upright along the sides of the pan. Add an extra drop or two of oil to any slices that don't adhere well. Add a second layer, staggering the slices to cover the gaps in the first layer.

4 To make the filling, add 1 tablespoon of the remaining oil to a large pan over high heat (adjusting the heat if needed) and sauté the leeks until browned and tender, about 20 minutes, stirring frequently. Deglaze with a few tablespoons of water whenever the leeks begin to stick and scrape the bottom of the pan to reincorporate any browned bits.

5 Add the zest and juice from 1 lemon (reserving the zest and juice from the other ½ lemon), and the agave and cook for about 5 minutes, or until the liquid evaporates. Add the soy cream, gluten-free flour, and ground flaxseed and simmer for about 15 minutes, or until the mixture thickens and reduces by about half. Season with salt and pepper and remove from the heat. Let cool for about 5 minutes while you prepare the aquafaba.

6 Add the aquafaba to a bowl and whip with a hand-held mixer on high speed for about 5 minutes, or until stiff, white peaks form, then fold into the leek cream until fully integrated. Pour the leek filling into the potato crust. Arrange the endives cut side up on top. Drizzle with the remaining oil and lemon juice.

7 Bake for 30 to 40 minutes, until the endives are browned and the potato crust is crispy and golden brown. Let cool for 5 minutes, then run a knife along the edges to loosen the quiche before removing the sides of the springform pan. Serve warm, garnishing with the remaining lemon zest for an extra burst of freshness.

TIP: To increase this recipe's fertility-boosting potential, you can add 2 teaspoons ashwagandha, vitex, or maca powder to the filling along with the soy cream.

White Bean Soup
FOR DIGESTION

Gluten-Free ✦ No Sugar Added ✦ Nut-Free

The spring equinox in late March marks the return of the sun. Plants like leek and watercress help us regain balance during this time of transition and shifting temperatures. This refreshing and nourishing chunky white bean and watercress soup is infused with the nutrients we need to help regenerate and revive us for the seasons ahead. Serve with a side of rice, which complements the amino acids in the beans to provide a complete-protein meal.

Serves 4 to 6 as a main or 6 to 8 as a side

- 2 quarts (2 L) vegetable broth or water, plus more as needed
- ¼ cup (60 ml) extra virgin olive oil, plus more for drizzling
- ¼ cup (60 ml) white wine or apple cider vinegar
- 2 cups (400 g) dried white beans such as cannellini or navy
- 4 red onions, diced
- 1 pound (450 g) waxy potatoes (such as red or Yukon Gold), peeled and diced
- 2 leeks, thoroughly rinsed, sliced
- 1 bunch (60 g) watercress, stemmed

1 Bring the broth to a boil in a large saucepan over high heat. Add the oil and wine, season with salt and pepper, then add the white beans. Lower the heat to medium and simmer gently for 45 to 60 minutes (or sometimes closer to 2 hours, depending on the type of white bean or if the dried beans are old), until the beans are tender and some start to split, but not break apart. When the beans are tender, check the liquid level and add more broth or water if you prefer a brothier soup.

2 Add the onions, potatoes, and leeks and continue to simmer, covered, for about 20 minutes, or until the vegetables are tender and the beans entirely softened. Season with salt and pepper and adjust the balance of richness and acidity by adding more oil and/or wine to taste.

3 Stir in the watercress, reserving a few leaves for serving, and cook for 2 to 3 minutes, just until wilted. Serve warm with an extra drizzle of oil, sprinkle of freshly ground black pepper, and garnish of fresh watercress leaves.

TIP: To make beans easier to digest, soak them overnight to soften them (this also reduces their cooking time!) and then drain the soaking water to reduce the concentration of oligosaccharides, a type of complex carbohydrate that can cause gas.

MAGICAL BENEFITS

Fiber ✦ The plentiful dietary fiber in beans, leeks, onions, and potatoes promotes regular bowel movements and nourishes beneficial gut bacteria.

Potassium ✦ Found in high concentrations in potatoes and beans, potassium supports muscle function, including the involuntary muscles involved in digestion.

Amylase and Protease ✦ Potatoes, white beans, and watercress contain amylase and protease, digestive enzymes that assist in breaking down complex carbohydrates and proteins, lessening the pancreas' workload and leading to less discomfort and bloating.

Lemon-Artichoke Pasta
FOR DETOX

Gluten-Free ✦ No Sugar Added ✦ Nut-Free

Pasta dishes are often associated with indulgence, but it all depends on the ingredients you use. This artichoke, lemon, and legume-based pasta not only celebrates the fresh flavors of early springtime, but is charged with cleansing magic, making this the kind of pasta best enjoyed in multiple helpings! For extra detox magic, serve with the Radish, Cucumber, and Hibiscus Salad (page 55) or the Mustard-Caper Potatoes and Radishes (page 51).

Serves 2 to 4 as a main

- 8 ounces (225 g) lentil or chickpea pasta
- 1 cup (170 g) oil-marinated artichoke hearts, quartered, plus ¼ cup (60 ml) of their oil
- Juice and grated zest of 1 lemon
- ½ teaspoon fresh thyme leaves
- 2 tablespoons nutritional yeast, optional

1 Bring a medium saucepan of water to a boil and cook the pasta according to the package instructions. Reserve a few tablespoons of the pasta water to help thicken the sauce, then drain and set aside.

2 Heat half of the artichoke oil in a large pan over medium heat, reserving the rest for serving. Add the artichoke hearts and sauté for about 5 minutes, or until slightly browned and crispy.

3 Add the pasta and mix. Add the lemon juice and reserved pasta water and toss to coat evenly, then season with salt and pepper. Divide among individual plates and garnish with a drizzle of the reserved oil and a sprinkling of the lemon zest, freshly ground black pepper, thyme, and nutritional yeast, if using. Serve warm.

TIP: If you have leftover artichoke pasta, you can turn it into a gratin! Toss the pasta with a little plant-based cream to rehydrate it, then transfer to an oven-safe dish. Sprinkle with a layer of gluten-free bread crumbs and drizzle with olive oil before baking at 350°F (180°C) for 15 to 20 minutes, until the top is golden brown and crispy.

MAGICAL BENEFITS

Cynarin and Silymarin ✦ Artichokes contain medicinal plant compounds such as cynarin, which promotes bile production to aid in liver function and digestion, and silymarin, which has antioxidant properties that may protect the liver and support its detoxifying capabilities.

Citric Acid ✦ Lemons contain citric acid, which may enhance liver function, help the body metabolize toxins, and even prevent kidney stones.

Potassium ✦ Potassium from the artichokes, legume-based pasta, and lemon supports kidney function and helps maintain the body's fluid balance.

Caramelized Zucchini and Peas with Citrus-Dill Sauce
FOR VISION

Gluten-Free ✦ Nut-Free

When it comes to eyesight, what you eat is more important than you might assume. Here, caramelized zucchini and peas are blanketed in a velvety citrus-dill cream, making for a saucy sauté that contains sight-boosting nutrients so you can see with clear vision. Adding the Adaptogenic Vinegar (page 192) while the zucchini caramelize infuses them with extra herbal magic and nicely offsets the richness of the Creamy Citrus-Dill Sauce. To make this a hearty meal, serve with a side of rice, quinoa, or polenta.

Serves 4 as a main or 4 to 6 as a side

3 tablespoons extra virgin olive oil

8 zucchini, cut into ¼-inch (6 mm) rounds

2 tablespoons Adaptogenic Vinegar (page 192) or Anti-Allergy Vinegar (page 68)

6 ounces (170 g) peas (such as sugar snap or English peas)

CREAMY CITRUS-DILL SAUCE

One 13.5-ounce (400 ml) can coconut cream

Grated zest of 1 lemon, plus ¼ cup plus 1 tablespoon (75 ml) lemon juice

3 tablespoons extra virgin olive oil

2 tablespoons agave

3 fresh dill sprigs, minced, plus more for serving

1 Heat the oil in a large pan over medium-high heat. Add the zucchini and sauté for about 30 minutes, stirring frequently and adjusting the temperature as needed to prevent burning. Deglaze with a splash of water whenever the zucchini begin to stick and scrape the bottom of the pan to reincorporate any browned bits, until they have reduced in size and are very tender and browned.

2 Increase the heat to high and drizzle with the vinegar, then stir to combine, scraping the bottom of the pan to stir in any flavorful browned bits. Cook for about 10 minutes, or until the zucchini is fully caramelized.

3 To make the creamy citrus-dill sauce, add the coconut cream, lemon zest, reserving some for serving, lemon juice, oil, agave, and dill to a bowl and whisk until smooth. Season with salt and pepper.

4 If serving directly from the pan, pour the sauce over the zucchini and toss to coat. Otherwise, transfer the zucchini to a serving dish before covering in the sauce.

5 Sprinkle the raw peas over the zucchini and garnish with extra fresh dill, lemon zest, and a sprinkle of freshly ground black pepper before serving.

TIP: For an autumn and winter-friendly version of this vision-supporting recipe, swap out the zucchini for beta carotenoid–rich carrots or sweet potatoes and use canned or frozen peas.

MAGICAL BENEFITS

Carotenoids ✦ Carotenoid-dense vegetables like peas and zucchini and herbs like dill help the body synthesize vitamin A, which contributes to maintaining the integrity of the eyes' photoreceptor cells, protecting against night blindness and other vision impairments.

Phenolic Acids ✦ Phenolic compounds, found in peas, zucchini, dill, and coconuts, may help protect the eyes from oxidative stress and age-related degeneration.

Vitamin E ✦ Found in coconut cream, vitamin E has been associated with a lower risk of cataracts and degeneration of the eye.

Mushrooms with Artichoke-Potato Purée
FOR DETOX

Gluten-Free ✦ No Sugar Added ✦ Nut-Free

During the cold winter months we tend to stay inside, move less, and often eat more! So when spring arrives, the body is in need of a rejuvenating boost. Eating foods such as artichokes, mushrooms, and potatoes, especially when infused with the detoxifying magic of dandelion roots, can give our bodies a "spring-clean." Dandelion roots can be foraged from pesticide-free areas in spring when roots are less bitter, or sourced from distributors like Mountain Rose Herbs. For a heartier meal, serve with a side of protein-rich quinoa or buckwheat.

Serves 2 to 4 as a main

- 2 quarts (2 L) vegetable broth or water
- ¼ cup plus 2 tablespoons (90 ml) olive oil, plus 1 tablespoon for serving
- 2 tablespoons dried dandelion root (ideally foraged from pesticide-free areas in spring when roots are less bitter, or sourced from distributors like Mountain Rose Herbs)
- 1 pound (450 g) starchy potatoes (such as Russet or Idaho), peeled and diced
- One 13.5-ounce (400 g) can or jar marinated artichoke hearts, drained
- 2 tablespoons lemon juice
- 1.3 pounds (600 g) shiitake mushrooms, stems trimmed, sliced
- 2 tablespoons white wine
- 1 tablespoon balsamic vinegar
- 4 to 6 fresh thyme sprigs, optional

1 Bring the broth and 2 tablespoons of the oil to a boil in a large saucepan over high heat, then add the dandelion root. Keep the broth at a rolling boil, uncovered, for about 20 minutes, then turn off the heat, cover the mixture, and let it infuse for another 20 minutes. Strain and reserve the liquid, discarding the roots.

2 Add the potatoes to the dandelion infusion and boil over medium heat for about 20 minutes, or until tender.

3 Combine the potatoes and dandelion infusion with the artichokes, lemon juice, and 2 tablespoons of the oil in a blender and blend on high until smooth, with the consistency of a very thick soup or thin purée, adding a few tablespoons of extra broth or water if needed. Season with salt and pepper.

4 Heat the remaining oil in a pan over medium-high heat until it sizzles. Add the mushrooms and sear, stirring regularly. Deglaze with the white wine whenever the mushrooms begin to stick and scrape the bottom of the pan to reincorporate any browned bits, until they have released their liquid, reduced in size by half, and turned golden brown, 15 to 20 minutes.

5 Divide the warm purée between individual plates and top with the mushrooms. Drizzle with the balsamic vinegar and oil and garnish with fresh thyme, if using, before serving.

TIP: You can make a soup with the leftovers by puréeing the mushrooms and sauce and then thinning the mixture with vegetable broth until the desired consistency is achieved.

MAGICAL BENEFITS

Triterpenoids ✦ Shiitake mushrooms contain high levels of triterpenoids, anti-inflammatory and antioxidant compounds that help the liver break down and eliminate toxins.

Taraxasterol ✦ Dandelion root contains compounds that stimulate the liver to produce bile, aiding in the breakdown of fats and promoting overall digestion. The diuretic properties of dandelion help the body flush out waste.

Fiber ✦ The soluble fiber in potatoes, artichokes, and mushrooms forms a gel that binds toxins for elimination via the liver and kidneys. They also contain insoluble fiber, which promotes regular bowel movements to aid waste and toxin removal.

Asparagus and Pea Quiche
FOR DIGESTION

Gluten-Free ✦ No Sugar Added ✦ Nut-Free

After months of winter cocooning, our digestive systems can use a regenerating boost. This egg-free quiche made with fresh asparagus, creamy peas and caramelized onions, and a crispy potato crust offers an enchanting combination of fresh spring flavors, gut-soothing magic, and a comfort blanket of cozy indulgence. For an even heartier meal, serve with a side of protein-rich amaranth, buckwheat, or quinoa.

1 Preheat the oven to 375°F (190°C).

2 **To make the potato crust,** grease the bottom and sides of a 9-inch (23 cm) springform pan with the oil and arrange the potato slices in concentric, slightly overlapping circles over the bottom of the pan. Add a second layer, staggering the slices to cover the gaps in the first layer.

3 To form the edges of the crust, press a layer of potato slices (edges touching but not overlapping) upright along the sides of the pan. Add an extra drop or two of oil to any slices that don't adhere well. Add a second layer, staggering the slices to cover the gaps in the first layer.

4 **To make the caramelized onion and pea cream,** heat the oil in a pan over medium heat until small bubbles begin to form. Add the onion and sauté, stirring occasionally, for 20 to 30 minutes, until caramelized.

5 Add the cream and peas and let the mixture simmer for 10 to 15 minutes, until the cream has reduced and thickened. Mixing well, stir in the gluten-free flour to further thicken and stabilize the cream. Season with salt and pepper, then pour the cream mixture evenly over the potato crust.

6 **To make the asparagus topping,** arrange the asparagus in a single parallel layer on top of the cream. Drizzle with the oil and season with salt and pepper.

7 Bake the quiche for 20 to 25 minutes, until the asparagus is tender and the edges of the potato crust are crispy and golden brown.

8 Let cool for 5 minutes, then run a knife along the edges to loosen the quiche before removing the sides of the springform pan. Serve warm with an extra drizzle of oil.

TIP: To increase the quiche's gut-regenerating power, consider adding 1 teaspoon chaga mushroom powder. Chaga mushrooms are rich in antioxidants, which help protect the gut lining from oxidative stress and damage.

Serves 4 to 6 as a main

POTATO CRUST

2 tablespoons extra virgin olive oil

3 waxy potatoes (such as red or Yukon Gold), peeled and cut into ⅛-inch (3 mm) slices

CARAMELIZED ONION AND PEA CREAM

2 tablespoons extra virgin olive oil

1 red onion, chopped

1¾ cups (420 ml) soy cream

1 cup (200 g) fresh, canned, or thawed frozen peas

2 tablespoons plus 2 teaspoons all-purpose gluten-free flour blend (see page 5)

ASPARAGUS TOPPING

½ bunch (250 g) asparagus, ends trimmed

1 tablespoon extra virgin olive oil, plus more for drizzling

MAGICAL BENEFITS

Vitamin B9 ✦ Although vitamin B9 (folate), found in high quantities in asparagus, peas, and soy, is best known for its benefits during pregnancy, it also helps the body repair connective tissue and the lining of the digestive tract.

Prebiotic Fiber ✦ The prebiotic fiber in vegetables like onions and asparagus nourishes good gut bacteria, renewing and healing the gut lining.

Isoflavones ✦ These antioxidant compounds, found in high concentrations in soy and other legumes, help reduce inflammation in the digestive system, soothing the gut lining.

Creamy Mushroom Pasta
FOR METABOLISM

Gluten-Free ✦ No Sugar Added ✦ Nut-Free

This creamy, naturally gluten-free buckwheat pasta dish is imbued with the metabolism-stimulating magic of mushrooms. The nutty robustness of the buckwheat is amplified by the savory richness of the mushrooms and the creamy sauce that packs every bite with indulgent flavor. Serve with a side of Squash and Asparagus Sauté (page 56) for an extra invigorating meal.

Serves 2 to 4 as a main

- 8 ounces (225 g) buckwheat pasta
- 2 tablespoons extra virgin olive oil
- 2 cups (200 g) shiitake or maitake mushrooms, sliced
- Half a 13.5-ounce (400 ml) can coconut cream
- 2 garlic cloves, minced

OPTIONAL GARNISHES
- Freshly ground black pepper
- Fresh basil or chives
- 2 tablespoons nutritional yeast

1 Bring a medium saucepan of water to a boil and cook the buckwheat pasta according to the package instructions. Reserve a few tablespoons of the pasta water to help thicken the sauce, then drain and set aside.

2 Heat the oil in a large pan over medium heat. Add the mushrooms and sauté, stirring occasionally, for 15 to 20 minutes, until they have reduced in size by half and are evenly browned.

3 Add the coconut cream and garlic. Still over medium heat, bring the mixture to a gentle simmer and continue cooking for about 15 minutes, until the mixture thickens and reduces by half. Season with salt and pepper. Stir in the pasta water, then add the pasta and toss until well coated.

4 Serve hot, garnishing with freshly ground black pepper, fresh basil, and/or nutritional yeast, if desired.

TIP: To give this recipe an extra metabolism-boosting punch, add a sprinkle of chili powder to the mushroom cream. Chiles contain capsaicin, a compound that has been studied for its metabolism-stimulating potential.

MAGICAL BENEFITS

Beta-Glucans ✦ Mushrooms, particularly varieties like shiitake and maitake, contain beta-glucans, a type of soluble fiber that may help regulate blood sugar levels and improve insulin sensitivity.

Complete Protein ✦ Like animal-based proteins, mushrooms and buckwheat contain all nine essential amino acids, so they are considered complete protein sources that offer long-term energy.

Riboflavin and Niacin ✦ Mushrooms and buckwheat are both good sources of vitamins B2 (riboflavin) and B3 (niacin), which help convert food into energy and regulate metabolism.

Adaptogenic Stuffed Zucchini
FOR STRESS RELIEF

Gluten-Free ✦ No Sugar Added ✦ Nut-Free

Zucchini stuffed with creamy caramelized shallots, mushrooms, and peas are the ideal canvas for a sprinkle of potent powdered rhodiola root, earthy ashwagandha root, or peppery-sweet holy basil, all of which contribute a dose of stress-relieving magic. Serve with a side of amaranth, buckwheat, quinoa, or lentils for extra protein.

Serves 4 as a main

- 4 round or 2 long zucchini
- 2 tablespoons extra virgin olive oil
- 10 to 12 shiitake, mini portobello, or oyster mushrooms, larger mushrooms cut into eighths, smaller mushrooms quartered
- 4 shallots, minced
- ¼ cup (60 ml) white wine or lemon juice
- 1 cup (240 ml) soy cream
- 2 tablespoons Adaptogenic Vinegar (page 192) or apple cider vinegar
- 2 teaspoons ashwagandha, rhodiola, or holy basil (tulsi) powder, optional
- 4 scallions, sliced
- ¼ cup (50 g) fresh or frozen peas

OPTIONAL GARNISHES

- Extra virgin olive oil
- Ground black pepper
- Sugar snap peas

1 Preheat the oven to 350°F (180°C).

2 Cut off the zucchini stems and, if using long zucchini, slice them in half lengthwise. Use a spoon to scoop out some of the flesh to make a hollow for the filling. Mince the zucchini flesh and seeds and set aside. Set the hollowed zucchini in a round 9-inch (23 cm) baking pan or on a rimmed baking sheet.

3 Heat the oil in a large pan over high heat. Add the minced zucchini, mushrooms, and shallots and sauté for 20 to 30 minutes, stirring frequently and adjusting the temperature as needed to prevent burning. Deglaze with the wine whenever the vegetables begin to stick and scrape the bottom of the pan to reincorporate any browned bits. Cook until the zucchini and shallots are tender, the mushrooms have reduced in size and become evenly browned, and the wine has reduced to a glaze. Season with salt and pepper.

4 Continuing to cook over high heat, stir in the cream and vinegar and cook for another 15 to 20 minutes, until the liquid thickens and reduces by half. Add the ashwagandha, rhodiola, or holy basil, if using, then gently fold in the scallions. Remove the pan from the heat and stir in the peas. Season with salt and pepper.

5 Carefully fill each hollowed zucchini with the creamy mushroom mixture. (If you have leftover filling, you can serve it on the side or save it for another use!) Bake for about 30 minutes, or until the zucchini skins begin to brown and turn crispy. Garnish with a drizzle of oil, a sprinkle of freshly ground black pepper, and/or a few fresh peas, if desired, before serving.

TIP: If you have leftovers, just purée everything in a blender and thin the mixture with a little vegetable broth or water to make a soup.

MAGICAL BENEFITS

B Vitamins ✦ Peas are packed with B vitamins, which help the body adapt to stress and convert food into energy.

Antioxidants ✦ Zucchini, scallions, mushrooms, and peas contain antioxidants that neutralize free radicals, which are often elevated during stressful periods.

Adaptogens ✦ Plants with adaptogenic properties, such as ashwagandha, rhodiola, and holy basil (tulsi), may help the body adapt to and cope with stressors, increase energy, and promote overall resilience by reducing oxidative stress.

Mushroom Pizza
FOR PASSION

Gluten-Free ◆ No Sugar Added

Desire depends on many factors, but we can support the hormones and neurotransmitters essential for a healthy libido by eating foods like this date-night-perfect mushroom pizza. The bright orange zest provides a citrusy (but not sour!) contrast to the umami flavors of the sautéed sliced mushrooms. Topped with cashew cheese, this pizza is a rich yet light meal imbued with aphrodisiac magic, especially when served before the Lilac Panna Cotta (page 60). Leftovers are ideal for the next morning!

Serves 2 as a main

GLUTEN-FREE PIZZA CRUST

3 cups (360 g) chickpea flour

¾ cup plus 1 tablespoon (100 g) arrowroot flour

1½ teaspoons garlic powder

1½ teaspoons pepper

1 teaspoon salt

⅓ cup (80 ml) extra virgin olive oil, plus 1 tablespoon for greasing

TOPPING

2 cups (200 g) chanterelle or shiitake mushrooms, sliced

2 cups (450 g) Cashew Cheese (page 229)

Grated zest of 1½ oranges (about 3 tablespoons)

Fresh basil or thyme, optional

MAGICAL BENEFITS

Sterols ◆ Mushrooms contain various sterols, which are compounds similar in structure to hormones that influence the body's hormonal systems and signaling pathways.

Vitamin D ◆ When mushrooms are exposed to sunlight or UV light during growth, they can produce vitamin D, which is known to play a role in regulating sex hormones.

Zinc ◆ Found in chickpeas and cashews, zinc plays a crucial role in regulating testosterone and estrogen levels.

1. Preheat the oven to 400°F (200°C).

2. **To make the gluten-free pizza crust,** add the chickpea flour, arrowroot flour, garlic powder, pepper, and salt, to a large bowl and whisk to combine. Add the ⅓ cup (80 ml) oil and 2½ cups (600 ml) water, whisking vigorously to prevent lumps. Add more water or chickpea flour as needed to achieve the consistency of thick pancake batter. Set aside.

3. Grease a large rimmed baking sheet, pizza pan, or oven-safe pan with the remaining oil. Pour the batter into the prepared pan, spreading it into an even layer about ⅛ inch to ¼ inch (3 to 6 mm) thick.

4. Bake for about 20 minutes, until the edges are golden brown and the center is set, then remove from the oven and set aside, leaving the oven on.

5. **To make the topping,** while the crust bakes, sauté the mushrooms in a large pan over high heat for about 20 minutes, stirring frequently and adjusting the temperature as needed to prevent burning, until they have released their moisture and become tender and lightly charred. Season with salt and pepper.

6. Spread the cashew cheese evenly over the parbaked crust, leaving about ½-inch (1.25 cm) border, then distribute the mushrooms on top of the cheese. Sprinkle about 2 tablespoons of the orange zest over the pizza (reserving the rest for serving) and season with salt and pepper.

7. Return the pizza to the oven and bake for an additional 30 minutes, until the edges are crispy and well browned. Garnish with the remaining zest and a sprinkle of fresh basil, if using, before slicing and serving.

TIP: To increase this recipe's aphrodisiac power, mix ½ teaspoon of a libido-supporting herb such as maca powder into the cashew cheese before spreading it over the crust.

Baked Asparagus with Almonds
FOR FERTILITY

Gluten-Free ✦ No Sugar Added

Plants and mushrooms are masters of fertility, scavenging the nutrients they need to survive and reproduce from the soil. When we consume them, these nutrients support our own reproductive processes. This oven-roasted asparagus, blanketed in a creamy shiitake sauce infused with fertility-supporting Herbal Vinegar (page 72) and topped with herby almond crumbs, is a perfect example. Serve with a side of complete-protein-rich quinoa.

Serves 4 to 6 as a side

- 16 shiitake mushrooms (about 8.75 ounces/250 g), finely chopped
- 2 tablespoons extra virgin olive oil
- 1 cup (240 ml) soy cream
- 1½ teaspoons Herbal Vinegar (page 72) or apple cider vinegar
- ¼ cup (30 g) almond flour
- ½ teaspoon herbes de Provence
- 1 bunch (500 g) asparagus, ends trimmed

1. Preheat the oven to 375°F (190°C).

2. Set aside about one eighth of the chopped mushrooms. Sauté the rest with 1 tablespoon of the oil in an oven-safe pan over high heat for about 15 minutes, stirring regularly, until they have released their liquid, reduced in size, and become tender, evenly browned, and crispy.

3. Add the soy cream and vinegar and simmer for about 15 minutes, or until the cream is reduced by half, then season with salt and pepper. Remove from the heat and set aside.

4. Mix together the almond flour and herbes de Provence in a small bowl and set aside.

5. Divide the asparagus spears between 4 to 6 mini baking dishes (5-inch/13 cm) or arrange them in a single layer in a 9-by-13-inch (23 by 33 cm) baking dish. Drizzle the remaining oil over the asparagus and toss gently to ensure the spears are well coated.

6. Pour the mushroom sauce over the asparagus, then sprinkle with the almond flour mixture. Top with the reserved chopped mushrooms and season with salt and pepper.

7. Bake for 20 to 25 minutes, until the asparagus spears are tender and the almond topping is golden brown. Serve warm.

TIP: To transform leftovers, just purée everything into a fertility-boosting cream of asparagus and mushroom soup!

MAGICAL BENEFITS

Selenium ✦ Selenium in the mushrooms and almonds plays a crucial role in sperm cell development and helps protect eggs from oxidative stress.

Vitamin E ✦ Almonds and soy are rich in vitamin E, and asparagus contains moderate levels. This antioxidant protects sperm and eggs from oxidative stress and supports tissue repair in reproductive organs.

Vitamin B9 ✦ Found in asparagus, soy, shiitake mushrooms, and almonds, vitamin B9 (folate) supports DNA synthesis and repair, essential for healthy eggs and fetal development.

Citrus, Sugar Snap Pea, and Endive Salad
FOR GLOWING SKIN

Gluten-Free ✦ No Sugar Added ✦ Nut-Free

This salad's magic focuses on supporting connective tissue, and it harnesses springtime sunshine to give you a sun-kissed glow from the inside out. Cooking the lemon slices turns them sweet and tender all the way through so you can eat and get the nutritional benefits from the normally bitter pith and peel. The Flower Vinaigrette (page 199), infused with complexion-supporting flowers and herbs, adds extra magic. This salad can be transformed into a heartier meal by mixing in protein-rich grains such as amaranth, buckwheat, or quinoa, or legumes such as lentils or white beans.

Serves 4 as a side

1 tablespoon extra virgin olive oil
2 lemons, seeded, thinly sliced
4 endives, chopped
1 bunch small radishes, halved
2 tablespoons balsamic vinegar
1 cup (150 g) sugar snap peas
¼ to ⅓ cup (60 ml to 80 ml) Flower Vinaigrette (page 199)
Fresh chopped basil or dill, optional

MAGICAL BENEFITS

Vitamin B3 ✦ This B vitamin (also known as niacin), found in peas, helps the body synthesize collagen and the blood vessels just beneath the skin to relax, improving blood flow and regulating melanin production to even skin tone.

Vitamin C ✦ This protective antioxidant found in peas, radishes, and citrus fruits (especially their peels!) is crucial for collagen production, repairing skin damage, and promoting a smoother and more even complexion.

Vitamin K ✦ This circulation-supporting vitamin found in endives, peas, and radishes plays a role in wound healing and may help reduce skin discoloration.

1 Add the oil to a large pan over high heat. Once it sizzles, add the lemon slices and sear for 10 to 15 minutes, until caramelized, stirring regularly. Deglaze with a splash of water whenever they begin to stick and scrape the bottom of the pan to reincorporate any browned bits.

2 Add the endives, radishes, and balsamic vinegar and continue to sauté over high heat, stirring regularly and adjusting the temperature as needed to prevent burning for about 15 minutes, until the vegetables are tender and browned, then season with salt and pepper.

3 Transfer the sautéed vegetables to a large serving bowl and add all but 6 to 8 of the sugar snap peas. Drizzle with the vinaigrette, using more if you prefer a more heavily dressed salad, and gently toss to coat evenly. Garnish with the reserved sugar snap peas and fresh chopped basil, if using, and serve warm.

TIP: If desired, you can substitute any vinaigrette or dressing you like for the Flower Vinaigrette (page 199).

Cucumber and Asparagus Salad
FOR INFLAMMATION RELIEF

Gluten-Free ✦ Nut-Free

Acute (short-term) inflammation is part of the body's normal healing response, but it can become problematic when it becomes chronic. A diet high in anti-inflammatory plants such as asparagus, cucumbers, and scallions is the first line of defense against long-term inflammation, and all three have a starring role in this fresh salad topped with a creamy lemon dressing! Serve as a side with the Adaptogenic Stuffed Zucchini (page 35).

1 To make the creamy lemon dressing, combine the coconut cream, two-thirds of the lemon zest, the lemon juice, oil, agave, and ginger in a bowl. Add the scallions, reserving some for serving, and mix well. Season with salt and pepper, then set aside.

2 To make the salad, combine the asparagus and cucumbers in a large bowl. Pour the dressing over the vegetables and toss until evenly coated.

3 Portion the salad onto individual plates or serve family style, garnishing with an extra drizzle of oil and a sprinkle of the remaining lemon zest, scallions, flaky salt, if using, and freshly ground black pepper.

TIP: To increase this recipe's anti-inflammatory actions, add 1 teaspoon ground turmeric and extra black pepper to the dressing.

Serves 2 to 4 as a side

CREAMY LEMON DRESSING

Half a 13.5-ounce (400 ml) can coconut cream or other plant-based cream

Grated zest of 1½ lemons, plus 3 tablespoons lemon juice

3 tablespoons extra virgin olive oil, plus more for drizzling

1 teaspoon agave

½ teaspoon grated fresh ginger or ⅛ teaspoon ground ginger

2 scallions, green parts only, finely chopped

SALAD

1 bunch asparagus, ends trimmed, thinly sliced

8 cocktail cucumbers (500 g), thinly sliced, or 1 large cucumber, diced

Flaky salt, optional

MAGICAL BENEFITS

Cucurbitacins ✦ Cucumbers contain cucurbitacins, a group of bioactive compounds that may help counter inflammation.

Lauric Acid ✦ Present in high concentrations in coconut cream, lauric acid has been associated with reducing overall inflammation by adjusting how the body responds to inflammatory triggers.

Quercetin ✦ Found in cucumbers, ginger, and scallions, this flavonoid has a variety of protective health benefits, notably an ability to reduce inflammation-causing chemicals in the body.

Balsamic Mushrooms and Radishes
FOR MOOD BALANCE

Gluten-Free ◆ No Sugar Added ◆ Nut-Free

A good mood starts in the gut. Some plant-based foods such as mushrooms and radishes (which transform from spicy to subtly sweet when cooked!) are particularly charged with gut-brain axis-supporting magic. Coated in a balsamic vinegar glaze, here they offer a balance of nutty richness and tangy bite. To make this salad a heartier main, serve with a grain such as amaranth, buckwheat, or quinoa.

Serves 2 as a main or 3 to 4 as a side

3 tablespoons extra virgin olive oil
1 pound (450 g) small radishes, halved
1 pound (450 g) shiitake mushrooms, stems trimmed
¼ cup (60 ml) balsamic vinegar
Flaky salt, optional
Minced fresh basil or chives, optional

1 Heat the oil in a large pan over medium heat, then add the radishes and mushrooms and sear for about 20 minutes, stirring regularly, until the radishes can be pierced with a fork, the mushrooms are tender, and both are evenly golden brown. Season with salt and pepper.

2 Increase the heat to high and add the balsamic vinegar, letting it sizzle for about 10 minutes, or until it reduces to a thick syrup that clings to the mushrooms and radishes. Serve warm or cold with a sprinkle of freshly ground black pepper, garnishing with the flaky salt and fresh basil, if using.

TIP: For another nourishing spin on this recipe, add some vegan kimchi to the radishes and mushrooms after taking them off the heat. The fermented kimchi is imbued with gut- (and thereby brain-) nourishing probiotics, prebiotics, and nutrients.

MAGICAL BENEFITS

GABA ◆ Mushrooms contain gamma-aminobutyric acid (GABA), a neurotransmitter that calms the central nervous system by balancing nerve signals. Low levels of GABA are often linked to depression.

Selenium ◆ Found in high concentrations in mushrooms, selenium helps to neutralize free radicals in the brain. It also plays a role in synthesizing mood-regulating neurotransmitters like serotonin.

Prebiotic Fiber ◆ Fiber-rich foods such as mushrooms and radishes support a healthy gut microbiome, which influences serotonin production via the gut-brain axis.

Lemony Lettuce Wedges
FOR HYDRATION

Gluten-Free ✦ *Nut-Free*

Staying hydrated means not only drinking adequate amounts of water but also getting enough electrolytes. One of the best ways to get enough of both is through electrolyte- and water-dense plants like the lettuce in this crisp wedge salad. Topped with a creamy lemon-mint dressing mixed with finely chopped cucumber, it's both refreshingly crunchy and hydrating.

1 Carefully cut the lettuce head in half lengthwise to serve two or into quarters lengthwise to serve four. Place the lettuce wedges on a serving platter or divide them between individual plates. Set aside.

2 To make the cucumber-mint dressing, add the coconut cream, cucumber, scallion, lemon zest, lemon juice, agave, oil, and mint to a bowl and whisk to combine. Season with salt and pepper.

3 Drizzle the dressing evenly over the lettuce wedges. Garnish with the extra mint, lemon zest, and freshly ground black pepper, then serve immediately while the lettuce is still crisp!

TIP: You can revive limp lettuce leaves by submerging them in an ice bath for 30 to 60 minutes. They'll crisp back up like magic!

Serves 2 to 4 as a side

1 head butter or Bibb lettuce

CUCUMBER-MINT DRESSING

Half a 13.5-ounce (400 ml) can coconut cream

½ cucumber, finely diced

1 scallion, green part only, thinly sliced

Grated zest and juice of 2 lemons, plus more zest for serving

2 tablespoons agave

1 tablespoon extra virgin olive oil

10 to 15 fresh mint leaves, minced, plus more for serving

MAGICAL BENEFITS

High Water Content ✦ Vegetables such as lettuce, especially iceberg, and cucumbers are made up of around 95 percent water, offering steady and long-lasting hydration as they're digested.

Electrolytes ✦ Minerals such as sodium, potassium, calcium, magnesium, chloride, phosphate, and bicarbonate—found in lettuce, cucumbers, lemons, and coconut—help regulate fluid balance, transmit nerve impulses, contract muscles, and maintain proper pH levels.

Asparagus and Artichoke Salad
FOR HEART SUPPORT

Gluten-Free

This ultra-simple citrusy salad is filled with heart-supporting magic. The crunch of raw asparagus contrasts with the tender marinated artichoke hearts and the creamy, zesty Citrus-Scallion Sauce (page 76). It's so refreshing, and so easy to make, that you might just fall in love with it at first bite! For a complete heart-supporting meal, serve this salad as a side for the Baked Purple Cauliflower and Potatoes with Rosemary Vinaigrette (page 214).

Serves 4 as a side

1 bunch asparagus, ends trimmed, cut into bite-size pieces

One 13.5-ounce (400 ml) can or jar marinated artichoke hearts, drained and quartered

1 lemon

¼ cup (60 ml) Citrus-Scallion Sauce (page 76)

Chopped pistachios

1 Add the asparagus and artichoke hearts to a large bowl. Zest the lemon directly over the vegetables, setting some zest to the side for serving. Add a squeeze of lemon juice if you like!

2 Pour on the Citrus-Scallion Sauce and gently toss to coat evenly. Season with salt and pepper. Just before serving, sprinkle with the chopped pistachios, extra freshly ground black pepper, and the rest of the lemon zest.

TIP: To keep asparagus spears crisp and fresh longer, store them like flowers: Cut off the bottom of the stems and place the spears upright in a glass with 1 to 2 inches (2.5 to 5 cm) of water. Refrigerated, this should keep the asparagus fresh for up to 1 week.

MAGICAL BENEFITS

Quercetin and Rutin ✦ Found in artichokes and pistachios, quercetin and rutin are powerful antioxidants that reduce inflammation and oxidative stress in blood vessels and help lower LDL (bad) cholesterol and increase HDL (good) cholesterol.

Citric Acid ✦ The citric acid found in lemon juice enhances the absorption of minerals, like calcium, that play a role in regulating heart rhythm, blood pressure, and clotting.

Potassium ✦ This macro mineral found in artichokes, asparagus, and pistachios helps regulate blood pressure by relaxing blood vessels and balancing sodium levels.

Mustard-Caper Potatoes and Radishes
FOR DETOX

Gluten-Free ✦ Nut-Free

Throughout the spring, nutrients in the soil become more bioavailable as temperatures gradually rise, making late spring the perfect time to reap the nutritional benefits of root vegetables such as potatoes and radishes. The potatoes, raw radishes, and mustard-caper sauce in this plant-based carpaccio salad all support the digestive system's natural cleansing actions. This dish pairs well with the Asparagus and Pea Quiche (page 31) or the Mushrooms with Artichoke-Potato Purée (page 28).

1 Heat the oil in a pan over high heat, then add the onions and sauté for about 20 minutes, stirring frequently and adjusting the heat as needed to prevent burning. Deglaze with a splash of water whenever the onions begin to stick and scrape the bottom of the pan to reincorporate any browned bits, until tender and caramelized.

2 Add the potatoes and a pinch of salt to a medium saucepan filled with water, place over high heat, and bring to a boil. Reduce the heat to medium and simmer the potatoes for about 15 minutes, until tender enough to be pierced with a fork. (Make sure not to overcook the potatoes. You want them to hold their form in the salad.)

3 Drain the potatoes, then immediately submerge them in a large bowl filled with ice water to stop the cooking process. Peel the skins using your hands or a small paring knife. Cut the potatoes into slices roughly the same thickness as the radishes. Transfer both the potatoes and radishes to a large bowl.

4 **To make the mustard-caper sauce,** add the yogurt, mayonnaise, mustard, about 1 teaspoon capers (reserving the rest for serving), agave, lemon zest, and lemon juice to a small bowl and whisk until smooth, then season with salt and pepper.

5 Pour the sauce over the potatoes and radishes and toss gently to coat. Garnish with the scallions, reserved capers, and extra freshly ground black pepper before serving.

TIP: If you have time, refrigerating the cooked potatoes for several hours before use will boost their resistant starch content by causing the structure of some of the starch molecules to change. Just don't leave cooked potatoes at room temperature, as bad bacteria can form.

Serves 2 to 4 as a side

1 tablespoon extra virgin olive oil

2 yellow onions, minced

1 pound (450 g) small red or fingerling potatoes

1 bunch small radishes, thinly sliced

2 scallions, thinly sliced

MUSTARD-CAPER SAUCE

2 tablespoons vegan yogurt or plant-based cream

2 tablespoons vegan mayonnaise

1 tablespoon Dijon mustard

2 to 3 teaspoons capers

1 tablespoon agave

Grated zest and juice of ½ lemon

MAGICAL BENEFITS

Insoluble Fiber and Resistant Starch ✦ Insoluble fiber, abundant in vegetables like potatoes and radishes, resists digestion, promoting intestinal cleansing. Resistant starch, found in potatoes, ferments in the large intestine, acting as a prebiotic for beneficial gut bacteria.

Glucosinolates ✦ Radishes help the body remove waste, break down fats, and absorb nutrients thanks to their sulfur-containing compounds known as glucosinolates, which also help protect the liver from damage.

Butyrate ✦ A short-chained fatty acid produced when foods like potatoes and radishes ferment in the gut, butyrate serves as an energy source for beneficial gut bacteria and has anti-inflammatory effects on the gut lining.

Spring • Mains & Sides

Raw Zucchini and Sprouted Pea Salad
FOR STRENGTH

Gluten-Free ✦ Nut-Free

Delicate young sprouts are packed with even more invigorating nutritive power than their full-grown counterparts; the process of sprouting increases their protein, vitamin, and mineral content dramatically. In this salad, spring greens such as watercress, peas, raw zucchini, and scallions are tossed in a creamy lemon dressing and topped with pea sprouts, making for a salad charged with energizing and invigorating benefits.

Serves 2 to 4 as a side

SALAD
4 ounces (115 g) watercress
1 cup (25 g) pea sprouts
7 ounces (200 g) fresh or thawed frozen peas
1 zucchini, thinly sliced
3 scallions, thinly sliced

CREAMY LEMON DRESSING
¼ cup (60 ml) extra virgin olive oil
2 tablespoons Anti-Allergy Vinegar (page 68) or apple cider vinegar
2 tablespoons plain soy yogurt or cream
Grated zest and juice of ½ lemon
1 teaspoon agave

1 **To make the salad,** place the watercress in a large bowl for family-style serving, reserving a few leaves for serving. Add the pea sprouts, peas, zucchini, and two-thirds of the scallions.

2 **To make the creamy lemon dressing,** whisk the oil, vinegar, yogurt, lemon zest and juice, and agave in a small bowl to combine.

3 Drizzle the dressing over the salad. Toss to coat, then garnish with the remaining scallions and watercress leaves and season with salt and pepper. Serve immediately.

TIP: If you're avoiding FODMAPs, replace the scallions with sprouts (like alfalfa or broccoli) or fresh herbs. If you have leftover dressing, you can use it as a dip for crudités!

MAGICAL BENEFITS

Vitamin K ✦ Watercress is an excellent source of vitamin K, which plays a role in muscle formation, repair, and proper function. Vitamin K also supports red blood cell production and may prevent calcium buildup in arteries.

Amino Acids ✦ Peas (a nearly complete protein) and soy (a complete protein), offer a balanced spectrum of amino acids, supporting muscle synthesis and energy production.

B Vitamins ✦ Zucchini, peas, and watercress contain B vitamins that play essential roles in energy production.

Radish, Cucumber, and Hibiscus Salad
FOR DETOX

Gluten-Free ✦ No Sugar Added

This crisp and rejuvenating salad supports the functions of the liver and kidneys, which are vital for detoxifying the body. The antioxidant-charged pigments in the radishes, cucumbers, and sprouts and the hibiscus petals in the Flower Vinaigrette (page 199) account for this salad's cleansing action. Serve alongside the Lemon-Artichoke Pasta (page 24) for a protein-filled spring dinner.

Combine the cucumber and radishes in a large bowl, drizzle with the Flower Vinaigrette and olive oil, and toss gently to coat. Season with salt and pepper. Garnish with the chopped pistachios and pea sprouts, and serve.

TIP: For another detox-supporting spin, soak the cucumbers and radishes in apple cider vinegar for 1 to 2 hours to increase their probiotic potential, which directly supports liver functions. The strained vinegar can be saved for use in other recipes. If desired, you can substitute any vinaigrette or dressing you like for the Flower Vinaigrette (page 199).

Serves 4 as a side

1 cucumber, thinly sliced

6 to 8 small radishes, or 3 to 4 larger daikon radishes (about 250 g), thinly sliced

2 tablespoons Flower Vinaigrette (page 199)

1 tablespoon extra virgin olive oil

3 tablespoons chopped pistachios

Small handful of pea sprouts

MAGICAL BENEFITS

Anthocyanins ✦ These pigment compounds, found in high concentrations in hibiscus flowers, have antioxidant and anti-inflammatory properties that may help protect the kidneys.

Quercetin ✦ Found in radishes, quercetin helps the liver break down and eliminate toxins. It also helps the body produce glutathione, a powerful antioxidant.

Chlorophyll ✦ The green color in pea sprouts comes from chlorophyll, a plant pigment with powerful antioxidant and detoxifying properties.

Squash and Asparagus Sauté
FOR ENERGY

Gluten-Free ✦ Nut-Free

The transition from spring to summer calls for optimizing our energy levels so we can make the most of the long days. This sauté of thinly sliced yellow squash and asparagus cooked in coconut milk and topped with pea sprouts is a celebration of the best of both seasons and is rich in the proteins and B vitamins that we need to boost our energy levels, especially when served with a complete-protein grain such as quinoa or buckwheat.

Serves 4 as a side

- 2 tablespoons extra virgin olive oil
- 2 shallots, thinly sliced
- 3 garlic cloves, thinly sliced
- 4 yellow squash, thinly sliced
- 1 bunch asparagus, ends trimmed, cut into 2-inch (5 cm) pieces
- Half a 13.5-ounce (400 ml) can coconut milk

LEMON-MUSTARD VINAIGRETTE

- 3 tablespoons balsamic vinegar
- 1 tablespoon Dijon mustard
- 1 teaspoon agave
- Grated zest and juice of ½ lemon
- Fresh pea sprouts

1. Heat the oil in a large pan over high heat until it sizzles, then add the shallots and sauté 5 to 10 minutes, adjusting the temperature as needed to prevent burning, until crispy. Add the garlic and fry until fragrant, about 1 minute, then add the squash and asparagus and sauté for about 30 minutes, stirring regularly. Deglaze with a splash of water whenever the vegetables begin to stick and scrape the bottom of the pan to reincorporate any browned bits, until tender and caramelized. Add the coconut milk and simmer for about 20 minutes, or until the liquid reduces by half and thickens into a creamy sauce. Season with salt and pepper.

2. **To make the lemon-mustard vinaigrette,** whisk the vinegar, mustard, agave, lemon zest, and lemon juice in a small bowl until smooth. Season with salt and pepper.

3. Pour the vinaigrette over the vegetables and toss gently to coat. Transfer to a serving dish or individual plates. Garnish with the fresh pea sprouts and serve warm or cold.

TIP: To amplify the energy-boosting magic, add 1 teaspoon of stimulating guarana or maca powder to the coconut milk as it simmers.

MAGICAL BENEFITS

Vitamin B6 ✦ This B vitamin also known as pyridoxine, found in asparagus, squash, and sprouts, helps convert food into glucose, which the body uses for energy.

Vitamin B3 ✦ Found in asparagus, squash, and sprouts, vitamin B3 (niacin) helps convert food into energy.

Vitamin C ✦ This antioxidant helps the body synthesize energy-boosting neurotransmitters such as dopamine and norepinephrine.

MAGICAL BENEFITS

Vitamin B9 ✦ Found in strawberries and chickpeas, this B vitamin, also known as folate, plays a crucial role in healthy egg and sperm production, and in healthy fetal development.

Diterpenoids ✦ The active compounds in vitex (chaste) berries interact with the pituitary gland to regulate sex hormones, particularly balancing estrogen and progesterone.

Quercetin ✦ This flavonoid, found in strawberries, is known primarily for its antioxidant and detox-supporting benefits, but it also plays a role in modulating estrogen levels.

Strawberry Cream Cupcakes
FOR FERTILITY

Gluten-Free ♦ Nut-Free

Hiding inside these fluffy cupcakes is a strawberry-cream filling bursting with fertility-supporting magic. Puréed strawberries are also incorporated directly into the batter along with aquafaba (the liquid from canned chickpeas) to create a spongy sweet cake perfect for topping with vanilla frosting. The cupcakes, filling, and icing can be made up to a day in advance, stored in airtight containers in the refrigerator, and assembled later.

1 Preheat the oven to 350°F (180°C). Grease the wells of a muffin pan with the oil or line them with paper liners.

2 To make the strawberry cupcakes, whisk together the gluten-free flour, baking soda, vitex berry powder, if using, and a pinch of salt in a large bowl. Set aside.

3 Using a food processor, purée the strawberries together with the sugar and aquafaba for about 5 minutes, or until smooth. In 4 batches, add the dry ingredients to the strawberry purée and pulse just until smooth and lump-free. Spoon the batter into the prepared muffin pan, filling each well about two-thirds full.

4 Bake for about 20 minutes, or until a toothpick inserted into the center of a cupcake comes out clean. Remove from the oven and allow the cupcakes to cool in the pan for about 10 minutes before transferring them to a wire rack to cool for another 20 minutes.

5 Once the cupcakes have cooled, slice off the tops and set them aside. Hollow out the center of each cupcake using a small spoon or a paring knife.

6 To make the strawberry cream filling, whisk the coconut cream, jam, and agave in a bowl until well combined.

7 Spoon the filling into the hollows of the cooled cupcakes, then replace the cupcake tops. Chill the cupcakes in the refrigerator for at least 30 minutes to let the filling set.

8 To make the vanilla frosting, using a stand mixer or handheld mixer, whip the chilled coconut cream with the vanilla extract on high speed for 5 to 10 minutes, until fluffy. Gradually add the powdered sugar and continue mixing for 2 to 3 more minutes, until smooth.

9 Add the frosting to a piping bag or a ziplock bag with ¼ inch (6 mm) cut off the tip, then pipe the frosting onto the top of each cupcake. These are best if eaten right away, but can be stored in the refrigerator and enjoyed within 2 days.

TIP: To amplify this recipe's magic, you can add ½ teaspoon of any other hormone-supporting or fertility-boosting powders, such as ashwagandha or maca, to the batter or filling in addition to the vitex powder. You can also play with the flavors by replacing the strawberry purée with puréed apple and the strawberry jam with melted chocolate or caramel.

Makes 12 cupcakes

STRAWBERRY CUPCAKES

2 teaspoons cold-pressed virgin coconut oil

2½ cups (300 g) all-purpose gluten-free flour blend (see page 5)

1 teaspoon baking soda

½ teaspoon vitex (chaste) berry powder, optional

8 ounces (225 g) fresh or thawed frozen strawberries

1 cup (200 g) cane sugar

½ cup (120 ml) aquafaba (see page 5), chilled

STRAWBERRY CREAM FILLING

Half a 13.5-ounce (400 ml) can coconut cream, chilled

½ cup (160 g) strawberry jam

2 tablespoons agave

VANILLA FROSTING

One 13.5-ounce (400 ml) can coconut cream, chilled

1 teaspoon vanilla extract or ½ teaspoon vanilla powder

½ cup (60 g) powdered sugar

Spring • Desserts

Lilac Panna Cotta
FOR PASSION

Gluten-Free ✦ Nut-Free

Flowers like lilacs are masters of aphrodisiac magic; the fragrant compounds that attract pollinators can also impact our libido. Here, the flowers are infused into soy milk that's then set with agar-agar (seaweed powder) to create an irresistibly floral panna cotta. Pair with the Mushroom Pizza (page 36) for an unforgettable date night!

Serves 4 to 6

- 1½ cups (360 ml) soy milk
- 2 tablespoons fresh, culinary-grade lilac flowers, plus more for serving
- 1⅛ to 1¼ teaspoons agar-agar powder
- ½ teaspoon vanilla extract or ¼ teaspoon vanilla powder
- 1 to 2 tablespoons agave

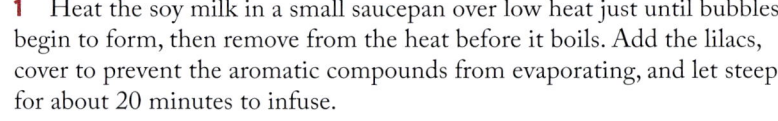

MAGICAL BENEFITS

Linalool ✦ This soothing aromatic compound found in fragrant flowers like lilacs calms the nervous system and reduces stress and anxiety, which are major inhibitors of sexual arousal.

Iodine ✦ Found in seaweed products such as agar-agar powder, this essential mineral influences thyroid hormones that play a role in regulating sex hormones, energy levels, and mood.

Phytoestrogens ✦ Soy products contain phytoestrogens, compounds that mimic the activity of estrogen in the body and can help boost libido. Phytoestrogens are considered safe when consumed in moderation.

1 Heat the soy milk in a small saucepan over low heat just until bubbles begin to form, then remove from the heat before it boils. Add the lilacs, cover to prevent the aromatic compounds from evaporating, and let steep for about 20 minutes to infuse.

2 Strain into a bowl through a fine-mesh strainer, discarding the flowers, then return the infused milk to the saucepan.

3 Mix the agar-agar powder (adding the larger amount if you prefer your panna cotta slightly firmer) with 1 teaspoon water in a small bowl to create a smooth paste, then add the paste and the vanilla to the milk, whisking vigorously until smooth.

4 Bring the milk to a gentle simmer over medium heat, stirring regularly for 5 to 10 minutes, to activate the gelling properties of the agar-agar powder. Add the agave, adjusting the sweetness to taste.

5 Remove from the heat and let the mixture cool for about 10 minutes, then divide between individual ramekins or glasses. Let the panna cotta set in the refrigerator for at least 4 hours, until fully firm.

6 Serve directly in their ramekins, or remove them by running a knife around the edge of the ramekins to loosen the panna cotta, then placing a small plate on top and, with one hand underneath the ramekin and one on top of the plate, inverting them. Garnish with a few fresh flower petals, if desired, and serve.

TIP: For similar aphrodisiac effects, you can substitute the lilac for culinary-grade flowers, such as rose petals, jasmine, blue lotus, or lavender.

MAGICAL BENEFITS

Vitamin C ✦ Strawberries, lemons, and amla (Indian gooseberry) are rich in vitamin C, which supports the production of mood- and cognition-supporting dopamine, serotonin, and norepinephrine.

Antioxidants ✦ Strawberries, lemons, and almonds contain a spectrum of antioxidants, which are linked to improved mood and cognitive performance.

Vitamin B2 ✦ Almonds contain riboflavin, a B vitamin that helps convert food into energy and supports neurological functions. Riboflavin deficiency has been associated with headaches and cognitive impairment.

Strawberry-Lemon Squares
FOR EUPHORIA

Gluten-Free

These cookies put a springtime spin on classic lemon squares. With a sweet swirl of strawberry in the tart filling and a crunchy almond butter crust, these gooey, citrusy treats are filled with mood-supporting magic. Medicinal benefits aside, the flavors alone will leave you feeling euphoric and craving more!

1 Preheat the oven to 350°F (180°C).

2 **To make the crust,** combine the almond flour, gluten-free flour, oil, sugar, arrowroot flour, and a pinch of salt in a bowl and mix until a crumbly dough is formed.

3 Line the bottom of a 9-by-13-inch (23 by 33 cm) baking dish with parchment paper, leaving enough excess paper to overhang two of the sides, then grease the paper and the sides of the pan. Press the dough into an even layer on the bottom of the pan and poke several holes in the center with a fork to prevent large bubbles from forming while it bakes.

4 Bake for about 20 minutes, or until the crust is golden, then remove from the oven and set aside for 5 to 10 minutes to cool slightly so that it isn't too hot when you pour in the filling.

5 Raise the oven temperature to 375°F (190°C).

6 **To make the lemon filling,** add the sugar, lemon zest, lemon juice, aquafaba, arrowroot flour, amla powder, and a pinch of salt to a blender and blend on high speed for about 3 minutes, or until a froth forms. Pour the filling over the parbaked crust and set aside while you prepare the strawberry topping.

7 **To make the strawberry swirl topping,** add the strawberries, sugar, and ginger to a clean blender and blend on medium speed for 3 to 5 minutes, until smooth. Drizzle over the lemon filling, using a toothpick or knife to draw swirls through the filling.

8 Place the baking pan back in the oven and bake for another 20 to 30 minutes, until the filling is set (meaning the liquid filling has partially infused into the crust and reduced to a jam-like custard that holds its form) and the top is lightly golden brown.

9 Remove from the oven and let cool for about 30 minutes. Using the overhanging parchment paper, lift the lemon cookie from the pan and onto a flat surface. Cut into squares of your desired size. Carefully remove the squares from the paper and dust with powdered sugar and extra lemon zest, if using. Enjoy right away, or store at room temperature in an airtight container for up to 2 days, in the refrigerator for up to 1 week, or in the freezer for up to 3 months!

TIP: For another take on this recipe, use puréed apricots, raspberries, or blueberries, in place of the strawberries.

Makes 12 to 15 squares

CRUST

2 cups (240 g) almond flour

1¼ cups (150 g) all-purpose gluten-free flour blend (see page 5)

½ cup (120 g) cold-pressed virgin coconut oil, melted, plus more for greasing

½ cup (100 g) cane sugar or ½ cup (120 ml) agave

⅓ cup plus 1 tablespoon (50 g) arrowroot flour

LEMON FILLING

1 cup (200 g) cane sugar

Grated zest of 1 lemon, plus ¾ cup (180 ml) lemon juice (from 4 to 5 lemons)

½ cup (120 ml) aquafaba (see page 5), chilled

2 tablespoons arrowroot flour, cornstarch, or all-purpose gluten-free flour blend (see page 5)

1 teaspoon amla (Indian gooseberry) powder, optional

STRAWBERRY SWIRL TOPPING

6 ounces (170 g) fresh or thawed frozen strawberries

½ cup (100 g) cane sugar

2 tablespoons fresh grated ginger

Powdered sugar and grated lemon zest, optional

Adaptogenic Chocolate Mousse
FOR ENERGY

Gluten-Free ♦ Nut-Free

This rich and creamy mousse is imbued with more than just the medicinal benefits of cacao. Hiding inside this simple and irresistible dessert is the energizing magic of guarana berries, which rival the caffeine content of coffee, as well the adaptogenic powers of rhodiola root and cordyceps mushrooms, particularly known for their ability to boost energy levels. You'll never even detect the medicinal powders thanks to the deep richness of the chocolate and whipped cream.

Serves 4 to 6

- 5.25 ounces (150 g) 70 to 90 percent dark chocolate, chopped
- 1 teaspoon cordyceps mushroom powder, optional
- 1 teaspoon rhodiola root powder, optional
- ½ teaspoon guarana powder or instant coffee, optional
- One 13.5-ounce (400 ml) can coconut cream, chilled

1 Set a heat-safe bowl over a small saucepan of water. Bring the water to a boil over high heat. Add the chocolate to the bowl and let it melt, stirring occasionally until smooth. Add the cordyceps mushroom powder, rhodiola powder, and guarana powder, if using, and a pinch of salt, and mix until smooth. Refrigerate for 10 minutes to slightly cool the chocolate while you prepare the whipped coconut cream.

2 Using a stand mixer or handheld mixer, whip the chilled coconut cream on high speed for about 10 minutes, or until fluffy. Once the chocolate has cooled but is still in liquid form, fold it into the coconut cream just until fully integrated. Divide the mousse between individual ramekins or glasses and refrigerate for at least 2 hours to set before serving.

TIP: You can use vegan white chocolate instead of dark, or garnish with antioxidant-packed berries such as dried goji berries or fresh blueberries, raspberries, or strawberries.

MAGICAL BENEFITS

Caffeine ♦ Guarana berries are similar to coffee beans in their caffeine content, but their caffeine is released more slowly for a sustained energy boost.

Salidroside ♦ This active compound in rhodiola root is known for its ability to help the body adapt to stress by regulating adrenal and cortisol levels.

Cordycepin | ♦ This adaptogen in cordyceps mushrooms enhances the body's ability to produce and store energy, thereby increasing stamina and endurance.

Chocolate Cake
FOR LUCID DREAMS

Gluten-Free ✦ Nut-Free

This chocolate cake is so irresistible it's hard to believe it can exist outside of a dream. Yet all it takes is a little culinary magic to render this sweet enchantment a reality. Beyond the layers of gooey chocolate cake and Adaptogenic Chocolate Mousse (page 64) drizzled in melted chocolate, this dessert is infused with mind-boosting and dream-inducing cacao (which is raw, unprocessed, and higher in antioxidants and nutrients than cocoa), chickpeas, rhodiola root, and cordyceps mushrooms.

1. Preheat the oven to 350°F (180°C). Grease a 9-inch (23 cm) springform pan with oil.

2. **To make the chocolate cake,** add the chocolate and the remaining oil to a heat-safe bowl placed over a small saucepan of water. Bring the water to a gentle simmer over high heat, then reduce the heat to medium-low to keep the water at a gentle simmer, stirring occasionally for about 10 minutes, until the chocolate and oil are completely melted and combined. Remove from the heat.

3. Whisk the coconut milk, brown sugar, aquafaba, and melted chocolate mixture in a large bowl until well combined. Add the gluten-free flour, cacao powder, and a pinch of salt. Stir until the batter is smooth and free of lumps.

4. Pour the batter into the prepared springform pan and bake for about 1 hour, or until a toothpick inserted into the center comes out clean. Remove from the oven and allow the cake to cool in the pan for about 20 minutes, then transfer the pan to the refrigerator to cool for another 20 minutes.

5. Spread the chocolate mousse over the cooled cake while it is still in the pan, then place the cake in the freezer for a final 20 minutes, or until the mousse is set.

6. Remove the cake from the freezer, run a knife around the edges to loosen it, then carefully unmold it. Using a butter knife or spatula, gently neaten the edges by smoothing the sides of the mousse. Place the cake in the refrigerator while preparing the chocolate drizzle.

7. **To make the chocolate drizzle,** add the chocolate to a heat-safe bowl set over a small saucepan of water. Bring the water to a gentle simmer over high heat and let the chocolate melt, stirring occasionally. Let the chocolate cool slightly before drizzling it over the cake.

8. Serve immediately, or store in an airtight container at room temperature for up to 3 days, in the refrigerator for up to 1 week, or in the freezer for up to 3 months.

TIP: For a quicker version of this recipe, you can leave out the chocolate mousse.

Serves 6 to 8

CHOCOLATE CAKE

10.5 ounces (300 g) 70 to 90 percent dark chocolate, chopped

½ cup (120 g) cold-pressed virgin coconut oil, melted, plus more for greasing

One 13.5-ounce (400 ml) can coconut milk

1⅓ cups (300 g) packed light brown sugar

1 cup (240 ml) aquafaba (see page 5), chilled

1¼ cups (150 g) all-purpose gluten-free flour blend (see page 5)

3 tablespoons cacao powder

2 cups (500 g) Adaptogenic Chocolate Mousse (page 64)

CHOCOLATE DRIZZLE

7 ounces (200 g) 70 to 90 percent dark chocolate, chopped

MAGICAL BENEFITS

Adaptogens ✦ The adaptogenic compounds in rhodiola and cordyceps can enhance sleep quality and reduce stress, thereby increasing REM sleep (the stage of sleep in which dreams occur).

Magnesium ✦ This essential mineral, found in high concentrations in cacao, helps balance brain chemicals, energy, and sleep.

Acetylcholine ✦ This neurotransmitter found in chickpeas is crucial for brain functions such as memory, learning, and attention. It also helps regulate sleep cycles, especially REM sleep.

Anti-Allergy Vinegar
FOR IMMUNITY

Gluten-Free ✦ No Sugar Added ✦ Nut-Free

Spring brings a surge of pollen along with its flowers and buds, causing uncomfortable symptoms for allergy sufferers. The plants in this subtly bitter-sweet herbal tincture have natural antihistamine properties to help calm allergy responses. Incorporate this versatile vinegar into recipes like Raw Zucchini and Sprouted Pea Salad (page 52) or Caramelized Zucchini and Peas with Citrus-Dill Sauce (page 27) to enjoy spring with fewer allergy symptoms. To use, dilute 1 to 2 teaspoons in water or juice and take daily, or add to salad dressings, soups, or sautés starting a month before allergy season begins.

Makes 4¼ cups (1 L)

4¼ cups (1 L) apple cider vinegar
½ cup (5 g) dried stinging nettle
½ cup (8 g) dried chamomile flowers
½ cup (25 g) dried green tea leaves
½ cup (25 g) dried licorice root

MAGICAL BENEFITS

Quercetin ✦ Stinging nettle contains various anti-allergy compounds, such as quercetin, that block the release of histamine from mast cells, a type of immune cell related to allergies and inflammation.

Apigenin ✦ Chamomile contains flavonoids such as apigenin, which helps calm inflammatory and allergic reactions by blocking the release of histamine from mast cells.

EGCG ✦ Green tea is rich in EGCG (epigallocatechin gallate), an antioxidant and anti-inflammatory compound that helps regulate the immune system and block histamines.

Glycyrrhizin ✦ Licorice contains glycyrrhizin, a compound that helps block histamines while also boosting adrenal function, further suppressing allergic reactions.

1 Combine the vinegar, nettle, chamomile, green tea, and licorice in a sterilized glass jar or other airtight container that can hold 6 cups (1.5 L) of liquid. Ensure the leaves are fully covered by the vinegar by weighing them down with a fermentation weight. If you don't have one, you can sterilize a rock that fits inside the jar's rim by boiling it for 10 minutes and use it to keep the plants submerged. This is essential, as any exposed plant matter can mold and spoil the tincture.

2 Seal the jar tightly to prevent evaporation and contamination and place it in a cool, dark place away from direct sunlight. Allow the mixture to steep for about 3 weeks, shaking the jar gently every few days to help circulate the vinegar around the plant matter and ensure that the plants' medicinal compounds are evenly extracted.

3 After the steeping period, strain the tincture through a fine-mesh strainer or cheesecloth, pressing down on the solids to extract as much liquid as possible, into clean, sterilized bottles or jars for storage, then discard the solids. Label the bottles with the contents and date, and store in a cool, dark place. The tincture should keep well for several months.

TIP: To accelerate the extraction process, you can use heat, although the tincture won't be as potent as a longer 3-week extraction. Combine the vinegar and plants in a heat-safe glass jar and place it, uncovered, in a saucepan filled with 2 to 3 inches (5 to 7.5 cm) of water, creating a bain-marie. Heat the water to just below boiling, 185°F to 205°F (85°C to 96°C), to avoid damaging the medicinal compounds. Let the tincture steep for 2 to 3 hours, checking the water level occasionally and topping it up as needed, to gently heat the vinegar and quickly extract the acid-soluble compounds.

Flower Syrup
FOR LIBIDO

Gluten-Free ✦ Nut-Free

Infused into this sweet agave syrup is the libido-boosting magic of flowers and plant roots. The irresistible power and scent of roses in this love potion will bring you into the euphoric state of relaxation where libido thrives. Add a spoonful of the syrup to tea, coffee, lemonade, or cocktails, or even drizzle it over pancakes.

Makes 2 cups (480 ml)

2 cups (480 ml) agave
½ cup (5 g) crushed dried rose petals
½ cup (5 g) crushed dried blue lotus flowers
2 tablespoons dried maca root, powdered or sliced

1. Combine the agave, rose petals, blue lotus flowers, and maca root in a small saucepan. Place the saucepan over medium heat and gently warm the mixture, stirring occasionally, until it just begins to simmer.

2. Lower the heat and allow the mixture to very gently bubble for 15 minutes, stirring occasionally, to infuse the medicinal compounds of the plants into the syrup, or until the petals turn pale. Remove the saucepan from the heat and let the syrup cool for about 15 minutes.

3. Once slightly cooled, strain the syrup through a fine-mesh strainer, pressing on the plants with a spoon to extract as much liquid as possible, then discard.

4. Transfer the syrup into a clean, sterilized bottle or jar for storage. Label the bottle with the contents and date and store the syrup in the refrigerator for up to 1 year.

TIP: To boost this libido-enhancing syrup, add 2 tablespoons each of dried tribulus, damiana, and/or ashwagandha. These adaptogens support desire and complement the other plants in flavor as well as aphrodisiac actions!

MAGICAL BENEFITS

Geraniol and Nerol ✦ Roses contain bioactive compounds like geraniol and nerol, which help reduce anxiety and promote relaxation by modulating neurotransmitters linked to mood, arousal, and libido.

Macamides ✦ These active compounds are concentrated in the roots of the maca plant. They may enhance libido and sexual function by acting as an adaptogen to support hormonal balance and endocrine function.

Apomorphine and Nuciferine ✦ The active compounds in blue lotus flowers include apomorphine, which interacts with dopamine receptors that play a role in libido, and nuciferine, which enhances mood and has calming effects.

Herbal Vinegar
FOR FERTILITY

Gluten-Free ✦ No Sugar Added ✦ Nut-Free

This vinegar contains powerful fertility-supporting vitex (chaste) berries, red clover, maca root, fenugreek seeds, and stinging nettle. With its nutty and sweet, herbal and floral flavors, this versatile vinegar can be used in salad dressings or any dish that calls for vinegar (like the Baked Asparagus with Almonds on page 39). To use, dilute 1 to 2 teaspoons in water or juice and take daily or as desired.

Makes 2 cups (480 ml)

- 2 cups (480 ml) apple cider vinegar
- ½ cup (50 g) dried maca root, powdered or sliced
- ½ cup (5 g) dried stinging nettle
- ½ cup (10 g) packed red clover flowers
- ¼ cup plus 2 tablespoons (50 g) dried vitex (chaste) berries
- 2 tablespoons fenugreek seeds

1 Combine the vinegar, maca root, nettle, red clover flowers, vitex berries, and fenugreek seeds in a sterilized glass jar or other airtight container that can hold 6 cups (1.5 L) of liquid. Ensure the plants are fully covered by the vinegar by weighing them down with a fermentation weight. If you don't have one, you can sterilize a rock that fits inside the jar's rim by boiling it for 10 minutes and use it to keep the plants submerged. This is essential, as any exposed plant matter can mold and spoil the tincture.

2 Seal the jar tightly to prevent evaporation and contamination and place it in a cool, dark place away from direct sunlight. Allow the mixture to steep for about 3 weeks, shaking the jar gently every few days to help circulate the vinegar around the plant matter and ensure that the plants' medicinal compounds are evenly extracted.

3 After the steeping period, strain the tincture through a fine-mesh strainer or cheesecloth, pressing down on the solids to extract as much liquid as possible, into clean, sterilized bottles or jars for storage, then discard the solids. Label the bottles with the contents and date, and store in a cool, dark place. The tincture should keep well for several months.

TIP: Red clover and stinging nettle are common spring forageables. If you have trouble finding maca root, vitex berries, or fenugreek seeds (which can often be found at grocery stores or specialty shops), you can substitute ½ cup (5 g) of red raspberry leaves, which are loaded with fragarine, a compound that tones and relaxes the muscles of the pelvic region, including the uterus.

MAGICAL BENEFITS

Diterpenoids ✦ This active compound in vitex, also known as chaste tree berries, supports hormone production, the menstrual cycle, and ovulation.

Isoflavones ✦ Red clover flowers are rich in isoflavones, a type of plant estrogen (phytoestrogen) that binds to estrogen receptors and helps regulate menstrual cycles and balance hormonal symptoms. Excess consumption, however, can cause imbalances.

Macamides ✦ Maca root's unique macamides have adaptogenic actions that support reproductive functions and hormone balance.

Diosgenin ✦ Fenugreek seeds contain a plant compound known as diosgenin, a type of phytoestrogen that supports reproductive functions by modulating hormone levels.

Lotus-Elderflower Liqueur
FOR EUPHORIA

Gluten-Free ✦ Nut-Free

Infused into this liqueur is the euphoric magic of elderflowers and blue lotus, both of which are revered in folk healing traditions for their mood-altering effects. The medicinal compounds in the blue lotus flowers turn the liqueur a violet-pink hue and give it a sweet floral flavor that makes it a magical base for a mood-boosting cocktail.

1 Combine the elderflower liqueur and blue lotus flowers in a clean glass jar or other airtight container and let infuse for at least 20 minutes, stirring occasionally, until the petals have lost their color.

2 Strain through a fine-mesh strainer or cheesecloth, pressing on the flowers to extract as much liquid as possible, into a clean, sterilized glass jar, then discard the solids. Since alcohol is a preservative, the liqueur can be stored for years.

3 To use, consume as a liqueur or mixed into a simple fizzy cocktail made with 1 part liqueur to 2 parts ginger ale or Turmeric Ginger Ale (page 138), plus ice, if using.

TIP: To give this tincture an energizing boost, consider adding ¼ cup (15 g) of ginseng root, rhodiola root, or caffeine-rich guarana berry powder.

Makes 2 cups (480 ml)

2 cups (480 ml) elderflower liqueur

1 cup (10 g) dried blue lotus flowers

Ginger ale or Turmeric Ginger Ale (page 138) for serving, optional

Ice for serving, optional

MAGICAL BENEFITS

Quercetin and Kaempferol ✦ Elderflowers contain antioxidant flavonoid compounds such as kaempferol and quercetin, which enhance serotonin and mood-regulating hormone levels.

Nuciferine and Apomorphine ✦ Blue lotus flowers contain active compounds that enhance mood. Nuciferine has relaxation-promoting effects, and apomorphine acts on dopamine receptors, increasing feelings of pleasure and well-being.

Citrus-Scallion Sauce
FOR SATIETY

Gluten-Free ✦ Nut-Free

This simple yet versatile, creamy sauce is bursting with tangy scallion flavor. It's also great for satisfying cravings and promoting feelings of fullness, pairing delightfully with vegetable sautés (like the Squash and Asparagus Sauté on page 56), salads (like the Asparagus and Artichoke Salad on page 48), and purées, or simply served as a dipping sauce.

Serves 4 to 6

One 13.5-ounce (400 ml) can coconut cream

⅛ to ¼ teaspoon agave syrup

3 scallions, minced

Grated zest and juice of 1 to 1½ lemons

Mix the coconut cream, agave, scallions, lemon zest, and lemon juice together in a bowl until well combined. Season with salt and pepper and adjust the lemon juice and agave to taste. Store in the refrigerator for up to 1 week.

TIP: If you like, substitute 2 shallots or 1 caramelized onion for the scallions. For extra satiety-supporting action, add 1 teaspoon of mucilage fiber–containing chia seeds.

MAGICAL BENEFITS

Lauric Acid ✦ Found in coconut oil, lauric acid stimulates the production of hormones that promote the feeling of fullness, aiding in weight management.

Healthy Fats ✦ The healthy fat content of coconut cream increases feelings of satiety by stimulating the release of hormones that signal the brain to suppress appetite and slow stomach emptying.

Mucilage ✦ This type of soluble fiber found in scallions forms a gel-like substance in the digestive tract that optimizes the absorption of nutrients and adds bulk for a feeling of fullness.

MAGICAL BENEFITS

Lignans ✦ Flaxseeds contain phytoestrogens (plant estrogens) known as lignans, which block synthetic chemicals with harmful estrogen-mimicking and endocrine- and hormone-disrupting effects.

Vitamin B6 ✦ Found in flax and potatoes, vitamin B6 supports estrogen-progesterone balance and plays a key role in reproductive and metabolic health.

Adaptogens ✦ Plants with adaptogenic properties, such as maca and ashwagandha roots, balance stress and reproductive hormones by modulating the hypothalamic-pituitary-adrenal (HPA) axis, which links the brain and adrenal glands.

Zucchini Quiche
FOR HORMONE BALANCE

Gluten-Free ◆ No Sugar Added ◆ Nut-Free

Certain plants possess remarkable abilities to help maintain hormonal harmony both in themselves and in us. This vibrant quiche is a feast for the taste buds, combining the sweetness of caramelized onions with the nuttiness of the chickpeas and flaxseeds that together replace eggs to form the filling. Hormone-balancing adaptogens like ashwagandha and maca blend in undetected in the rich and savory filling. To make this an even heartier main, pair with a protein-rich grain like amaranth, buckwheat, or quinoa, or with the Baby Greens and Radish Salad (page 110).

1 Preheat the oven to 350°F (180°C).

2 **To make the filling,** add the oil to a saucepan set over medium-high heat. Add the onions and sauté for 15 to 20 minutes, stirring frequently and adjusting the temperature as needed to prevent burning. Deglaze with a splash of the vinegar whenever the onions begin to stick and scrape the bottom of the pan to reincorporate any browned bits and draw out the onions' natural sugars to help them caramelize.

3 Add the coconut cream, increase the heat to high, and cook for about 10 minutes, or until the cream has reduced by half. Season with salt and pepper. Add the arrowroot flour, ground flaxseed, ashwagandha powder, and maca powder, if using, and mix well. Continue cooking for about 10 minutes, or until the sauce thickens, then remove from the heat and set aside while you prepare the aquafaba.

4 Add the aquafaba to a bowl and whip with a hand-held mixer on high speed for about 10 minutes, or until stiff white peaks form, then fold into the coconut cream until fully integrated.

5 **To make the potato crust,** grease the bottom and sides of a 9-inch (23 cm) springform pan with the oil and arrange the potato slices in concentric, slightly overlapping circles over the bottom of the pan. Add a second layer, staggering the slices to cover the gaps in the first layer.

6 To form the edges of the crust, press a layer of potato slices (edges touching but not overlapping) upright along the sides of the pan. Add an extra drop or two of oil to any slices that don't adhere well. Add a second layer, staggering the slices to cover the gaps in the first layer.

7 Pour the onion-cream filling into the crust and spread evenly.

8 **To make the topping,** place the zucchini slices in slightly overlapping concentric circles on top of the filling, drizzle with the oil, and sprinkle with salt and pepper.

9 Bake for 30 to 40 minutes, until the potatoes are cooked through and a little crispy and the zucchini is tender. Let cool for 5 minutes, then run a knife along the edges to loosen the quiche before removing the sides of the springform pan. Serve warm.

TIP: If you cut the potato slices too thick and they're not flexible enough to line the edges of the pan, just microwave them for about 1 minute to make them flexible and easy to work with.

Serves 4 to 6 as a main

FILLING

2 tablespoons extra virgin olive oil

3 red onions, chopped

2 tablespoons apple cider vinegar

One 13.5-ounce (400 ml) can coconut cream

3 tablespoons arrowroot flour

1 tablespoon ground flaxseed

2 teaspoons ashwagandha powder, optional

2 teaspoons maca powder, optional

½ cup (120 ml) aquafaba (see page 5), chilled

POTATO CRUST

1 tablespoon extra virgin olive oil

1 pound (450 g) waxy potatoes (such as red or Yukon Gold), peeled and cut into ⅛-inch (3 mm) slices

TOPPING

4 zucchini and/or yellow squash, thinly sliced

1 tablespoon extra virgin olive oil

Lion's Mane Cakes
FOR COGNITION

Gluten-Free ◆ No Sugar Added ◆ Nut-Free

Medicinal mushrooms are nature's health powerhouses, but lion's mane (*Hericium erinaceus*) stand out for their brain-boosting properties. They also bring a delicate, tender texture and a subtly sweet flavor that mimics crab meat. Fittingly, the crab is a symbol of wisdom, which is the magic served in this plant-based take on crispy crab cakes. Golden on the outside with a moist, tender center, these patties deliver potent brain support and a satisfying crunch in every bite.

Serves 4 as a main

- ¼ cup (60 ml) extra virgin olive oil
- 7 ounces (200 g) lion's mane mushrooms or white button mushrooms, finely chopped
- 1 small red onion, minced
- 4 small radishes, minced
- 2 scallions, minced
- 4 tablespoons dried gluten-free bread crumbs
- 2 tablespoons apple cider vinegar
- 2 tablespoons vegan mayonnaise
- 2 teaspoons vegan prepared horseradish
- 1 tablespoon arrowroot flour or cornstarch
- 2 tablespoons fresh parsley or cilantro leaves, optional
- Lemon wedges, for serving

1 Heat 2 tablespoons of the oil in a large pan set over medium heat. Add the mushrooms and sauté, stirring occasionally, until they release their moisture and become golden brown, 15 to 20 minutes, increasing the temperature to high near the end of the cooking time to give them a sear.

2 Transfer the mushrooms to a bowl and add the onion, radishes, scallions, half of the bread crumbs, apple cider vinegar, mayonnaise, horseradish, and arrowroot flour. Season with salt and pepper and mix well.

3 Spread the remaining bread crumbs in a thin layer over a plate. Divide the mushroom mixture into 4 portions and shape them into patties. Coat both sides of each patty with the bread crumbs, pressing gently to help the crumbs adhere. This will make the patties extra crispy.

4 Return the pan to medium heat and add the remaining oil. Cook the patties for 3 to 4 minutes on each side, until they develop a golden crust.

5 Garnish the "crab" cakes with the parsley, if using, and serve them warm with lemon wedges on the side.

TIP: To amplify the anti-inflammatory benefits, add 1 teaspoon of fresh grated (or powdered) turmeric to the patty mixture.

MAGICAL BENEFITS

Nerve Growth Factor ◆ Lion's mane mushrooms are rich in compounds that help the body stimulate nerve growth factor, which supports the growth of nerve and brain cells, neuroplasticity, and cognitive function.

Antioxidants ◆ Mushrooms like lion's mane are rich in antioxidants with anti-inflammatory effects targeting the brain, helping to combat oxidative stress and inflammation linked to neurodegenerative diseases and cognitive decline.

Hericenones and Erinacines ◆ These active compounds in lion's mane support the systems involved in the production and balance of serotonin and dopamine, which play crucial roles in mood regulation, memory, and overall cognitive function.

Blueberry Pizza
FOR HEART SUPPORT

Gluten-Free ✦ No Sugar Added ✦ Nut-Free

Who says that heart-healthy foods can't come in the form of a pizza? This summery pizza takes a crispy flatbread crust and transforms it into a sweet-and-savory delight. The balsamic caramelized onions and tangy blueberries, the crunch of the golden crust, the rich sweetness of the onions, and the bright, juicy pops of fruit are sure to make you fall in love!

1   Preheat the oven to 400°F (200°C). Grease 2 rimmed baking sheets or line them with parchment paper.

2   **To make the flatbread pizza,** mix the gluten-free flour, corn flour, arrowroot flour, garlic powder, salt, and pepper together in a bowl. Add the oil and, while mixing, gradually incorporate just enough water to achieve a thin pancake batter–like consistency, starting with 1½ cups (360 ml) and adding up to 1 cup (240 ml) more, a few tablespoons at a time.

3   Spread the batter onto the prepared baking sheets, creating two 10- to 12-inch (25 to 30 cm) pizza crusts. Bake for 20 minutes, until the edges are light golden brown. Remove from the oven and set aside. Increase the oven temperature to 430°F (220°C).

4   **To make the onion-blueberry topping,** while the crust bakes, add the oil to a large pan and sauté the onions over medium-high heat for 15 to 20 minutes, until caramelized, stirring frequently and adjusting the temperature as needed to prevent burning. Deglaze with a splash of water whenever the onions begin to stick and scrape the bottom of the pan to reincorporate any browned bits.

5   Add the coconut milk, reduce the heat, and let simmer for about 10 minutes, or until it has the consistency of a thick, spreadable sauce. Season with salt and pepper.

6   Spread the onion mixture evenly over the pizzas, leaving a perimeter around the edges for the crust. Sprinkle the blueberries evenly over the top. Bake the pizzas for 10 minutes, or until the blueberries are slightly softened and the crust is deep golden brown.

7   Garnish with fresh basil leaves, an extra drizzle of olive oil, and a sprinkle of freshly ground black pepper. Enjoy straight from the oven or cold!

TIP: The cooking process destroys some of the blueberries' antioxidants but enhances others. Consider sprinkling with a few fresh blueberries just before serving to get their full antioxidant profile.

Serves 2 to 4 as a main

FLATBREAD PIZZA

1 cup (120 g) all-purpose gluten-free flour blend (see page 5)

1 cup (120 g) fine corn flour or cornmeal

¼ cup (30 g) arrowroot flour

1 teaspoon garlic powder

½ teaspoon salt

¼ teaspoon pepper

¼ cup plus 2 tablespoons (90 ml) extra virgin olive oil, plus more for drizzling

ONION-BLUEBERRY TOPPING

2 tablespoons extra virgin olive oil

3 onions, thinly sliced

¼ cup plus 2 tablespoons (90 ml) coconut milk

⅔ cup (110 g) blueberries

¼ cup (5 g) fresh basil leaves

MAGICAL BENEFITS

Anthocyanins ✦ Blueberries are rich in antioxidants, particularly anthocyanins, which help combat the LDL (bad) cholesterol that contributes to plaque buildup in arteries.

Allicin ✦ Released when onions are crushed or chopped, this sulfur-containing compound can help lower LDL cholesterol levels by reducing its production in the liver and promoting its removal from the body.

Quercetin ✦ Quercetin, found in blueberries and onions, may aid in blood vessel relaxation (vasodilation), improving blood flow and regulating blood pressure.

Summer • Mains & Sides

Rainbow Antioxidant Roots
FOR IMMUNITY

Gluten-Free ✦ Nut-Free

This warm salad showcases beets and radishes, seared to bring out their natural sweetness. The antioxidant-packed dressing is made from the Hawthorn-Hibiscus Tonic (page 257) that is infused with immune system–supporting magic, but apple cider vinegar can be substituted if you like. To make this a heartier main, pair it with a protein-rich and antioxidant-filled grain such as amaranth, buckwheat, or quinoa.

Serves 4 as a main or 6 as a side

1 tablespoon extra virgin olive oil
1 onion, chopped
8 small beets
8 small, colorful radishes
1 apple, chopped

HIBISCUS-SCALLION DRESSING

2 tablespoons Hawthorn-Hibiscus Tonic (page 257) or apple cider vinegar
2 tablespoons agave
1 tablespoon extra-virgin olive oil
1 inch (2.5 cm) piece of ginger, grated
2 scallions, diced
5 fresh mint, basil, dill, or chive sprigs, minced

> **MAGICAL BENEFITS**
>
> **Glucosinolates** ✦ Chopping or chewing radishes breaks down glucosinolates, compounds in cruciferous vegetables that help protect them from pests, into bioactive compounds with antioxidant and anti-inflammatory effects.
>
> **Natural Nitrates** ✦ Unlike harmful nitrates found in processed foods, the natural nitrates found in beets act as a natural vasodilator and anti-inflammatory, potentially inducing cancer cell death.
>
> **Betanins** ✦ These antioxidant pigments give beets their deep red color, neutralize free radicals, decrease inflammation, and may help inhibit cancer cell growth.

1 Heat the oil in a large pan over medium-high heat. Add the onion and cook for 15 to 20 minutes, until caramelized, stirring frequently and adjusting the temperature as needed to prevent burning. Deglaze with a splash of water whenever the onions begin to stick and scrape the bottom of the pan to reincorporate any browned bits.

2 While the onion cooks, bring a large saucepan of water to a boil over high heat. Boil the beets for about 15 minutes, or until just beginning to soften, then blanch in cold water and peel. Add the beets to the radish mixture and continue to sauté for another 10 minutes, until tender enough to be easily pierced with a fork.

3 When the onions are caramelized, increase the heat to high and add the radishes and apple. Sauté for 5 to 10 minutes, until the radishes begin to brown, then lower the heat to medium.

4 **To make the hibiscus-scallion dressing,** while the vegetables cook, whisk together the Hawthorn-Hibiscus Tonic, agave, oil, ginger, and scallions in a small bowl. Season with salt and pepper.

5 Pour the dressing into the pan with the vegetables and stir well to coat. Cook for about 10 minutes, stirring occasionally, until the dressing caramelizes and forms a glaze, ensuring the flavors meld, then sprinkle half of the mint leaves over the vegetables and stir gently to incorporate.

6 Transfer the salad to a serving dish. Garnish with the remaining fresh mint, and serve.

TIP: To increase the protective actions of this culinary magic, add broccoli or brussels sprouts to the mix, as these are also good sources of glucosinolates.

Corn Chowder
FOR SATIETY

Gluten-Free ✦ No Sugar Added ✦ Nut-Free

Sometimes the key to healthy weight maintenance comes in the form of an indulgent chowder. Made with corn, squash, and coconut milk, this chowder is filled with fiber, healthy fats, and nutrients to help you feel full and nourished. To make this soup a heartier main, pair it with a filling protein-rich grain like amaranth, buckwheat, or quinoa.

1 Heat ¼ cup (60 ml) of the oil in a large saucepan over medium heat. Add the squash and sauté for 15 to 20 minutes, until softened and slightly golden brown. Add the corn and continue to sauté for 2 to 3 minutes, until tender.

2 Pour in the vegetable broth, coconut milk, and white balsamic vinegar. Stir in most of the basil, reserving some for serving, then bring the mixture to a gentle simmer. Simmer for about 10 minutes to cook the corn and meld the flavors. Season with salt and pepper and adjust the richness and acidity with more oil and/or vinegar to taste.

3 Divide the chowder between individual bowls or serve family style. Drizzle individual portions with the remaining oil and garnish with the reserved basil and a sprinkle of freshly ground black pepper to make the flavors of that first bite stand out!

TIP: You can purée the soup with a blender or an immersion blender if you prefer a creamier texture.

Serves 4 as a main or 6 as a side

¼ cup (60 ml) plus 1 tablespoon extra virgin olive oil

2 yellow squash, thinly sliced

4 ears fresh corn, kernels cut from the cobs, or about 4 cups (650 g) thawed frozen or canned corn kernels

4¼ cups (1 L) vegetable broth or water

One 13.5-ounce (400 ml) can coconut milk

2 tablespoons white balsamic vinegar or apple cider vinegar

1 cup (20 g) fresh chopped basil

MAGICAL BENEFITS

Healthy Fats ✦ Coconut cream provides satiety-promoting medium-chain triglycerides (MCTs), while olive oil offers healthy monounsaturated fats, both aiding fullness cues.

Magnesium ✦ Yellow squash, corn, and coconut all contain this essential mineral, which plays a role in energy production, blood sugar regulation, and muscle function, contributing to hunger management and satiety.

Dietary Fiber ✦ Corn and yellow squash are high in fiber, which adds bulk, slows digestion, and supports lasting feelings of fullness.

Savory Fruit Sauté
FOR RESTFUL SLEEP

Gluten-Free ✦ *No Sugar Added* ✦ *Nut-Free*

At times, it can feel like deep and restful sleep can be achieved only with a sleeping spell of fairytale proportions. Sleep is a complicated process that requires multiple systems in the body to align. Although fruit might be an unusual ingredient in a savory dish, the combination is delicious. The interplay of flavors and textures—the tender squash, the lightly charred cherries, and the nutty, fluffy quinoa—make this dish as satisfying as it is sleep-supporting, and for a truly restful sleeping spell, pair the dish with a cup of TranquiliTea (page 262)!

Serves 4 as a main

- 2 tablespoons extra virgin olive oil
- 2 yellow squash, thinly sliced
- 2 garlic cloves, minced
- 4 plums, pitted, halved, and sliced
- 1 cup (210 g) tart cherries, halved and pitted
- 3 tablespoons balsamic vinegar
- 2 cups (400 g) cooked quinoa
- Fresh basil leaves

1 Heat the oil in a large pan over medium-high heat. Add the yellow squash and cook for 10 to 15 minutes, stirring often. Deglaze with a splash of water whenever the squash begins to stick and scrape the bottom of the pan to reincorporate any browned bits, until the squash has reduced in size by half and become tender, slightly crispy, and golden brown at the edges.

2 Once the squash is caramelized to your liking, add the garlic and sauté for 1 minute until fragrant. Reduce the heat to medium and add all but a few of the plum slices and halved cherries, reserving some for serving. Season with salt and pepper. Cook for an additional 5 to 10 minutes, until the fruit has browned slightly but still maintain their shape.

3 Increase the heat to high and add the balsamic vinegar. Cook for 2 to 3 minutes to create a glaze before removing the pan from the heat.

4 Spread the quinoa over a serving dish and top with the sautéed squash and fruit, or serve the quinoa on the side. Garnish with the fresh basil and reserved plum slices and cherries, and serve.

TIP: If you like, you can substitute other tryptophan-dense grains or legumes, such as chickpeas, brown rice, or lentils, for the quinoa.

MAGICAL BENEFITS

Melatonin ✦ This hormone and antioxidant, found in foods like tart cherries, helps regulate circadian rhythms by signaling the brain to prepare for sleep and improve sleep quality.

Magnesium ✦ Found in yellow squash, magnesium activates the relaxation-inducing parasympathetic nervous system and reduces stress. It also helps convert tryptophan, an essential amino acid needed for protein synthesis, to serotonin, then to melatonin.

Potassium ✦ This important mineral present in yellow squash and plums supports muscle relaxation, which is essential for falling asleep and maintaining deep sleep stages.

Sunny Summer Pasta
FOR EUPHORIA

Gluten-Free ✦ *No Sugar Added* ✦ *Nut-Free*

While pasta is always a good idea, this one brings an extra dose of joy! Protein-packed chickpea pasta is enveloped in a light but creamy coconut sauce brightened with lemon zest and mixed with caramelized yellow squash and corn. For a euphoric pairing, serve the Strawberry-Lemon Squares (page 63) for dessert.

1 Add the oil to a large pan and cook the squash over high heat for 10 to 15 minutes, until the squash is reduced in size by half, tender yet slightly crispy, and golden brown at the edges. Stir regularly. Deglaze with a splash of water whenever the squash begins to stick and scrape the bottom of the pan to reincorporate any browned bits.

2 Add the corn and sauté for another 10 minutes, or until tender, adding the lemon juice little by little to prevent sticking and scraping any browned bits from the bottom of the pan.

3 Reduce the heat to medium, add the coconut milk, and let it simmer for 10 to 15 minutes, until thickened. Stir in half of the lemon zest, reserving the rest for serving. Season with salt and pepper.

4 While the sauce cooks, bring a large saucepan of salted water to a boil over high heat and cook the pasta according to the package instructions. Reserve a few tablespoons of the pasta water to help thicken the sauce, then drain.

5 Stir the pasta and reserved cooking water into the squash and corn sauce, then divide the pasta between individual plates. Garnish with the reserved lemon zest and Cashew Cheese, if using, before serving.

TIP: To save time, instead of making the cashew cheese, simply garnish with chopped cashews! If leaving out the cashew cheese to make this recipe nut-free, try garnishing it with a sprinkle of nutritional yeast instead.

Serves 2 as a main

- 2 tablespoons extra virgin olive oil
- 2 or 3 small yellow squash, sliced
- 3 ears fresh corn, kernels cut from the cobs, or about 3 cups (500 g) thawed frozen or canned corn kernels
- Juice and grated zest of 2 lemons
- ¾ cup (180 ml) canned coconut milk
- 4 ounces (115 g) chickpea pasta
- ½ cup (110 g) Cashew Cheese (page 229) for serving, optional

MAGICAL BENEFITS

Choline ✦ Found in high quantities in chickpeas, corn, and squash, choline helps to produce acetylcholine, a neurotransmitter involved in mood regulation, memory, and muscle control.

Complex Carbohydrates ✦ Starch and fiber-based carbs in the squash, corn, and chickpeas help regulate mood by providing the brain with a steady release of glucose and supporting the production of the neurotransmitters crucial for mood, memory, and learning.

Tryptophan ✦ This amino acid found in foods like chickpeas and cashews is used by the body to produce mood-lifting serotonin.

Roasted Eggplant
FOR COGNITION

Gluten-Free ✦ Nut-Free

Packed with antioxidants that protect brain cells, this recipe harnesses the power of eggplant to support mental clarity. The eggplant is infused with vinegar and olive oil before being roasted, to cut through the natural bitterness from its beneficial chlorogenic acids. For an even deeper flavor, the eggplant is baked twice: first, to achieve velvety tenderness, then to crisp the caramelized onion and bread crumb topping. A bed of protein-rich amaranth (which can be substituted with buckwheat or quinoa if you like) soaks up the flavorful sauce while fueling both body and mind.

Serves 4 as a main

- 2 eggplants, halved lengthwise
- ¾ cup (180 ml) apple cider vinegar
- ½ cup plus 2 tablespoons (150 ml) extra virgin olive oil
- ¼ cup (60 ml) agave
- 3 large white onions, chopped
- ½ cup (60 g) dried gluten-free bread crumbs
- ¼ cup (5 g) fresh basil leaves
- ¾ cup (140 g) amaranth

MAGICAL BENEFITS

Chlorogenic Acid ✦ Found in eggplants, this antioxidant provides anti-inflammatory benefits that help protect nerve and brain cells, support blood flow, and regulate neurotransmitters, and may aid in mood, memory, and cognition.

Anthocyanins ✦ Deep-purple plants like eggplants are rich in these dietary antioxidants, which protect brain cells from oxidative stress and inflammation.

Nasunin ✦ An antioxidant found in the skin of eggplants, nasunin is known for its neuroprotective effects, including its ability to help maintain the integrity of cell membranes in the brain.

1 Preheat the oven to 400°F (200°C).

2 Cut a crosshatch pattern into the cut side of each eggplant half. (This will allow the sauce to penetrate and flavor the eggplant more deeply.) Place the eggplant halves cut side up in a large oven-safe pan or baking dish. Pour the vinegar evenly over the eggplant, followed by ¼ cup (60 ml) of the oil and the agave.

3 Bake for 30 to 40 minutes, until the eggplants' flesh is tender and golden, then remove from the oven, leaving the oven on.

4 While the eggplants bake, add 2 tablespoons of the oil to a large pan and sauté the onions over medium-high heat for 15 to 20 minutes, until caramelized, stirring frequently. Deglaze with a splash of water whenever the onions begin to stick and scrape the bottom of the pan to reincorporate any browned bits.

5 Top the eggplant with the caramelized onions. Season with salt and pepper, then top with the bread crumbs, and finish by drizzling the remaining oil evenly across the bread crumbs to help them crisp. Return to the oven for an additional 15 minutes, or until the bread crumb topping is crisp and golden brown.

6 While the eggplant bakes, prepare the amaranth. In a medium saucepan, combine the amaranth with enough salted water (about 1½ cups/360 ml) to cover by about ½ inch (1.25 cm). Bring to a boil, then reduce heat to medium, cover, and simmer for 15 to 20 minutes. Remove from the heat and let sit, covered, for 5 minutes.

7 Fluff the amaranth with a fork, then spread it in a serving dish and top with the eggplant, or serve the eggplant directly from the baking dish with the amaranth on the side. Serve hot with an extra sprinkle of salt and freshly ground black pepper.

TIP: If you enjoy eggplants but struggle with their histamines, remove their skin! While the skin contains many powerful antioxidants, it also contains compounds that may trigger an inflammatory reaction for those with sensitivities.

Pesto Avocado Salad
FOR HORMONE BALANCE

Gluten-Free

Revered by the Aztecs for their fertility-enhancing and aphrodisiac properties, avocados were central to rituals celebrating vitality and potency. Inspired by this ancient wisdom, this simple but hearty salad combines creamy avocado slices with the zesty nut-and-herb-based Magic Pesto (page 137). An extra drizzle of lemon juice and olive oil enhances the pesto's flavor, while scallions and protein-rich chia seeds add brightness and crunch. To make this a heartier main, serve it with a protein-rich grain like amaranth, buckwheat, or quinoa.

1 Whisk together the Magic Pesto, oil, and lemon juice in a small bowl until combined.

2 Divide the avocado slices between individual plates, then drizzle with the dressing and garnish with the scallions and chia seeds, a final drizzle of extra virgin olive oil, and some freshly ground black pepper.

TIP: If you like, you can purée all the ingredients into a creamy dressing that can be used on salads or pasta, or served alongside raw or cooked vegetables. This is a great way to use up any leftovers!

Serves 2 as a main or 4 as a side

¼ cup (60 g) Magic Pesto (page 137)

2 tablespoons extra virgin olive oil, plus more for serving

2 tablespoons lemon juice

2 avocados, halved, pitted, and sliced

Thinly sliced scallions

Chia seeds

MAGICAL BENEFITS

Monounsaturated Fats ✦ Avocados and extra virgin olive oil are rich in monounsaturated fats, which support hormone production and balance, including of sex hormones essential for fertility.

Zinc ✦ This trace mineral present in walnuts is key for the production and regulation of reproductive hormones such as testosterone, estrogen, and progesterone.

Omega-3 Fatty Acids ✦ Found in chia seeds, walnuts, and almonds, these healthy fats support reproductive health by calming inflammation, protecting cells, and helping hormones work properly.

Shielding Succotash
FOR PROTECTION

Gluten-Free ✦ *Nut-Free*

This vibrant succotash draws inspiration from the traditional Native American dish *msíckquatash,* named from the Algonquian word for broken corn kernels. Packed with antioxidants and protective nutrients, this summery variation highlights the natural sweetness of corn and bell peppers, balanced by caramelized onions and a splash of lemon.

Serves 6 as a side

2 tablespoons extra virgin olive oil

3 white onions, finely chopped

4 bell peppers, preferably a mix of yellow, orange, and red, diced

2 ears fresh corn, kernels cut from the cobs, or about 2 cups (325 g) thawed frozen or canned corn kernels

Grated zest and juice of ½ lemon

1 tablespoon agave

1 Heat the oil in a large pan over high heat. Add the onions and sauté for about 15 to 20 minutes, until caramelized, stirring frequently and adjusting the temperature as needed to prevent burning. Deglaze with a splash of water whenever they begin to stick and scrape the bottom of the pan to reincorporate any browned bits.

2 Add the peppers and corn and continue sautéing for another 10 to 15 minutes, until tender and speckled brown.

3 Stir in the lemon zest, lemon juice, and agave and season with salt and pepper. Serve warm or cold.

TIP: For a heartier version of this recipe that adheres even more closely to traditional Native American succotash, add cooked beans—black, lima, navy, or cannellini beans are all suitable.

MAGICAL BENEFITS

Quercetin ✦ Found in onions, bell peppers, and corn, this protective antioxidant has anti-inflammatory and immune-supporting properties that may help prevent DNA damage.

Carotenoids ✦ These pigments, including beta-carotene, give bell peppers and corn their vibrant colors, provide immunity-supporting antioxidant and anti-inflammatory benefits, and protect DNA from oxidative damage.

Vitamin C ✦ This potent antioxidant plays a crucial role in helping to neutralize free-radicals, unstable molecules that can cause cellular damage.

Honeydew-Basil Salad
FOR HYDRATION

Gluten-Free ✦ *Nut-Free*

During the hot days of summer, it's important to drink extra water, but you can also stay hydrated by consuming high-water-content plants like the juicy honeydew melon slices in this salad, which pair perfectly with the peppery basil. The melon's sweetness is offset by the sharp lime vinaigrette. For added protein, top with a sprinkle of Cashew Cheese (page 229) or a few spoonfuls of soft tofu for a nut-free option.

1 **To make the lime dressing,** whisk together the lime zest, lime juice, vinegar, oil, and agave in a small bowl. Season with salt and pepper.

2 **To make the salad,** divide the melon slices between 4 individual plates, or 1 large serving plate to serve family style. Drizzle the dressing evenly over the melon slices. Top with the basil and cashew cheese, if using. Sprinkle with flaky salt, if using, and freshly ground black pepper before serving.

TIP: To increase this recipe's hydrating power, add some sliced watermelon. And for more antioxidants and detox support, add a few cooled boiled beet slices.

Serves 4 as a side

LIME DRESSING

Grated zest and juice of 2 limes

2 tablespoons apple cider vinegar

2 tablespoons extra virgin olive oil

½ teaspoon agave

SALAD

1 honeydew melon, rind cut away, seeded, and cut into ½-inch (1.25 cm) slices

1 cup (20 g) fresh basil leaves

¾ cup (170 g) Cashew Cheese (page 229) for serving, optional

Flaky salt, optional

MAGICAL BENEFITS

High Water Content ✦ Many hydrating foods, like melons, are around 90 percent water. While drinking water is essential, eating water-rich fruits and vegetables as well makes it easier to stay hydrated.

Electrolytes ✦ Potassium and magnesium—electrolytes abundant in melons and present in smaller amounts in limes—help the kidneys regulate sodium and fluid levels in the blood while supporting muscle and cardiovascular health.

Blueberry-Beet Salad
FOR COGNITION

Gluten-Free ✦ No Sugar Added ✦ Nut-Free

Since the brain has fewer internal, self-generated antioxidant defenses compared to other organs, consuming antioxidant-rich plants—like the blueberries, beets, arugula, and chia seeds in this salad—is key for neurological health. The vinaigrette is made from Adaptogenic Vinegar (page 192), which is infused with brain-supportive herbs.

Serves 4 as a side

6 cups (140 g) arugula

2 raw beets, thinly sliced

1 cup (150 g) fresh blueberries, plus more for serving

¼ cup (40 g) chia seeds or hemp seeds, plus more for serving

¼ cup (60 ml) extra virgin olive oil

¼ to ½ cup (60 to 120 ml) Adaptogenic Vinegar (page 192) or apple cider vinegar

1 Combine the arugula, beets, and blueberries in a large salad bowl, then sprinkle with the chia seeds.

2 Just before serving, whisk together the oil and vinegar and drizzle evenly with the vinaigrette. Season with salt and pepper. Start with a smaller portion and add more according to taste.

3 Toss gently to ensure even distribution of the ingredients and vinaigrette, then divide the salad among individual plates and garnish with extra blueberries and seeds. Garnish with freshly ground pepper and serve.

TIP: If you anticipate having leftovers, serve the vinegar on the side and refrigerate any leftover salad and vinegar separately. This can help to avoid food waste, as the leftover salad will stay fresh and crisp instead of going soggy.

MAGICAL BENEFITS

Natural Nitrates ✦ Unlike harmful nitrates in processed foods, the natural nitrates in beets and arugula support brain health by enhancing oxygen and nutrient delivery.

Anthocyanins ✦ Abundant in blueberries, these antioxidants support neuronal signaling, boost blood flow to the brain, and reduce oxidative damage and inflammation.

Omega-3 Fatty Acids ✦ ALA, a type of omega-3 fatty acid found in chia and hemp seeds, is essential for brain cell health and communication, helping to reduce neural inflammation associated with cognitive disorders such as dementia.

Cucumber-Fennel Salad
FOR DIGESTION

Gluten-Free ◆ Nut-Free

This fresh and crisp salad features the cooling crunch of cucumbers and fennel coated in a zesty lemon-dill dressing. Perfect as a side for a dish like the Zucchini Quiche (page 81) or the Corn Chowder (page 89), this salad is especially delightful during the hot summer months, helping to soothe the digestive system and body as a whole. For an extra gut-soothing effect, chill the salad for 20 minutes before serving. This will allow the vinegar in the dressing to begin breaking down some of the fiber, making it easier to digest.

1 To make the lemon-dill vinaigrette, whisk together the oil, lemon zest, lemon juice, and agave in a small bowl. Season with salt and pepper and adjust the acidity and sweetness with more lemon juice and/or agave to taste.

2 To make the salad, combine the cucumbers and fennel in a large bowl. Add the vinaigrette and toss gently to coat. Garnish with the dill and lemon zest and finish with a sprinkle of salt and freshly ground black pepper.

TIP: To imbue the salad with even more digestive benefits, consider adding whole or ground fennel seeds to the dressing. The seed of the fennel plant has even higher anethole concentrations than the bulb or dill!

Serves 6 as a side

LEMON-DILL VINAIGRETTE
¼ cup (60 ml) extra virgin olive oil
Grated zest and juice of 1 lemon
1 to 2 teaspoons agave

SALAD
4 cocktail cucumbers or 1 large cucumber, thinly sliced
1 fennel bulb, cored and very thinly sliced
4 fresh dill sprigs, divided into fronds
Grated zest of 1 lemon

MAGICAL BENEFITS

Anethole ◆ This compound found in fennel and dill acts as a natural defense mechanism in plants to deter herbivores while attracting pollinators. Anethole relaxes our digestive tract muscles, easing indigestion, bloating, and gas.

Fiber ◆ Fennel is rich in both soluble and insoluble fiber, which help prevent constipation.

High Water Content ◆ Water-rich cucumbers and fennel gently hydrate the intestines. This helps support regular, easy-to-pass bowel movements, providing digestive benefits that complement drinking water.

Lemony Okra and Squash
FOR DIGESTION

Gluten-Free ◆ *No Sugar Added* ◆ *Nut-Free*

Certain plants, like okra, have a unique ability to retain moisture through their mucilage, a gel-like substance that soothes and protects the digestive system. Roasting turns infamously slimy okra into a delightfully crispy complement to the tender, caramelized yellow squash. Lemon zest and basil lift and refresh the dish. Serve as a side with the Corn Chowder (page 89) or, to make this a heartier main, toss it with a warm, protein-rich grain like amaranth, buckwheat, or quinoa.

Serves 4 as a main or 4 to 6 as a side

- 4 yellow squash, cut into ¼-inch (6 mm) slices
- 8 ounces (225 g) okra, sliced
- 2 tablespoons extra virgin olive oil
- One 1-inch (2.5 cm) piece of fresh ginger, grated
- Grated zest and juice of 1 lemon, plus more zest for serving
- 4 fresh basil leaves, minced

1. Preheat the oven to 400°F (200°C).

2. Add the squash and okra to a large bowl with the oil, ginger, lemon zest, and lemon juice, and toss until evenly coated.

3. Once the oven is hot, spread the vegetable mixture in a single layer on a rimmed baking sheet. Roast for 20 to 30 minutes, until the vegetables are tender and slightly golden, turning them halfway through to ensure even roasting.

4. Remove from the oven and transfer to a serving dish or individual plates. Sprinkle with the basil and garnish with the extra lemon zest, a sprinkle of salt, and freshly ground black pepper. Serve warm.

TIP: For extra digestion-supporting magic (and crunch!), consider sprinkling with a few teaspoons of mucilage fiber–filled chia seeds just before serving.

MAGICAL BENEFITS

Mucilage ◆ Okra contains mucilage, a type of soluble fiber that draws water into the gut, soothing and protecting the digestive tract and aiding digestion.

Soluble Fiber ◆ Okra and squash are rich in soluble fiber, which forms a gel-like substance in the gut. This softens stool, slows digestion, and aids nutrient absorption, helping prevent constipation.

Insoluble Fiber ◆ Okra and squash also contain insoluble fiber, which adds bulk to stool and stimulates intestinal contractions to promote regularity.

Raw Corn and Squash Salad
FOR GLOWING SKIN

Gluten-Free

Connective tissues are the body's structural glue, forming everything from skin and hair to ligaments and bones. This light yet satisfying golden-hued salad focuses on your skin, nourishing to give it a healthy, radiant glow. Each bite offers a refreshing crunch, with the sweetness of fresh corn and the crisp, delicate flavor of thinly sliced raw yellow squash balanced by basil and a hint of bright lemon zest in a vinaigrette made with Magic Pesto (page 137).

1 **To make the magic pesto vinaigrette,** whisk together the Magic Pesto, oil, and lemon juice in a small bowl. Season with salt.

2 **To make the salad,** add the corn and squash to a large salad bowl. Add the vinaigrette and toss gently to coat. Garnish with the basil leaves and sprinkle with the lemon zest before serving.

TIP: If you like, instead of serving the vegetables raw, you can sauté the corn and squash in extra virgin olive oil for 5 to 10 minutes. This will render the dish easier to digest, although some of its vitamin C will be destroyed during the cooking process.

Serves 4 as a side

MAGIC PESTO VINAIGRETTE

¼ cup (60 g) Magic Pesto (page 137)

3 tablespoons extra virgin olive oil

2 tablespoons lemon juice, plus grated zest for serving

SALAD

4 ears fresh corn, kernels cut from the cobs, or about 4 cups (650 g) thawed frozen or canned corn kernels

2 yellow squash, thinly sliced

Fresh basil leaves

MAGICAL BENEFITS

Manganese ◆ This trace mineral found in corn, yellow squash, and basil is used by the body to produce collagen and other structural molecules necessary for healthy tendons and ligaments.

Carotenoids ◆ These antioxidant pigments convert to vitamin A, which supports collagen formation, skin health, and immune function. They also protect connective tissues by neutralizing free radicals and preventing damaging oxidative stress.

Vitamin C ◆ Plants like basil, corn, and yellow squash are rich in vitamin C, an antioxidant crucial for the structural formation and repair of skin, tendons, ligaments, and blood vessels.

Baby Greens and Radish Salad
FOR DIGESTION

Gluten-Free ✦ *Nut-Free*

This side salad combines the peppery snap of radishes, the sweetness of spring onions, and the tender, earthy bite of baby greens. Tossed in the refreshing and versatile Simple Dressing (page 133), a tangy, shallot-and-garlic vinaigrette, it's perfect as a palate-awakening starter or a light, cooling accompaniment. This salad also pairs beautifully with digestion-friendly mains like the Asparagus and Pea Quiche (page 31) or the Corn Chowder (page 89).

Serves 4 as a side

4 cups (120 g) loosely packed mixed baby greens

8 small radishes, thinly sliced

4 spring onions, white parts only, thinly sliced

¼ to ⅓ cup (60 to 80 ml) Simple Dressing (page 133)

1 Combine the greens, radishes, and spring onions in a large salad bowl.

2 Drizzle the Simple Dressing over the salad and toss gently to coat. Season with salt and pepper. Serve immediately.

TIP: For an extra boost to digestion, try adding slices of fruits like papaya, pineapple, mango, avocado, banana, or kiwi, all of which contain natural enzymes that help break down food and support overall digestion.

MAGICAL BENEFITS

Insoluble Fiber ✦ Spring onions, radishes, and baby greens provide fiber, primarily insoluble, that supports regularity, prevents constipation, and promotes a healthy gut microbiome.

Prebiotic Fiber ✦ Spring onions, garlic, and radishes contain prebiotic fibers that feed beneficial gut bacteria and ferment in the colon, producing short-chain fatty acids and other compounds that support the health of the intestinal lining.

Organosulfur ✦ These sulfur-containing compounds in garlic and onions, and to a lesser extent radishes, stimulate bile production, which aids in fat digestion.

Peach and Flower Salad
FOR SUN PROTECTION

Gluten-Free ✦ Nut-Free

What's a better accompaniment for sunny summer days than a protective salad of sun-kissed peaches and a rainbow of edible flowers? The tangy-sweet, hibiscus-infused Flower Vinaigrette (page 199) ties together the peppery crispness of watercress and the delicate pansies and roses, and all work together to shield your skin from free-radical sun damage. This light salad is a beautiful side for the energizing Lentil-Chard Plant Parcels (page 19).

1 Divide the watercress between individual plates. Top with the peach slices, then sprinkle with the edible flowers.

2 Drizzle each portion with the vinaigrette, then sprinkle with salt and freshly ground black pepper. Serve immediately.

TIP: You can sometimes find edible flowers at well-stocked grocery stores or farmers markets, but you can also consider foraging them! There are edible flowers hiding everywhere—maybe even in your own backyard. Just make sure to forage from areas free from pesticides and pollutants, and away from roadways.

Serves 2 to 4 as a side

2 handfuls (about 100 g) watercress, stems removed, leaves chopped into bite-size pieces

4 peaches, pitted and cut into ½-inch (1.25 cm) slices

1 cup (20 g) loosely packed culinary-grade pansies, roses, violets, marigolds, or white clover flowers

¼ cup (60 ml) Flower Vinaigrette (page 199), or 2 tablespoons extra virgin olive oil plus 2 tablespoons balsamic vinegar

MAGICAL BENEFITS

Antioxidants ✦ The vibrant colors of many flowers reflect their richness in vitamins like A, C, and E, and antioxidants like polyphenols, flavonoids, and anthocyanins, which all help protect skin cells against free-radical damage and support connective tissue repair.

Vitamin K ✦ Found in watercress and edible flowers like pansies, vitamin K supports skin healing and helps reduce redness and irritation by promoting healthy blood flow.

Chilled Melon-Cucumber Soup
FOR INFLAMMATION RELIEF

Gluten-Free ✦ No Sugar Added ✦ Nut-Free

While inflammation is a crucial part of the body's natural defenses against disease, too much or chronic inflammation can wreak havoc. This raw, chilled summer soup is a cooling antidote to the heat—both outside and within. The natural sweetness of cantaloupe blends with the hydrating cucumber, while basil and mint add a refreshing burst of flavor to create a silky, soothing soup. The chilling period helps the flavors develop and meld. Serve on hot summer nights alongside the Pesto Avocado Salad (page 97) or the Sunny Summer Pasta (page 93).

Serves 4 to 6 as a side

- 1 cantaloupe, rind cut away, seeded, and chopped
- 1 cucumber, chopped
- ½ white onion, chopped
- Grated zest and juice of 1 lemon
- 1 to 2 tablespoons white balsamic vinegar or apple cider vinegar
- 2 tablespoons extra virgin olive oil
- 8 to 10 fresh basil leaves
- 6 to 8 fresh mint leaves

1 Combine the cantaloupe, cucumber, onion, lemon zest, lemon juice, vinegar, 1 tablespoon of the oil, and about half of the basil and mint leaves in a blender or food processor and blend until smooth. (If you prefer a chunkier texture, pulse the mixture a few times to leave some small pieces.) Season with salt and pepper and adjust the acidity with more white balsamic vinegar to taste.

2 Chill for at least 2 hours or up to 1 day, then divide the soup among individual bowls. Drizzle with the remaining oil and garnish with the remaining basil and mint. Serve.

TIP: For a twist on this recipe, substitute the cantaloupe with watermelon, honeydew melon, or tomatoes, all of which contain a spectrum of beta-carotenoids, flavonoids, and considerable concentrations of vitamin C.

MAGICAL BENEFITS

Flavonoids ✦ Abundant in fruits, vegetables, and teas, flavonoids protect cells from damage, calm oxidative stress, and support the body's natural anti-inflammatory processes.

Vitamin C ✦ A potent antioxidant found in melons (but sensitive to heat), vitamin C combats inflammation by neutralizing cell-damaging free radicals.

Vitamin A ✦ Derived from the antioxidant pigment beta-carotene found in cantaloupe, vitamin A regulates immune responses and balances cytokine production to help prevent excessive inflammatory reactions.

Potato-Beet Salad
FOR HEART SUPPORT

Gluten-Free ✦ Nut-Free

This salad possesses a spectrum of healing antioxidants that specifically nourish the heart in all its functions. The beets' earthy sweetness and the buttery texture of the rainbow potatoes are balanced by a caper dressing infused with the protective magic of the Hawthorn-Hibiscus Tonic (page 257). This dish can be served as a substitute for a typical potato salad, or as a colorful accompaniment to the Blueberry Pizza (page 85). To make it a heartier main, serve it with a protein-rich grain like amaranth, buckwheat, or quinoa.

1 Bring a pot of salted water to a boil over high heat. Add the potatoes and beets and boil for 20 to 30 minutes, until tender enough to be pierced with a fork. Drain, then blanch the vegetables under cold water to cool them and make removing the peels easier.

2 Peel and place the potatoes and beets in a large bowl.

3 **To make the caper-hibiscus sauce,** while the vegetables boil, combine the coconut milk, mayonnaise, scallions, capers, Hawthorn-Hibiscus Tonic, and agave in a small bowl and whisk until thoroughly combined. Season with salt and pepper and adjust the sweetness and acidity with more agave and/or Hawthorn-Hibiscus Tonic to taste.

4 Pour the sauce over the potatoes and beets, gently stirring to coat evenly without breaking up the potatoes too much. Garnish with the dill and sprinkle with freshly ground black pepper just before serving.

TIP: This heart-supporting recipe can be modified to nourish another kind of vitality. To incorporate some libido-supporting magic, boil the beets and potatoes in 2 quarts (2 L) water that has been infused with 1 tablespoon dried maca root, ginseng root, tribulus terrestris plant, damiana leaves, or epimedium leaves, or about ½ teaspoon of each if using a blend. All of these plants stimulate actions related to arousal by balancing and stimulating sex hormones.

Serves 4 as a main or 6 as a side

1 pound (450 g) small rainbow potatoes

1 pound (450 g) small beets

2 scallions, minced

CAPER-HIBISCUS SAUCE

½ cup (120 ml) coconut milk or plant-based yogurt

3 tablespoons vegan mayonnaise

2 scallions, minced

2 tablespoons capers

2 tablespoon Hawthorn-Hibiscus Tonic (page 257) or apple cider vinegar

1½ teaspoons to 1 tablespoon agave

5 fresh dill sprigs, divided into fronds, or basil or chives, minced

MAGICAL BENEFITS

Betanins and Betacyanins ✦ Found in beets, these pigments with powerful antioxidant actions guard cardiovascular cells from oxidative stress and damage.

Natural Nitrates ✦ Unlike harmful nitrates found in processed foods, the natural nitrates in beets boost nitric oxide production to relax blood vessels, improve blood flow, and potentially lower blood pressure.

Chlorogenic Acid ✦ Found in capers, hibiscus, potatoes, and scallions, chlorogenic acid helps regulate blood pressure and reduce the risk of cardiovascular disease.

Tomato and Beet Soup
FOR STRENGTH

Gluten-Free ✦ Nut-Free

Inspired by the colors of a late summer sunset, this nutrient-packed soup supports muscle recovery and repair and features the rich reds of tomatoes, the earthy magentas of beets, and the glowing yellows and oranges of bell peppers. Verdant, sweet, and silky, it gets a subtle kick from fresh ginger and curry powder. For a heartier main, serve the soup with a protein-rich grain, or pair with the Shielding Succotash (page 98) for a complete meal.

Serves 4 to 6 as a main or 6 to 8 as a side

- 2 tablespoons extra virgin olive oil, plus more for drizzling
- 4 heirloom tomatoes, chopped
- 4 small beets and their greens, separated, chopped
- 3 onions, chopped
- 2 bell peppers, diced
- 1 small head of garlic (about 8 to 10 cloves), chopped
- ¼ cup (60 ml) red wine vinegar or apple cider vinegar
- One 2- to 3-inch (5 to 7.5 cm) piece of fresh ginger, grated
- 1½ to 2 teaspoons curry powder
- ¼ to ½ teaspoon ground cumin
- 2 quarts (2 L) vegetable broth or water
- ¼ cup (60 g) cold-pressed virgin coconut oil, melted
- Fresh herbs such as basil, thyme, or dill
- Coconut milk, optional

1 Heat the olive oil in a pot over medium heat. Stir in the tomatoes, beets, onions, bell peppers, and garlic and sauté for 20 to 30 minutes, until the onions are translucent and the peppers are tender. Stir frequently. Deglaze with the vinegar whenever the vegetables begin to stick and scrape the bottom of the pan to reincorporate any browned bits.

2 Stir in the ginger, curry powder, and cumin, then add the beet greens and pour in the vegetable broth and coconut oil. Increase the heat to high to bring the mixture to a boil, then reduce the heat to medium and cover to gently simmer. Simmer for at least 30 minutes to allow the flavors to meld. Season with salt and pepper and adjust the acidity and richness with more vinegar and/or olive oil to taste.

3 Divide the soup between individual bowls. Garnish with a sprinkle of fresh herbs, a drizzle of extra virgin olive oil, and a swirl of coconut milk, if using.

TIP: This soup is highly versatile, so feel free to vary the vegetables based on seasonal availability. If you have allergies, are following an elimination diet, or are sensitive to histamines—naturally occurring compounds in foods like tomatoes that can trigger reactions in some individuals—you can easily replace high-histamine tomatoes with magnesium-dense chard, kale, or collard greens.

MAGICAL BENEFITS

Allicin ✦ Garlic contains allicin, a sulfur compound with antioxidant and anti-inflammatory properties that may help reduce muscle inflammation caused by strenuous exercise.

Magnesium ✦ Tomatoes are a good source of magnesium, which aids muscle contraction, relaxation, and energy production. A deficiency can lead to cramps, spasms, and reduced exercise performance.

Natural Nitrates ✦ Unlike the harmful nitrates found in processed foods, the natural nitrates found in beets improve blood flow by dilating blood vessels and enhancing performance and recovery by ensuring muscles receive sufficient oxygen and nutrients during exercise.

Lychee-Cherry Soup
FOR CALM

Gluten-Free ◆ Nut-Free

This chilled fruit soup is a magic spell for those sweltering days when only a cold treat will bring relief. Infused with calming flower magic, it also supports the body's relaxation response. The juicy lychees and cherries meld with the refreshing mint and citrus notes of iced lemon balm tea. Serve following the Cucumber-Fennel Salad (page 105) or the Honeydew-Basil Salad (page 101) on a hot summer evening.

1 To make a concentrated lemon balm infusion, steep 10 to 12 of the fresh lemon balm leaves in ½ cup (120 ml) of hot water for 10 minutes, then strain, cover (to prevent volatile medicinal compounds from escaping), and refrigerate until completely cool.

2 Once the tea is cool, stir in the lychees and their syrup, cherries, lemon zest, and lemon juice.

3 Refrigerate for 1 to 2 hours, until chilled, then transfer the soup to the freezer for 20 to 30 minutes, until very cold. Garnish with the remaining herbs, and serve.

TIP: For an even more refreshing slushy version, separate the fruit from the liquid. Refrigerate the fruit and freeze the liquid for 2 to 4 hours, stirring occasionally to break up ice crystals as they form. Once the liquid reaches a slushy consistency, stir in the refrigerated fruit and serve immediately.

Serves 4 to 6

15 to 20 fresh lemon balm, vervain, or mint sprigs, leaves only

2 cups (about one 20-ounce or 590 ml can) lychees in syrup

1 pound (450 g) cherries, halved and pitted

Grated zest and juice of ½ lemon

MAGICAL BENEFITS

Linalool ◆ This active compound found in herbs such as lemon balm, vervain, and mint calms anxiety by interacting with GABA receptors and reducing excitatory signals.

Anthocyanins ◆ These antioxidant pigments in cherries help regulate mood-related neurotransmitters like serotonin, dopamine, and GABA by reducing oxidative stress and inflammation.

Vitamin C ◆ This antioxidant vitamin supports mood by reducing oxidative stress, supporting the production of mood-balancing neurotransmitters, and helping regulate the stress hormone cortisol.

Nectarine and Berry Galette
FOR ENERGY

Gluten-Free

Toward the end of summertime, long days and sun-warmed soil yield tangy blackberries and nectarines bursting with branch-ripened sweetness. This galette blends these seasonal energizing nutrients with a marzipan filling that practically melts into the fruit as it bakes, to make a dessert that is as indulgent as it is revitalizing. I like to use nectarines and blackberries, but you can also substitute any kind of stone fruit, such as peaches, or berry, such as blueberries.

Serves 4 to 6

MARZIPAN FILLING

¾ cup (170 g) packed light brown sugar

½ cup (60 g) almond flour

¼ cup (60 ml) coconut cream

CRUST

2 cups plus 1 tablespoon (250 g) all-purpose gluten-free flour blend (see page 5), plus more for dusting

1 cup plus 2 tablespoons (220 g) cane sugar

1 cup (120 g) almond flour

⅔ cup (80 g) arrowroot flour

¾ cup (180 ml) coconut cream

¼ cup plus 2 tablespoons (90 ml) extra virgin olive oil

3 nectarines, sliced

1 cup (140 g) blackberries

¼ cup (55 g) packed light brown sugar

Plant-based vanilla ice cream for serving, optional

1 Preheat the oven to 400°F (200°C). Line a rimmed baking sheet with parchment paper.

2 **To make the marzipan filling,** whisk together the brown sugar, almond flour, and coconut cream in a bowl until smooth, with the consistency of a thick cake batter. Set aside.

3 **To make the crust,** whisk together the gluten-free flour, sugar, almond flour, and arrowroot flour in a large bowl. Form a well in the dry ingredients, add the coconut cream and oil, and mix until a dense and sticky dough forms. Form the dough into a disk, wrap in plastic wrap, and refrigerate for about 30 minutes.

4 Once the dough is chilled, roll it into a circle ⅛- to ¼-inch (3 to 6 mm) thick on a well-floured surface, then carefully transfer it to the prepared baking sheet.

5 Spread the marzipan filling over the center of the dough, leaving a 2-inch (5 cm) border to fold over the filling. Arrange the nectarines and blackberries evenly over the marzipan. Sprinkle the brown sugar over the fruit. Working around the dough in a circle, fold the edges partway over the fruit, gently pinching the dough together where it overlaps. (Some of the filling in the middle of the galette should still be visible.)

6 Bake for about 30 minutes, until the filling is bubbling, the fruit is caramelized, and the crust is golden brown.

7 Allow the galette to cool slightly before slicing. Serve it warm with a scoop of plant-based ice cream, if desired.

TIP: This galette works just as well (and offers similar health benefits) with other seasonal fruits, like apples and figs in autumn, pears and kumquats in winter, strawberries and raspberries in spring, and apricots and cherries in summer.

MAGICAL BENEFITS

Monounsaturated Fats ✦ Almonds are rich in healthy monounsaturated fats, which are metabolized more slowly than carbohydrates, providing sustained energy.

MCTs ✦ Coconut contains medium-chain triglycerides (MCTs), a good type of saturated fat that's easier to digest and more quickly turned into energy than longer-chain fats.

Dietary Fiber ✦ Blackberries and nectarines, high in both soluble and insoluble fiber, slow digestion and gradually release glucose to support stable blood sugar and sustained energy.

Almond-Cherry Clafoutis
FOR RECOVERY

Gluten-Free

The body is in a perpetual state of recovery as it repairs and renews damaged cells to keep you healthy. To help with that is a classic French dessert, the clafoutis! Traditionally made with eggs and dairy, clafoutis is a baked dessert with a soft, custard-like texture, studded with cherries. This vegan gluten-free version is every bit as good, all the while harnessing a spectrum of antioxidants in the juicy cherries, creamy almonds, earthy flaxseeds, and zesty lemon. Let us eat cake!

1 Preheat the oven to 350°F (180°C). Grease a 9-by-13-inch (23 by 33 cm) baking dish or 6 individual ramekins with oil.

2 In a large bowl, mix the ground flaxseed with ¼ cup plus 2 tablespoons (90 ml) water until a smooth paste forms. Set aside.

3 In a separate bowl, whip the aquafaba with a hand-held mixer on high speed for 5 to 10 minutes, until it forms stiff, white, glossy peaks.

4 Add the sugar, coconut oil, lemon zest, and lemon juice to the bowl with the flaxseed paste and, using the hand-held mixer, whip on high for a few minutes, until smooth. Mix in the almond flour until thoroughly integrated.

5 Gently fold in the whipped aquafaba until the batter is well combined and smooth, then gently fold in the cherries, making sure they are evenly distributed. Pour the batter into the prepared baking dish or divide it between the ramekins.

6 Bake for about 40 minutes (or about 20 minutes, if using ramekins), or until the clafoutis is set and golden brown on top. You can test for doneness by inserting a toothpick into the center. It should come out clean when the cake is fully cooked.

7 Serve warm or cooled with a scoop of plant-based ice cream, if desired. Store on the counter for up to 2 days or in the refrigerator for up to 5 days.

TIP: You can use any fruit in clafoutis, making this a seasonally versatile dessert. For other fruit options that contain anthocyanins, try blueberries, blackberries, plums, or figs.

Serves 4 to 6

2 tablespoons ground flaxseed

½ cup (120 ml) aquafaba (see page 5), chilled

¾ cup (150 g) cane sugar

¼ cup plus 2 tablespoons (90 g) cold-pressed virgin coconut oil, melted, plus more for greasing

Grated zest and juice of 1 lemon

1⅓ cups (160 g) almond flour

1 pound (450 g) cherries, halved and pitted

Plant-based vanilla ice cream for serving, optional

MAGICAL BENEFITS

Lignans ✦ Found in plants like flaxseeds, lignans act as antioxidants, safeguarding cells against potential damage from free radicals.

Anthocyanins ✦ Cherries are rich in anthocyanins, antioxidant pigments that help reduce oxidative stress and inflammation.

Vitamin E ✦ This powerful fat-soluble antioxidant found in almonds and flaxseeds protects cell membranes from free-radical-induced oxidative stress.

Ginger-Lychee Slushy
FOR DIGESTION

Gluten-Free ◆ *Nut-Free*

This slushy offers a cooling escape from the heat along with relief for the digestive system. The sweet and floral lychees blend harmoniously with the warmth of fresh ginger. Its icy texture, with help from ginger's soothing properties, cools digestive fires. Light, nourishing, and effortlessly easy, serve on hot days and nights or as a refreshing finale to heartier meals.

Serves 2 to 4

2 cups (about one 20-ounce/590 ml can) lychees in syrup

1 to 3 teaspoons grated fresh ginger

1 teaspoon agave, optional

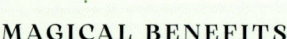

MAGICAL BENEFITS

Gingerol ◆ This active compound in ginger reduces nausea by affecting serotonin receptors in the gut, modulating nausea-related neurotransmitters, and speeding up gastric emptying.

Soluble Fiber ◆ The soluble fiber in lychee forms a gel-like substance in the gut, slowing digestion, aiding nutrient absorption, and promoting overall digestive health.

1 Set a few lychees aside for serving. Pour the rest of the lychees and syrup into a freezer-safe container and freeze for 4 to 6 hours, until icy but not frozen solid.

2 Once icy, purée the lychees in a blender along with the ginger, using a greater amount if you prefer a more intense ginger flavor, and agave, if using, until slushy.

3 Pour into glasses, garnish with the reserved lychees, and serve immediately, or store the slushy in an airtight container in the freezer for up to 6 months. If stored in the freezer, let the slushy sit for about 30 minutes at room temperature and re-blend just before serving.

TIP: Want to give this slushy a creamier texture and flavor, while also making it easier to digest by breaking down some of the fiber in the lychees? Add 1 to 1½ cups (240 to 360 ml) frozen coconut cream to the blender with the other ingredients and purée until smooth.

Rose and Peach Cupcakes
FOR GLOWING SKIN

Gluten-Free ✦ Nut-Free

These soft, fluffy cupcakes, made with sweet peach purée and a blend of oat and arrowroot flours, are a craveable remedy for the effects of UV exposure. Topped with a delicate pink rose-infused icing, they combine the nourishing power of fruits, flowers, grains, and roots into a dessert that helps your skin glow and recover from summer's heat.

Makes 12 cupcakes

CUPCAKES
1¼ cups (275 g) packed light brown sugar

½ cup (100 g) cane sugar

3 peaches, pitted and puréed

3 tablespoons oat milk

2 tablespoons cold-pressed virgin coconut oil, melted, plus more for greasing

½ cup (120 ml) aquafaba (see page 5), chilled

1 teaspoon apple cider vinegar

2 cups plus 1 tablespoon (250 g) gluten-free oat flour or all-purpose gluten-free flour blend (see page 5)

2 tablespoons arrowroot flour

½ teaspoon baking powder

ROSE ICING
1 cup (120 g) powdered sugar

2 teaspoons edible rose powder or ¼ teaspoon culinary rose extract

1 Preheat the oven to 350°F (180°C). Grease the wells of a muffin pan with oil or line them with paper liners.

2 To make the cupcakes, combine the brown sugar, cane sugar, puréed peaches, almond milk, and oil in a large bowl. Mix until well combined.

3 Add the aquafaba to a separate bowl and whip with a hand-held mixer on high speed for 5 to 10 minutes. About halfway through, start pouring in the vinegar a drop at a time while continuing to whip, until glossy, stiff peaks are formed. Then gently fold the whipped aquafaba into the wet ingredients until just combined.

4 In another bowl, sift together the gluten-free oat flour, arrowroot flour, and baking powder. Gradually add the dry ingredients to the wet ingredients, stirring continuously, until the batter is smooth.

5 Spoon the batter evenly into the prepared muffin pan, filling each well about two-thirds full. Bake for about 20 minutes, or until the tops are golden brown and a toothpick inserted into the center comes out clean. Remove from the oven and allow the cupcakes to cool in the pan for about 10 minutes, then transfer them to a wire rack to cool completely before icing.

6 To make the rose icing, combine the powdered sugar and rose powder in a bowl. (If the powdered sugar is clumped, sift it through a fine-mesh strainer to prevent lumps in the icing.) Stir in up to 3 tablespoons water, 1 tablespoon at a time, until the icing is smooth and spreadable.

7 Once the cupcakes are cooled, spread approximately 1½ teaspoons of the icing on top of each. Allow the icing to set, 15 to 20 minutes, before serving.

TIP: To imbue this sweet enchantment with even more skin-supporting magic, add 1 teaspoon of a medicinal herb powder like vitamin C-rich amla, horsetail (packed with silica), tremella mushroom (full of collagen-stimulating peptides), or connective tissue-nourishing gotu kola.

MAGICAL BENEFITS

Citronellol and Geraniol ✦ Found in roses, these antioxidants hydrate the skin, protect it from oxidative stress, reduce inflammation, and indirectly support collagen integrity and tissue repair.

Silica ✦ This mineral found in oats supports connective tissues by helping the body synthesize collagen and maintain the structural framework that holds tissues together.

Beta-Carotene ✦ This precursor to vitamin A found in peaches and roses protects skin from damage, supports new skin cell growth, and helps keep the complexion smooth and even.

Balancing Chia Lemonade
FOR SATIETY

Gluten-Free ✦ Nut-Free

This lemonade challenges the idea that all fibrous and filling foods are heavy and dense. It blends the sour brightness of citrus with the gentle warmth of ginger. The lightly hydrated chia seeds add a delicate, silky texture that enhances each sip. Sweetened with a touch of agave and garnished with fresh mint, this elixir quenches both thirst and hunger while helping you feel balanced and revitalized.

Makes about 4¼ cups (1 L)

- 2 tablespoons chia seeds
- 4 cups (1 L) filtered water
- Juice of 4 to 5 lemons (about 1 cup/240 ml), plus lemon slices for serving
- 1 teaspoon grated fresh ginger
- 1½ teaspoons to 2 tablespoons agave
- Fresh mint leaves, optional

1 In a glass or small bowl, combine the chia seeds with ½ cup (120 ml) of the filtered water. Stir well, then set aside for about 10 minutes, or until the chia seeds have absorbed the water and formed a gel.

2 Add the lemon juice, ginger, and the remaining filtered water to a pitcher. Add the agave according to your desired level of sweetness, and stir well. Finally, pour the chia seed gel into the pitcher and stir thoroughly to evenly distribute the seeds.

3 Refrigerate the lemonade for at least 1 to 2 hours to allow the flavors to meld and the chia seeds to hydrate fully. Stir well just before serving over ice, garnishing with lemon slices and/or mint leaves, if using. Store in an airtight container for up to 5 days.

TIP: You can transform this recipe into something totally new with virtually no extra effort by making chia seed lemonade popsicles! Pour the lemonade into popsicle molds or glasses with popsicle sticks and freeze for 4 to 6 hours, until solid.

MAGICAL BENEFITS

Fiber ✦ The soluble fiber in chia seeds forms a gel to ease bowel movements, while the insoluble fiber adds bulk, supporting digestion.

Natural Citric Acid ✦ Natural citric acid sources like lemons stimulate the production of gastric acid and digestive enzymes, aiding nutrient absorption.

Mucilage ✦ Chia seeds expand and form a gel as they absorb water, promoting fullness, easing acid reflux, and drawing water into the intestines to prevent constipation.

Simple Dressing
FOR IMMUNITY

Gluten-Free ✦ *Nut-Free*

This is your new go-to, good-for-everything salad dressing, with tangy cider vinegar, smooth olive oil, and a bit of garlic and shallot for savory depth. It can be served on salads, grains, or legumes, or as a dip for vegetables. Its magic both amplifies the flavor of other dishes—such as the Baby Greens and Radish Salad (page 110) or the Cucumber-Fennel Salad (page 105)—and offers protective immune-boosting and antioxidant properties.

1 Combine the shallots and garlic in a small bowl or jar. Stir in the vinegar and let sit for about 10 minutes to allow the shallot and garlic flavors to infuse into the vinegar, then add the oil and season with salt and pepper.

2 Add the agave, starting with 1 tablespoon and adjusting to taste. Once you're satisfied with the flavor, stir or shake well to emulsify, then transfer the vinaigrette to an airtight container or bottle.

3 The vinaigrette can be stored at room temperature for up to 2 weeks, refrigerated for up to 6 months, or frozen for up to 1 year. Before using, let the dressing come to room temperature and give it a good shake to re-emulsify.

TIPS: For added flavor and immunity protection, consider adding fresh herbs like rosemary, basil, or thyme. If you have trouble tolerating FODMAPs, you can swap out the garlic and shallots for the green parts of scallions or leeks, both of which provide onion flavor but are lower in FODMAPs.

Makes about 1¼ cups (300 ml)

2 shallots, minced
2 garlic cloves, minced
¼ cup (60 ml) apple cider vinegar
1 cup (240 ml) extra virgin olive oil
1 to 2 tablespoons agave

MAGICAL BENEFITS

Allicin ✦ Garlic and shallots contain allicin, which has antioxidant, antimicrobial, and anti-inflammatory properties.

Monounsaturated Fats ✦ Extra virgin olive oil, rich in monounsaturated fats (which are liquid at room temperature) and polyphenols (natural plant compounds that protect cells from damage), acts as an anti-inflammatory agent and supports a healthy gut microbiome.

Iced Rose Latte
FOR EUPHORIA

Gluten-Free ✦ Nut-Free

Whereas coffee lattes are meant to provide energy, flower lattes like this one are purely for pleasure. The almond milk brings creaminess and a subtly nutty flavor, while the soy milk contributes protein and supports mood. Infused with the delicate, floral aromas of powdered rose petals, this latte offers a whiff of bliss with every sip.

Makes 2 cups (480 ml)

- 1 cup (240 ml) oat milk
- 1 cup (240 ml) soy milk
- 2 teaspoons culinary grade rose powder, or 2 tablespoons dried rose petals
- 1 to 2 tablespoons agave
- Ice for serving

1 Combine the oat milk, soy milk, rose powder, and agave in a blender and blend until smooth. Adjust the sweetness by adding more agave to taste.

2 Pour into individual glasses, add some ice, and serve immediately.

TIP: You can turn this iced latte into a granita by adding 1 to 1½ cups (240 to 360 g) of ice (depending on how thick or icy you prefer it) to the blender with the milk mixture and blending until you reach a slushy texture. For a hot latte, use warmed plant milk.

MAGICAL BENEFITS

Isoflavones ✦ Soybeans contain isoflavones that interact with estrogen receptors in the brain and can positively affect mood.

Complete Protein ✦ As a complete protein, soy provides all the amino acids necessary for building neurotransmitters like serotonin and dopamine, both of which are crucial for mood regulation.

Rose Essential Oils ✦ Roses contain essential oils rich in aromatic compounds like citronellol, geraniol, and phenylethanol, which may influence dopamine and serotonin activity to promote calmness and reduce anxiety.

Magic Pesto
FOR RECOVERY

Gluten-Free

The magic of this pesto comes from the protective properties of its plant-based ingredients. Made with peppery arugula, fragrant basil, and walnuts and almond flour in place of the traditional pine nuts and Parmesan cheese, this versatile pesto goes with pretty much every savory vegetable dish you can dream of, like the Pesto Avocado Salad (page 97).

1 Combine the basil, arugula, oil, walnuts, almond flour, agave, lemon zest, and lemon juice in a blender or food processor and blend until smooth and creamy. Season with salt and pepper.

2 Serve right away, or transfer to an airtight container or jar and refrigerate for 1 to 2 weeks, or divide between smaller containers or ice cube trays and freeze for up to 1 year.

TIP: If basil isn't in season, you can substitute kale, more arugula, carrot greens, or beet greens.

Makes about 2½ cups (580 g)

2 cups (40 g) fresh basil leaves

1 cup (25 g) arugula

1 cup (240 ml) extra virgin olive oil

1 cup (120 g) walnuts

¾ cup plus 1 tablespoon (100 g) almond flour

1 to 2 tablespoons agave

Grated zest and juice of 1 lemon

MAGICAL BENEFITS

Antioxidants ✦ All the ingredients in this pesto contain antioxidants, including a spectrum of flavonoids and polyphenols, which help combat oxidative stress and cellular damage.

Anti-Inflammatories ✦ Compounds in basil, almonds, walnuts, and olive oil have anti-inflammatory effects that support immune function and overall health.

Omega-3 Fatty Acids ✦ Walnuts are rich in ALA, a type of omega-3 that reduces inflammation, supports heart health by lowering cholesterol and blood pressure, and aids brain function.

Turmeric Ginger Ale
FOR INFLAMMATION RELIEF

Gluten-Free ✦ Nut-Free

For centuries, ginger and turmeric have been revered around the world for their culinary and medicinal uses. When combined, their anti-inflammatory powers are amplified. This golden, spiced syrup, infused with the warmth of ginger and the earthy notes of turmeric root, transforms into a fizzy refresher when mixed with sparkling water and poured over ice. Lightly sweetened with agave syrup, it's a delightful way to cool the fires of inflammation—or to simply cool off on a hot day or summer night.

Makes 2 cups (480 ml) syrup

SYRUP

1 cup (200 g) cane sugar

1 cup (240 ml) filtered water

½ cup (120 ml) agave

¼ cup (25 g) thinly sliced fresh ginger

¼ cup (25 g) thinly sliced fresh turmeric or 1¼ teaspoons ground turmeric

1 teaspoon black peppercorns

Ice cubes, for serving

Sparkling water, for serving

1   **To make the syrup,** combine the sugar, filtered water, agave, ginger, turmeric, and peppercorns in a saucepan set over medium heat.

2   Bring the mixture to a gentle simmer, stirring until the sugar has completely dissolved, then reduce the heat to low and let simmer for 10 to 15 minutes to allow the flavors of the ginger and turmeric to infuse into the syrup.

3   Let cool slightly, then strain the syrup through a fine-mesh strainer or cheesecloth. Discard the solids and pour the syrup into an airtight, sterilized glass jar or bottle. Store in the refrigerator for up to 3 months.

4   To serve, fill a glass with ice cubes, add 1 tablespoon of the syrup, top up the glass with sparkling water, and stir gently to combine.

TIP: To enhance the anti-inflammatory powers of the ginger and turmeric, add ½ teaspoon lion's mane mushroom powder, which has brain-supporting compounds that combat neuro-inflammation.

MAGICAL BENEFITS

Curcumin ✦ This active compound in the root of the turmeric plant has anti-inflammatory and antioxidant properties that neutralize harmful free radicals, especially when combined with the piperine in black pepper.

Gingerol ✦ Ginger's bioactive compound, gingerol, provides anti-inflammatory and antioxidant benefits, and may help reduce oxidative stress.

MAGICAL BENEFITS

Vitamin A ✦ This vitamin, present in high quantities in pumpkin and sweet potato, helps regulate the immune system and maintain healthy mucosal membranes, which play a crucial role in fighting infection.

Polyphenols ✦ These powerful antioxidants, abundant in cranberries, grapes, and red wine, reduce inflammation, combat free radicals, and protect cells from oxidative stress.

Vitamin D ✦ Mushrooms are among the richest plant-based sources of vitamin D, which helps boost the immune system's ability to fight illness.

Whole Roasted Pumpkin
FOR IMMUNITY

Gluten-Free ◆ No Sugar Added

This whole stuffed pumpkin is the perfect vessel for sharing protective magic with loved ones as an autumn celebration centerpiece. As it roasts, the pumpkin's shell seals in the savory-sweet flavors and immunity-bolstering nutrients of the tender vegetables, dried and fresh fruits, meaty mushrooms, and crisp chestnuts in the filling. Use a large Cinderella pumpkin for feasts or a smaller sugar pumpkin for intimate gatherings.

1. Preheat the oven to 400°F (200°C).

2. Use a serrated knife to carve a wide circular opening around the stem of the pumpkin, as if you're preparing a jack-o'-lantern, leaving the stem attached to the "lid." Set the lid aside and scoop out the seeds and stringy pulp from inside the pumpkin. (You can rinse and dry the seeds and roast them later for an easy snack.)

3. Rub 1 tablespoon of the oil and a few pinches of salt and pepper around the inside of the hollowed-out pumpkin. Rub the remaining oil over the outside to create a glossy finish after roasting.

4. **To make the rosemary-garlic bread cubes,** spread the bread cubes evenly over a rimmed baking sheet. Drizzle with the oil, sprinkle with the rosemary and garlic powder, and season with salt and pepper. Roast for 10 to 15 minutes, until browned and crispy, turning them once halfway through to ensure even cooking. Remove from the oven and set aside.

5. **To make the vegetable stuffing,** add the oil to a large pan over medium-high heat, then stir in the onions, sweet potato, mushrooms, chestnuts, and garlic. Cook for about 30 minutes, or until tender, stirring frequently. Deglaze with the red wine whenever the vegetables begin to stick and scrape the bottom of the pan to reincorporate any browned bits. Remove from the heat and mix in the apples, grapes, cranberries, and bread cubes. Season with salt and pepper.

6. Place the hollowed pumpkin on a rimmed baking sheet or in a large oven-safe pan and fill it with the vegetable stuffing. Don't be afraid to pack it in, but if there's too much stuffing to fit, you can bake the rest in a separate baking dish.

7. Wrap the pumpkin "lid" with foil so it doesn't burn, and place it on the baking sheet with the pumpkin. Roast for about 1 hour, or until the outside becomes speckled brown and the stuffing is crispy and browned on top. Transfer the pumpkin to a serving dish, set the lid on top, and serve, using a sharp knife to cut slices from the pumpkin as you would from a cake and a large serving spoon to scoop up the stuffing.

TIP: If you have leftovers, turn them into a gratin! Remove the leftover stuffing and scoop out the pumpkin flesh (discarding the skin and stem if using a tough-skinned variety like Cinderella), then spread the mixture evenly in a greased baking dish or loaf pan. Top with gluten-free bread crumbs or almond flour, and bake at 350°F (180°C) for 45 to 60 minutes, until the topping is crispy and golden brown.

Serves 4 to 6 as a main

- 1 Cinderella pumpkin (or sugar pumpkin, harvest moon, porcelain doll, or red kuri)
- 2 tablespoons extra virgin olive oil

ROSEMARY-GARLIC BREAD CUBES

- ½ loaf (about 250 g) sliced gluten-free bread, cut into ½-inch (1.25 cm) cubes
- 2 tablespoons extra virgin olive oil
- 3 fresh rosemary sprigs, leaves minced
- 1½ teaspoons garlic powder

VEGETABLE STUFFING

- 3 tablespoons extra virgin olive oil
- 2 red onions, chopped
- 1 large sweet potato, peeled and cut into ½- to ¾-inch (1.25 to 2 cm) cubes
- 4 ounces (115 g) white button mushrooms
- 3.5 ounces (100 g) peeled and roasted whole chestnuts, roughly chopped
- 3 garlic cloves, minced
- ½ cup (120 ml) red wine
- 2 apples, cored and diced
- 1 cup (150 g) seedless grapes
- ½ cup (60 g) unsweetened dried cranberries

Golden Cauliflower with Scallion-Ginger Cream
FOR INFLAMMATION RELIEF

Gluten-Free ♦ Nut-Free

These roasted cauliflower florets, infused with turmeric and ginger, make for a warmly spiced meal suffused with soothing, anti-inflammatory benefits. A creamy scallion-ginger sauce is both refreshing and velvety and complements the crispy, golden-hued florets. The sauce can be used as a dressing for the Cucumber and Asparagus Salad (page 43) or as an alternative to the sauce for the Creamy Mushrooms and Beets (page 152). To make this a heartier main, serve it with a protein-rich grain such as amaranth, buckwheat, or quinoa.

Serves 2 to 4 as a main or 6 as a side

TURMERIC-GINGER CAULIFLOWER

¼ cup (60 ml) extra virgin olive oil

3 tablespoons apple cider vinegar

1 tablespoon agave

1 tablespoon Dijon mustard

1 tablespoon grated fresh ginger

1½ teaspoons grated fresh turmeric or ½ teaspoon ground turmeric

2 medium or 1 large cauliflower (1½ to 2 pounds/700 to 900 g), cut into bite-size florets

SCALLION-GINGER CREAM

1 cup (240 ml) coconut milk or soy cream

3 scallions, finely chopped

1 teaspoon grated fresh ginger

1 teaspoon extra virgin olive oil

Grated zest and juice of ½ lemon

1 Preheat the oven to 400°F (200°C).

2 **To make the turmeric-ginger cauliflower,** add the oil, vinegar, agave, mustard, ginger, and turmeric to a large bowl and whisk to combine, then season with salt and pepper. Add the cauliflower and stir gently until it is evenly coated.

3 Spread the cauliflower in one layer on a rimmed baking sheet and roast for 30 to 40 minutes, until the florets can be easily pierced with a fork and are browned and crispy. Transfer to a serving bowl or platter.

4 **To make the scallion-ginger cream,** in a clean bowl, mix together the coconut milk, scallions, ginger, oil, lemon zest, and lemon juice, and season with salt and pepper.

5 Drizzle the cream directly over the cauliflower or serve it on the side for dipping. Garnish with extra freshly ground black pepper just before serving.

TIP: You can either transform any leftover cauliflower and sauce into a purée or a soup by thinning it out with vegetable broth, or you can make it into a simple gratin by spreading the cauliflower in a baking dish, topping it with the leftover cream, and re-baking it for about 20 minutes, or until golden brown on top.

MAGICAL BENEFITS

Curcumin ♦ This active ingredient in turmeric regulates inflammation by reducing oxidative stress.

Gingerol ♦ This primary bioactive compound in ginger may reduce inflammation by regulating inflammation levels, potentially easing symptoms of autoimmune conditions.

Piperine ♦ The active compound in black pepper, piperine enhances the absorption of curcumin and gingerol by up to 2,000 percent, significantly amplifying their anti-inflammatory effects.

Comforting Potato and Corn Soup
FOR DIGESTION

Gluten-Free ◆ No Sugar Added ◆ Nut-Free

As summer's warmth fades into autumn's brisk embrace, our bodies naturally seek nourishment. This indulgent soup both comforts the soul and supports digestive health, making it an ideal companion for the months ahead. The tender potatoes and sweet corn kernels provide robust texture contrasting the silky coconut milk. This soup can be prepared ahead of time and frozen for up to a year. Serve with a side of grains, beans, or lentils for a heartier meal.

1   Heat the oil in a pot over medium heat. Add the onions and cook until caramelized, about 15 minutes. Deglaze with a splash of water whenever they begin to stick and scrape the bottom of the pot to reincorporate any browned bits.

2   Add the potatoes and corn, then pour in the broth, coconut milk, and vinegar, and season with salt and pepper. Stir well to combine.

3   Increase the heat to high to bring the soup to a boil, then reduce the heat to medium-low and simmer uncovered for about 20 minutes, or until the potatoes can be pierced easily with a fork.

4   Serve hot, drizzling individual portions with more oil, sprinkling with freshly ground black pepper, and garnishing with the fresh thyme and chopped bell pepper, if using, for a burst of color and crunch!

TIP: If you prefer a smoother soup, you can blend it to your preferred consistency after the vegetables are cooked, adding more vegetable broth or water to thin it out if desired.

Serves 4 as a main or 6 to 8 as a side

2 tablespoons extra virgin olive oil, plus more for drizzling

3 onions, chopped

1 pound (450 g) waxy potatoes (such as red or Yukon Gold), peeled and cut into 1- to 1½-inch (2.5 to 4 cm) pieces

2 cups (325 g) fresh or thawed frozen corn (about 2 ears)

4¼ cups (1 L) vegetable broth or water

One 13.5-ounce (400 ml) can coconut milk

3 tablespoons apple cider vinegar

Fresh thyme leaves or chopped chives

1 bell pepper, minced, optional

MAGICAL BENEFITS

Fiber ◆ Potatoes and corn are rich in dietary fiber, which promotes regular bowel movements and nourishes beneficial gut bacteria.

Resistant Starch ◆ Found in potatoes and corn, resistant starch bypasses absorption in the small intestine to support beneficial bacteria in the colon.

MCTs ◆ Coconut cream contains medium-chain triglycerides (MCTs), which support a balanced gut microbiome and healthy gut lining and help regulate inflammation.

Greens with Coconut Cream
FOR EUPHORIA

Gluten-Free ♦ No Sugar Added ♦ Nut-Free

This comforting sauté of tender kale and chard bathed in a creamy, garlicky sauce will brighten your mood on rainy autumn days. Dark leafy greens are gently simmered in plant-based cream and mixed with sweet-tart raw apples and nutty sunflower seeds to offset the greens' bitterness. To serve this as a main, pair it with a protein-rich grain like amaranth, buckwheat, or quinoa, or for an even more euphoric meal, serve as a side with the mood-boosting Sunny Summer Pasta (page 93).

Serves 4 as a main or 6 as a side

3 tablespoons extra virgin olive oil
1 large onion, chopped
2 garlic cloves, minced
4 chard leaves, chopped
4 kale leaves, stems removed, chopped
One 13.5-ounce (400 ml) can coconut milk
4 apples, cored and chopped
2 tablespoons sunflower seeds

1 Heat the oil in a large pan over medium heat. Add the onion and cook for about 15 minutes, or until softened and golden brown. Deglaze with a splash of water whenever the onions begin to stick and scrape the bottom of the pan to reincorporate any browned bits.

2 Add the garlic and cook until fragrant, about 1 minute. Stir in the chard and kale and cook for about 5 more minutes, or until wilted. Increase the heat to medium-high and stir in the coconut milk. Bring to a gentle simmer and cook for 10 to 15 minutes, until the cream has reduced by half and thickened into a sauce that clings to the back of a spoon. Season with salt and pepper.

3 Remove from the heat and mix in the apples, reserving a handful for serving. Transfer to a large serving dish or serve directly from the pan, garnishing with the sunflower seeds and reserved apples just before serving.

TIP: This recipe can also be made into a dip! After cooking, simply add all the ingredients to a blender and blend until smooth.

MAGICAL BENEFITS

Magnesium ♦ Sunflower seeds, kale, and chard contain magnesium, which plays a role in mood regulation and stress by supporting the synthesis of serotonin, dopamine, and GABA neurotransmitters.

Vitamin B9 ♦ Dark leafy greens like kale and chard are good sources of vitamin B9 (folate), which is important for the production of neurotransmitters like serotonin.

Tryptophan ♦ Found in foods like sunflower seeds, tryptophan is a precursor to serotonin, the "feel-good" neurotransmitter linked to mood, sleep, and cognition.

Buckwheat and Fungi Risotto
FOR SATIETY

Gluten-Free ◆ No Sugar Added ◆ Nut-Free

This ultra-satiating mushroom risotto envelops you with its earthy aroma and velvety texture. Nutty, toasted buckwheat grains replace the traditional rice for a heartier, protein-packed base that pairs perfectly with seared mushrooms. Using a variety brings a wider array of flavors and nutrients to the risotto. Each bite provides comfort and the long-lasting energy you need to fuel autumnal outdoor activities. Serve with a side of Smoky-Sweet Glazed Mushrooms (page 234) for an even more protein-packed meal.

1 Heat 2 tablespoons of the oil in a large sauté pan or wide pot over high heat. Add the onions and shallots and cook for 10 to 15 minutes, until translucent, stirring frequently and adjusting the temperature as needed to prevent burning. Deglaze with a splash of water whenever they begin to stick and scrape the bottom of the pan to reincorporate any browned bits.

2 Add the buckwheat and cook, stirring often, for about 5 minutes, or until lightly toasted. Add the wine and apple cider vinegar and continue cooking until the buckwheat has absorbed the liquid, stirring often, then slowly integrate the vegetable broth or water by adding a few tablespoons at a time, stirring often and letting the grains absorb the liquid between additions. Continue until all the liquid has been absorbed and the buckwheat is tender, 15 to 20 minutes. Season with salt and pepper.

3 While the buckwheat cooks, slice the mushrooms, leaving a few whole for serving. Add all the mushrooms to a pan with the remaining oil and sear over high heat until the mushrooms shrink and brown, 10 to 15 minutes. Remove the whole mushrooms from the pan and set aside.

4 Mix the rest of the mushrooms into the buckwheat risotto. Divide the risotto between individual dishes and top with the whole mushrooms. Before serving, garnish with an extra drizzle of oil and a sprinkle of salt and freshly ground black pepper.

TIP: Leftover risotto? Turn it into a salad! Toss with the Creamy Citrus Vinaigrette (page 258), some hardy greens like kale or frisée, and your choice of other seasonal vegetables, and you'll have a completely revamped recipe!

Serves 4 as a main or 6 to 8 as a side

¼ cup (60 ml) extra virgin olive oil, plus more for drizzling

2 onions, minced

2 shallots, minced

1½ cups (270 g) buckwheat

½ cup (120 ml) white or red wine

3 tablespoons apple cider vinegar

4¼ cups (1 L) vegetable broth or water

10 ounces (280 g) assorted mushrooms such as white button, shiitake, and oyster

MAGICAL BENEFITS

Complete Protein ◆ Buckwheat contains all the essential amino acids and is therefore considered a complete protein, providing long-lasting energy and satiety.

Acetic Acid ◆ This active ingredient in apple cider vinegar increases satiety by slowing gastric emptying and reducing blood sugar spikes, helping prevent energy crashes followed by cravings.

Fiber ◆ Fiber-filled foods like buckwheat, onions, and mushrooms promote feelings of fullness by adding bulk to meals and slowing digestion.

Creamy Mushrooms and Beets
FOR STRONG BONES

Gluten-Free ✦ No Sugar Added ✦ Nut-Free

Crispy shiitake mushrooms complement tender, jewel-toned beets in this comforting and bone-fortifying meal. Adding the mushroom cooking oil to the creamy sauce preserves the mushrooms' fat-soluble nutrients and amps up the sauce's mushroom flavor. To serve this as a main, pair it with a protein-rich grain such as amaranth, buckwheat, or quinoa.

Serves 4 as a main or 6 to 8 as a side

- 1 pound (450 g) beets
- 2 tablespoons extra virgin olive oil
- 1 pound (450 g) fresh shiitake mushrooms, stems trimmed

SCALLION-ROSEMARY CREAM

- 1½ cups (360 ml) soy cream
- 3 scallions, minced, plus more for serving
- Grated zest and juice of ½ lemon
- 1 tablespoon extra virgin olive oil
- 1 rosemary sprig, leaves minced, plus more for serving

1 Bring a large saucepan of salted water to a boil over high heat. Add the beets and boil for 20 to 30 minutes, until tender enough to be pierced with a fork, then drain and immediately submerge in cold water to cool them and make removing the peels easier. Peel and slice the beets, then set them aside.

2 Add the oil to a searing-hot pan over high heat. Once it sizzles add the shiitakes. After 2 minutes, lower the heat to medium-high and let the shiitakes fry, occasionally flattening them with a spatula until they release their water and become crispy, 10 to 15 minutes, turning them halfway through to ensure that they brown evenly. Use a slotted spoon to transfer the mushrooms to a plate, leaving the oil in the pan.

3 **To make the scallion-rosemary cream,** whisk together the soy cream, scallions, lemon zest, lemon juice, oil, and rosemary in a bowl. Carefully pour in the mushroom cooking oil and mix until smooth. Season with salt and pepper.

4 Divide the sauce between individual plates, top with the fried shiitakes and beet slices, and garnish with the extra rosemary and scallions. Season with salt and pepper, and serve.

TIP: If you place the shiitakes gill side up in direct sunlight for several hours before cooking them, their vitamin D content will increase dramatically!

MAGICAL BENEFITS

Vitamin D2 ✦ This fat-soluble vitamin found in shiitakes is essential for absorbing calcium and phosphorus, thereby playing a key role in bone formation.

Calcium ✦ A mineral essential for building strong bones with the help of vitamin D, calcium also keeps the heart beating steadily and helps muscles contract and nerves communicate smoothly.

Phosphorus ✦ Found in soy and mushrooms, phosphorus supports bones, teeth, and cell membranes and is essential for synthesizing the DNA and RNA needed for cell growth and repair.

Beet-Leek Quiche
FOR DEFENSE

Gluten-Free ◆ No Sugar Added ◆ Nut-Free

This root vegetable quiche features a crispy and golden sweet potato crust (which can be made with waxy red or Yukon Gold potatoes instead, if you prefer) stuffed with a creamy onion-and-leek filling. Topped with tender beets, it offers a harmonious balance of earthy sweetness and immunity-supporting antioxidants, sulfur compounds, and protective pigments. Serve with a protein-rich grain such as amaranth, buckwheat, or quinoa for a heartier meal with even more immune system-supporting nutrients.

1 Preheat the oven to 350°F (180°C).

2 **To make the sweet potato crust,** microwave the sweet potato slices for 2 to 3 minutes, until they are flexible enough to bend slightly. Grease the bottom and sides of a 9-inch (23 cm) springform pan with the oil and arrange the sweet potato slices in concentric, slightly overlapping circles over the bottom of the pan. Add a second layer, staggering the slices to cover the gaps in the first layer.

3 To form the edges of the crust, cut the remaining sweet potato slices into half-moons, then press them along the sides of the pan, with their edges slightly overlapping and the straight side along the bottom. Add an extra drop or two of oil to any slices that don't adhere well. Add a second layer of half-moon slices, staggering them to cover any gaps in the first layer. Set the crust aside.

4 **To make the onion-leek cream filling,** add 2 tablespoons of the oil to a large pan and sauté the leeks and onion over high heat for 15 to 20 minutes, stirring frequently and adjusting the temperature as needed to prevent burning. Deglaze with a splash of water whenever they begin to stick and scrape the bottom of the pan to reincorporate any browned bits, until the vegetables have cooked down and become tender and lightly caramelized.

5 Lower the heat to medium, add the coconut cream, and simmer gently for about 15 minutes, or until the cream has reduced by half and thickened enough to coat the back of a spoon. Season with salt and pepper.

6 Add the arrowroot flour and ground flaxseed and stir thoroughly to combine. Continue to stir the mixture for about 10 minutes, or until it thickens, then pour the filling into the sweet potato crust and spread it evenly.

7 Bring a pot of water to a boil over high heat. Add the beets and boil for 20 to 30 minutes, until tender enough to be pierced with a fork, then drain and immediately submerge in cold water to cool them and make removing the peels easier. Peel, then slice in half and gently press the beets into the cream mixture, with the flat, cut side facing up. Arrange the reserved leek slices in between the beets. Drizzle the remaining oil over the top and sprinkle with salt and pepper.

8 Bake for about 30 minutes, or until the sweet potato crust is soft and slightly browned at the edges and the filling has set. Let cool for 5 minutes, then run a knife along the edges to loosen the quiche before removing the sides of the springform pan. Serve warm or let cool completely before serving.

TIP: This quiche is a great canvas for other autumnal ingredients! If you like, try substituting beta-carotene-rich purple potatoes for the sweet potatoes and sliced rainbow carrots for the beets.

Serves 4 as a main or 6 to 8 as a side

SWEET POTATO CRUST

2 sweet potatoes, peeled and cut into ⅛-inch (3 mm) slices

2 tablespoons extra virgin olive oil

ONION-LEEK CREAM FILLING

3 tablespoons extra virgin olive oil

2 leeks, thoroughly rinsed, a few ⅛-inch (3 mm) crosswise slices reserved for serving, the rest minced

1 onion, minced

One 13.5-ounce (400 ml) can coconut cream or other plant-based cream

2 tablespoons arrowroot flour or cornstarch

1 tablespoon ground flaxseed

6 small beets

MAGICAL BENEFITS

Beta-Carotene ◆ Carotenoids in beets and sweet potatoes act as antioxidants, reducing the free radicals linked to degenerative diseases. Once converted to vitamin A in the body, they also support immune function.

Sulfur Compounds ◆ Vegetables from the allium family like leeks and onions are rich in sulfur compounds that protect against free radical damage and combat the growth of cancerous cells.

Linolenic Acid ◆ Flaxseeds are high in alpha-linolenic acid (ALA), an omega-3 fatty acid known for its immune-modulating, anti-inflammatory, and potential anti-tumor effects.

Stewed Cabbage with Apple-Mustard Cream
FOR DETOX

Gluten-Free ♦ No Sugar Added ♦ Nut-Free

One of the first signs that your body's natural cleansing systems aren't functioning at their peak is a lack of energy. This hearty and detox-supporting stew can help with that. It features the unexpected heat of mustard and the natural sweetness of apples, which complement the earthy cabbage and potatoes. Perfect for brisk autumn days, this dish delivers both warmth and vitality in every bite. To serve this as a main, pair it with a protein-rich grain such as amaranth, buckwheat, or quinoa, or serve as a side with the Caramelized Onion, Potato, and Bean Gratin (page 206) or the Cabbage and Potato Gratin (page 210).

Serves 4 as a main or 6 as a side

3 tablespoons extra virgin olive oil

1 small purple cabbage, cored and cut into about eight 1- to 2-inch (2.5 to 5 cm) wedges

2 large onions, chopped

8 ounces (225 g) small, waxy potatoes (such as red or Yukon Gold), peeled and halved

¼ cups plus 2 tablespoons (90 ml) white wine

One 13.5-ounce (400 ml) can coconut milk

3 tablespoons Dijon mustard

3 tart apples (such as Granny Smith or Braeburn), cored and cubed

1 Heat the oil in a wide pot over high heat. Add the cabbage in two batches and sear each side for about 5 minutes, or until browned. Remove from the pot, sprinkle both sides of each wedge with salt and pepper to taste, and set aside.

2 Add the onions and potatoes and reduce the heat to medium-high. Sauté for 15 to 20 minutes, stirring frequently. Deglaze with the wine whenever the vegetables begin to stick and scrape the bottom of the pot to reincorporate any browned bits, until the vegetables have reduced in size and are evenly browned. Mix in the coconut milk and mustard and season with salt and pepper.

3 Reduce the heat to low and place the cabbage wedges back on top of the vegetable sauté. Cover the pot with a lid and let the vegetables gently simmer for 30 to 40 minutes to allow the flavors to meld, until the cabbage is tender enough to be pierced with a fork. Let cool for a few minutes, then sprinkle with the apple pieces just before serving.

TIP: If you have leftovers, purée all the vegetables with broth until smooth for a velvety cabbage soup. You can also chop up the leftover vegetables into smaller pieces, spread them in a baking dish, top with gluten-free bread crumbs, and roast at 350°F (180°C) for about 30 minutes, until golden brown and crispy.

MAGICAL BENEFITS

Glucosinolates ♦ This sulfur-rich compound found in cruciferous plants like cabbage activates enzymes that directly help the liver eliminate toxins.

Myrosinase ♦ This enzyme found in mustard increases the bioavailability of glucosinolates, in turn boosting the detox benefits of the cabbage in this recipe.

Phenolic Acids ♦ These natural antioxidants found in apples, cabbage, and potatoes shield liver cells from harmful toxins and support overall liver function.

Pectin ♦ Apples are concentrated sources of pectin, which is a chelating agent, meaning it binds to toxins and helps flush them from the body.

Broccolini with Puréed Eggplant
FOR COGNITION

Gluten-Free ◆ No Sugar Added ◆ Nut-Free

The brain, unlike other organs that generate their own damage-repairing antioxidants, relies primarily on dietary sources of antioxidants—such as those in this creamy eggplant purée with roasted sweet-and-sour broccolini. Apple cider vinegar and ginger give the baba ghanoush–inspired purée brightness and warmth, while caramelized broccolini adds a nutty, crisp-tender textural contrast (broccoli florets work, too!). To serve this as a main, pair it with rice, lentils, or a protein-rich grain like amaranth, buckwheat, or quinoa.

1 Preheat the oven to 400°F (200°C).

2 Place the eggplant halves cut sides up on a rimmed baking sheet and drizzle evenly with 2 tablespoons of the oil. Once the oven is hot, roast for 30 to 40 minutes, until the flesh is tender and browned and the skin is slightly crisped.

3 Place the broccolini in a single layer on a second rimmed baking sheet. Drizzle the broccolini with 2 tablespoons of the apple cider vinegar followed by another 2 tablespoons of the remaining oil and toss to coat evenly. Season with salt and pepper. Set the baking sheet on a separate rack in the oven and roast for about 20 minutes, or until the broccolini is slightly browned and tender enough to be pierced with a fork and the eggplant skin is evenly browned and wrinkled, with flesh soft enough to scoop out easily with a spoon.

4 Remove from the oven, transfer the eggplants to a separate plate, and let them cool enough to handle, 5 to 10 minutes, then scoop the flesh into a blender or food processor, discarding the skins. Add the coconut cream, the remaining apple cider vinegar, ginger, lion's mane powder, and 1 tablespoon of the remaining oil to the blender or food processor and blend until smooth and creamy. Season with salt and pepper.

5 Divide the purée between individual plates or spread it over a large serving platter. Arrange the broccolini on top, and serve warm with a drizzle of the remaining oil and a sprinkle of freshly ground black pepper.

TIP: If you have leftover eggplant purée, you can also serve it as a dip! Pair with multigrain crackers or crudités for an appetizer. The eggplant purée freezes well and can be stored in an airtight container for up to 1 year.

Serves 4 as a main or 6 to 8 as a side

2 eggplants, halved lengthwise

¼ cup plus 2 tablespoons (90 ml) extra virgin olive oil

1 bunch broccolini or broccoli, florets separated

¼ cup (60 ml) apple cider vinegar

One 13.5-ounce (400 ml) can coconut cream

1 tablespoon grated fresh ginger

1 tablespoon lion's mane mushroom powder

MAGICAL BENEFITS

Nasunin ◆ An antioxidant in eggplant skin, nasunin protects brain cells from oxidative damage and inflammation and binds to metals that accumulate in the brain, aiding in their removal.

Chlorogenic Acid ◆ Found in eggplant and broccoli, chlorogenic acid has antioxidant and anti-inflammatory properties, protecting liver and kidney cells and enhancing blood flow to the brain.

Hericenones and Erinacines ◆ Found in lion's mane mushrooms, these bioactive compounds stimulate the production of nerve growth factor, promoting neuron repair and regeneration while protecting brain cells from oxidative damage and inflammation.

Sweet Potato Kale Salad with Magic Pesto
FOR CIRCULATION

Gluten-Free

This circulatory-system supporting salad combines caramelized roasted sweet potato and crunchy sliced almonds with a base of super nutrient-charged raw kale. A dressing made from a combination of Magic Pesto (page 137) and Flower Vinaigrette (page 199) brings an herbaceous tang and its own unique healing magic thanks to the circulatory system–supporting antioxidants in the greens and hibiscus flowers. Serve as a side with the Baked Purple Cauliflower and Potatoes with Rosemary Vinaigrette (page 214) for extra heart support.

Serves 4 to 6 as a side

1 sweet potato, peeled and cut into ½- to ¾-inch (1.25 to 2 cm) cubes

3 tablespoons extra virgin olive oil

1 cup (240 g) Magic Pesto (page 137)

¼ cup (60 ml) Flower Vinaigrette (page 199) or 2 tablespoons extra virgin olive oil plus 2 tablespoons apple cider vinegar

1 bunch kale, stems removed, leaves torn into bite-size pieces

¼ cup (30 g) sliced almonds

1. Preheat the oven to 400°F (200°C).

2. Place the sweet potato cubes on a rimmed baking sheet. Drizzle with the oil, season with salt and pepper, and toss to coat evenly. Spread the cubes in a single layer and roast until tender, about 30 minutes, stirring halfway through to ensure they cook evenly. Set aside to cool slightly while you prepare the dressing and salad.

3. Whisk together the Magic Pesto with the Flower Vinaigrette in a small bowl.

4. Add the kale to a large bowl and massage the leaves with your fingers for a 2 to 3 minutes to soften the fibers, then pour in the dressing and toss to coat thoroughly.

5. Transfer the kale to a serving platter or divide among individual plates. Top with the roasted sweet potato and sliced almonds and serve.

TIP: If you like, you can substitute other root vegetables, such as parsnips, beets, or celery root, for the sweet potato.

MAGICAL BENEFITS

Vitamin K ✦ This circulation-supporting vitamin, abundant in kale and basil, promotes healthy blood clotting, arteries, and blood flow.

Potassium ✦ This mineral found in sweet potatoes helps to regulate blood pressure by balancing sodium levels and promoting vasodilation, the relaxation of the blood vessel walls.

Magnesium ✦ Found in almonds, kale, and basil, this mineral is vital for blood-flow regulation. It helps to relax and dilate blood vessels, reducing the risk of hypertension.

Maple-Roasted Roots
FOR IMMUNITY

Gluten-Free ✦ *Nut-Free*

Autumn gives us an abundance of nutrient-dense produce, such as the rainbow carrots and parsnips in this side dish, to help strengthen our bodies for the draining winter months ahead. The natural sweetness of the carrots and earthy depth of the parsnips are accentuated by a sticky balsamic-vinegar-and-maple glaze. And sprinkling with citrusy ground amla and nutty reishi mushroom powder adds an extra layer of immune-boosting magic.

1 Preheat the oven to 400°F (200°C). Grease a baking dish or oven-safe pan with the oil.

2 Bring a large saucepan of water to a boil over high heat. Add the carrots and parsnips and let the water return to a rolling boil, then reduce the heat to medium. Simmer gently for about 15 minutes, or until the vegetables can be pierced with a fork with some slight resistance, then immediately drain and pat them dry with a paper towel.

3 To make the maple-balsamic glaze, whisk together the vinegar, oil, maple syrup, mustard, and amla powder and reishi powder, if using, in a small bowl. Season with salt and pepper.

4 Place the carrots and parsnips in a single layer on the prepared baking dish. Drizzle with the glaze and toss gently to coat.

5 Roast for about 30 minutes, or until the vegetables are browned and meltingly tender with a little crisping at their ends, turning them once or twice during roasting to ensure even browning. Remove from the oven and serve immediately.

TIP: *For an elevated presentation, serve the roots on a layer of the sauce from the Caramelized Zucchini and Peas with Citrus-Dill Sauce (page 27).*

Serves 4 to 6 as a side

1 tablespoon extra virgin olive oil
8 rainbow carrots, peeled
8 parsnips, peeled

MAPLE-BALSAMIC GLAZE

3 tablespoons balsamic vinegar
2 tablespoons extra virgin olive oil
2 tablespoons maple syrup
1 tablespoon Dijon mustard
1 teaspoon amla (Indian gooseberry) powder, optional
1 teaspoon reishi mushroom powder, optional

MAGICAL BENEFITS

Triterpenes ✦ Reishi mushrooms contain triterpenes, bioactive compounds that stimulate immune cells such as macrophages and T cells, enhancing the body's defense against infection.

Polyphenols ✦ These antioxidant and anti-inflammatory compounds, found in high concentrations in olive oil and amla berries, neutralize damaging environmental toxins and reduce oxidative stress.

Beta-Carotene ✦ The body transforms the antioxidant beta-carotene, found in carrots, especially darker varieties, into vitamin A, which supports the development and function of immune cells.

Squash and Parsnip Soup
FOR DETOX

Gluten-Free ◆ No Sugar Added ◆ Nut-Free

Autumn is an ideal time to prepare our bodies and immune systems for the colder days and longer nights ahead. In this soup, sweet red kuri squash—with its vivid orange edible skin and flavor reminiscent of chestnuts—complements nutty parsnips. Both are simmered in an herbal broth made from detox-supporting plants that give the soup a subtle earthy flavor. Rich and creamy, it can be served alongside fiber-filled legumes or a protein-rich grain like amaranth, buckwheat, or quinoa for extra detox support.

Serves 4 as a main or 6 to 8 as a side

4¼ cups (1 L) vegetable broth or water

3 tablespoons goldenrod flowers, dandelion root, artichoke leaves, or milk thistle

¼ cup (60 ml) extra virgin olive oil, plus more for drizzling

2 onions, chopped

1 unpeeled red kuri squash or peeled butternut squash, seeded and cubed

2 to 3 parsnips (300 g), peeled and chopped

1 tablespoon grated fresh ginger

2 garlic cloves, minced

One 13.5-ounce (400 ml) can coconut milk

2 to 4 tablespoons white wine or apple cider vinegar

1. Add the vegetable broth to a pot and bring to a boil over high heat. Once boiling, turn off the heat and add the goldenrod flowers. Cover and let infuse for 10 minutes, stirring occasionally. Strain, discarding the solids and setting the broth aside.

2. In the now-empty pot, heat ¼ cup (60 ml) of the oil over medium heat. Add the onions and cook, stirring occasionally, until translucent, 10 to 15 minutes, then stir in the squash, parsnips, ginger, and garlic. Add the broth plus just enough water to cover the vegetables.

3. Increase the heat to medium-high to bring the broth to a gentle boil, then reduce the heat to medium-low and simmer uncovered for about 20 minutes, or until the vegetables are tender.

4. Stir in the coconut milk and wine, then carefully transfer to a blender and blend until smooth. Season with salt and pepper and adjust the richness and acidity with more oil and/or wine to taste.

5. Serve hot, garnished with an extra drizzle of oil. Leftover soup can be cooled and refrigerated for up to 4 days or frozen for up to 6 months.

TIP: For an extra detox-supporting boost, add a handful of fresh cilantro or parsley leaves to the soup just before serving. Both herbs bind to toxins and heavy metals and help eliminate them from the body.

MAGICAL BENEFITS

Vitamin B5 ◆ Parsnips provide vitamin B5, which the body uses to synthesize enzymes that support liver function and fat metabolization.

Potassium ◆ Parsnips and red kuri squash are rich in potassium, which regulates fluid and electrolyte balance, supports kidney function, and aids in toxin elimination.

Vitamin A ◆ Converted from the beta-carotenoids in squash, this vitamin protects liver cells from damage, regulates the function and regeneration of liver cells, and facilitates bile production.

Smoky-Sweet Brussels Sprouts
FOR DEFENSE

Gluten-Free

This culinary spell for defense brings together earthy brussels sprouts and a smoky, sweet-and-sour glaze of paprika, balsamic vinegar, and maple syrup. A topping of toasted pecans and dried cranberries adds crunch and chew. As the brussels sprouts roast, their edges turn irresistibly crispy, while the balsamic-maple coating reduces into a glossy glaze. Serve alongside the Whole Roasted Pumpkin (page 143) for a decadent feast that offers double the defense against oxidative stress.

1 Heat 2 tablespoons of the oil in a large pan over medium-high heat until it sizzles. Add the brussels sprouts and cook, stirring occasionally, for 20 to 30 minutes, adjusting the temperature as needed to prevent burning, until tender inside and crispy and lightly seared on the outside. Season with salt and pepper.

2 While the brussels sprouts cook, add the cranberries and ¾ cup (75 g) pecans to a small pan with the remaining oil and sauté over medium heat until slightly browned, stirring frequently to prevent burning (which can happen suddenly), 5 to 10 minutes. Season with a pinch of salt and pepper, then stir into the brussels sprouts.

3 Whisk together the balsamic vinegar, maple syrup, and smoked paprika in a small bowl. Pour the glaze over the sprouts and increase the heat to high. Cook, stirring often, until the glaze reduces and caramelizes, about 10 minutes. Garnish with the remaining pecans and serve warm.

TIP: For easier digestion, add some chopped fennel to the pan along with the brussels sprouts. Fennel contains anethole, a digestion-stimulating enzyme that helps the body break down the fiber in cruciferous vegetables.

Serves 4 as a main or 6 to 8 as a side

3 tablespoons extra virgin olive oil

2.25 pounds (1 kg) brussels sprouts, stems trimmed and loose outer leaves removed, halved

1 cup (120 g) unsweetened dried cranberries

¾ cup (75 g) chopped pecans, plus ½ cup (50 g) pecan halves for serving

½ cup (120 ml) balsamic vinegar

¼ cup (60 ml) maple syrup

1½ teaspoons smoked paprika

MAGICAL BENEFITS

Glucosinolates ✦ These natural compounds in cruciferous vegetables like brussels sprouts protect plants from pests, and when chewed, break down into powerful antioxidants that help reduce oxidative stress.

Vitamin B9 ✦ Abundant in brussels sprouts, vitamin B9 (folate) supports DNA repair and cell division, helping prevent the kinds of mutations that can lead to cancer.

Fiber ✦ The dietary fiber in brussels sprouts, cranberries, and pecans binds to harmful substances in the gut to help the body eliminate them, while also nourishing beneficial gut bacteria.

Illumination Squash Soup
FOR GLOWING SKIN

Gluten-Free ♦ Nut-Free

This light and warming soup doubles as a spell for luminous skin. Its healing powers lie in the skin-and immunity-supporting antioxidants that give the butternut squash, carrots, and sweet potatoes their bright orange color. It's perfect as a side for the Buckwheat and Fungi Risotto (page 151). To serve as a main, pair it with a protein-rich grain such as amaranth, buckwheat, or quinoa, or with gluten-free bread.

Serves 4 to 6 as a main or 6 to 8 as a side

- 2 quarts (2 L) vegetable broth, or 2 quarts (2 L) water plus 2 vegetable bouillon cubes
- 1 small butternut squash, peeled, seeded, and chopped
- 6 carrots, peeled and chopped
- 2 large sweet potatoes, peeled and chopped
- 1 red onion, chopped
- One 13.5-ounce (400 ml) can coconut milk
- ¼ to ⅓ cup (60 to 80 ml) extra virgin olive oil, plus more for drizzling
- 3 to 4 tablespoons apple cider vinegar
- 1 tablespoon grated fresh ginger
- 1½ to 2 teaspoons agave

1 Pour the broth into a pot and bring to a boil over high heat. Add the squash, carrots, sweet potatoes, onion, coconut milk, oil, vinegar, ginger, and agave and reduce the heat to medium-low.

2 Simmer uncovered for 20 to 30 minutes, until the vegetables are tender enough to be pierced with a fork, then carefully transfer the soup to a blender and purée until silky smooth. Season with salt and pepper and adjust the richness, acidity, and sweetness with more oil, vinegar, and/or agave to taste.

3 Serve hot, drizzling individual portions with more oil. Leftovers can be cooled and refrigerated for up to 4 days or frozen for up to 6 months.

TIP: For an extra layer of richness and depth, caramelize the chopped red onion in 2 tablespoons of olive oil directly in the pot before adding the other vegetables and liquid, adding a splash of water as needed to prevent sticking and scraping up the browned bits from the bottom to enhance the flavor.

MAGICAL BENEFITS

Vitamin A ♦ Converted from the beta-carotene abundant in sweet potatoes, butternut squash, and carrots, this antioxidant vitamin supports collagen production and helps protect and repair skin from free radical damage.

Vitamin C ♦ This antioxidant vitamin found in butternut squash, carrots, and sweet potatoes stimulates the synthesis of collagen and the repair of connective tissues like skin, tendons, bones, and hair. It also protects skin from free radical damage.

Vitamin E ♦ This antioxidant supports healthy skin, hormone production, immune function, and inflammation levels, and protects the skin from damage.

Kale and Cabbage Coleslaw
FOR DETOX

Gluten-Free ◆ Nut-Free

This autumnal coleslaw is a great ally for the body's natural detoxification systems, harnessing the stimulating and cleansing power of crisp white and red cabbage, the pleasant bitterness of kale, and the sharp bite of red onion. Meanwhile, notes of apple cider vinegar, floral orange, lemon zest, and citrusy coriander elevate the dressing. Serve as a side with the Crispy Kohlrabi Steaks (page 222).

1 Thinly shred the white and red cabbage using a mandoline or sharp knife, then chop the shreds into smaller pieces. Combine with the onion and kale in a large bowl.

2 Whisk together the mayonnaise, vinegar, orange zest, orange juice, lemon zest, lemon juice, agave, and coriander in a small bowl. Season with salt and pepper.

3 Pour the dressing over the cabbage mixture and use tongs or your clean hands to toss until the vegetables are thoroughly coated. Refrigerate for at least 30 minutes to allow the flavors to meld and the cabbage to soften slightly.

4 Toss the coleslaw again just before serving to redistribute the dressing. Garnish with the fresh dill, and serve.

TIP: This is a highly versatile recipe. To customize it and expand its medicinal benefits, try adding antioxidant-rich shredded brussels sprouts, carrots, beets, radishes, and/or toasted nuts or seeds.

Serves 4 to 6 as a side

- 1 small white cabbage
- 1 small red cabbage
- 1 red onion, finely chopped
- 4 kale leaves, stems removed, leaves thinly sliced
- 1 cup (240 ml) vegan mayonnaise
- 3 tablespoons apple cider vinegar
- Grated zest and juice of ½ orange
- Grated zest and juice of ½ lemon
- 1 teaspoon agave
- 1 teaspoon ground coriander or black cumin seeds (nigella sativa), optional
- Fresh dill or parsley leaves

MAGICAL BENEFITS

Glucosinolates ◆ These sulfur-containing compounds, which contribute to the bitter taste of cabbage and kale, break down into liver-supporting antioxidants when digested.

Glutathione ◆ Cabbage and kale contain compounds that help the body make glutathione, a powerful antioxidant that protects the liver and indirectly supports kidney function.

Potassium ◆ Found in cabbage, onions, and kale, potassium helps keep sodium levels in check, thereby easing strain on kidneys, improving their function, and aiding in detoxification.

Balsamic-Roasted Onions
FOR IMMUNITY

Gluten-Free ✦ No Sugar Added ✦ Nut-Free

Many antioxidants double as pigments, so the vibrant colors of produce often reveal the presence of important nutrients. This is the case with these roasted red onions, which are packed with nutrients that support gut, heart, and immune system health. Covered in a balsamic-vinegar glaze and baked until tender and caramelized, they practically melt in your mouth. Serve as a side with the Beet-Leek Quiche (page 155) or the Buckwheat and Fungi Risotto (page 151).

Serves 4 to 8 as a side

¼ cup (60 ml) extra virgin olive oil
8 red onions, peeled and halved
½ cup (120 ml) balsamic vinegar
2 teaspoons salt
1 teaspoon pepper

1 Preheat the oven to 350°F (180°C).

2 Grease an oven-safe pan with 1 tablespoon of the oil, then add the onions cut side up. Pour the vinegar evenly over the onions, followed by the remaining oil. Sprinkle the onion halves with the salt and pepper.

3 Once the oven is hot, roast the onions for about 1 hour without moving them, or until their juices and the vinegar have reduced to a glaze and the onions are tender and caramelized. Let cool for about 5 minutes, then serve, spooning some of the balsamic glaze over each portion.

TIP: Save the onion skins, which contain high concentrations of nutritious antioxidant pigments like quercetin, for future vegetable broths. Just freeze them (along with other scraps like carrot peels, beet greens, and vegetable ends) until you're ready to make the broth, then boil, discarding the vegetable solids after straining.

MAGICAL BENEFITS

Quercetin ✦ Red onions contain over twenty-five antioxidant pigments, the most notable of which is quercetin, which neutralizes free radicals, reduces inflammation, and supports balanced immune function.

Onionin A ✦ This sulfur-based compound in onions has potent anti-inflammatory properties that protect the heart and potentially prevent cancerous cell mutations.

Prebiotics ✦ Rich in prebiotic fiber, onions nourish gut microbes, which break down these fibers into short-chain fatty acids that support gut health and immunity and reduce digestive inflammation.

MAGICAL BENEFITS

Monounsaturated Fats ✦ Found in olive oil, pumpkin seeds, and pecans, these healthy fats balance hormones, reduce inflammation, and improve blood flow and reproductive organ function.

Fiber ✦ Found in apples, cranberries, pecans, and pumpkin seeds, dietary fiber helps eliminate excess and synthetic estrogens that can disrupt hormones.

Cordycepin ✦ Cordyceps mushrooms are adaptogens and contain the bioactive compound cordycepin, which helps the body adapt to stress and thereby protect against stress-related hormonal disruption.

Mixed Greens Salad with Candied Pecans
FOR FERTILITY

Gluten-Free

From the omega-3 fatty acid–filled nuts to the antioxidant-packed mushroom, this superfood salad brims with the magic of rebirth. The crisp, sweet apples and tart cranberries complement the crunchy candied pecans. Earthy cordyceps mushroom powder adds depth to both the pecans' candied coating and the tangy mustard vinaigrette. Opt for raw pumpkin seeds, which are higher in antioxidants and healthy fats than when they are roasted. Serve as a side with the Zucchini Quiche (page 81) for a complete hormone-supporting meal.

1. Preheat the oven to 350°F (180°C). Grease a rimmed baking sheet with oil.

2. Add the mixed baby greens, kale, apples, pumpkin seeds, and dried cranberries to a large salad bowl and toss to combine.

3. **To make the candied cordyceps pecans,** place the pecans in a bowl, then add the oil and agave and toss until the pecans are thoroughly coated. Mix in the cordyceps powder and cinnamon and season with salt and pepper.

4. Spread the pecans evenly over the prepared baking sheet and roast for 10 to 15 minutes, stirring every few minutes, until the pecans begin to brown and the sugars caramelize, checking frequently near the end of cooking to ensure they don't burn. Set aside to cool.

5. **To make the cordyceps-mustard vinaigrette,** add the oil, vinegar, mustard, agave, and cordyceps powder to a small bowl or jar and whisk or shake until well combined. Season with salt and pepper.

6. Drizzle the vinaigrette over the salad and toss to coat evenly. Top with the candied pecans and reserved apple pieces, garnish with the remaining pumpkin seeds and cranberries, and serve.

TIP: You can source cordyceps powder at farmers markets, herbal shops, or online herbal and fungi retailers. If you want to make the salad in advance or think you may have leftovers, serve the dressing on the side and refrigerate the salad and vinaigrette separately to prevent soggy greens.

Serves 4 to 6 as a side

- 4 cups (120 g) loosely packed mixed baby greens
- 4 kale leaves, stems removed, chopped
- 3 apples (Gala, Honeycrisp, McIntosh, or Pink Lady), cored and cubed, a few pieces reserved for serving
- 2 tablespoons unsweetened dried cranberries, plus 1 tablespoon for serving
- 2 tablespoons raw pumpkin seeds, plus 1 tablespoon for serving

CANDIED CORDYCEPS PECANS

- 2 cups (200 g) pecan halves
- 1 tablespoon extra virgin olive oil, plus more for greasing
- 1 tablespoon agave
- 1 teaspoon cordyceps powder
- ⅛ teaspoon ground cinnamon

CORDYCEPS-MUSTARD VINAIGRETTE

- 3 tablespoons extra virgin olive oil
- 2 tablespoons apple cider vinegar
- 1 tablespoon Dijon mustard
- 1 teaspoon agave
- 1 teaspoon cordyceps powder

Ghostly Stuffed Squash
FOR DEFENSE

Gluten-Free ✦ No Sugar Added ✦ Nut-Free

Even the most ghostly white vegetables, like the white acorn squash in this recipe, contain powerful antioxidants that support everything from heart health to anti-cancerous actions. As the squash roasts, its tender, subtly sweet flesh absorbs the flavors of the caramelized onions, potatoes, and coconut, creating a dish that is as comforting as it is protective. To serve this as a main, pair it with a protein-rich grain like amaranth, buckwheat, or quinoa.

Serves 2 as a main or 4 as a side

- ¼ cup (60 ml) extra virgin olive oil, plus more for drizzling
- 2 to 3 white acorn squash or other small squash, halved and seeded
- 2 white onions, chopped
- 1 pound (450 g) small, waxy potatoes (such as red or Yukon Gold), peeled and diced
- One 13.5-ounce (400 ml) can coconut milk or soy cream

1. Preheat the oven to 350°F (180°C).

2. Rub 2 tablespoons of the oil over the skin of the squash halves, then place them cut side up in a large oven-safe pan or baking dish. Using a paring knife, cut a crosshatch pattern about ½-inch (1.25 cm) deep into the flesh to allow the filling to more deeply flavor the squash halves as they cook.

3. Heat the remaining oil in a separate pan over high heat, then add the onions and potatoes. Cook for 10 to 15 minutes, adjusting the temperature as needed to prevent burning, until the potatoes are soft and the onions have begun to caramelize, stirring frequently. Deglaze with a splash of water whenever they begin to stick and scrape the bottom of the pan to reincorporate any browned bits. Season with salt and pepper.

4. Reduce the heat to medium and add the coconut milk. Simmer for 10 to 15 minutes, until the liquid is reduced by half and thick enough to coat the back of a spoon. Divide the filling between the squash halves.

5. Roast the stuffed squash for 20 to 30 minutes, until the squash is tender and the filling is lightly browned on top. Allow the squash to cool for about 5 minutes, then garnish with an extra drizzle of oil and serve.

TIP: Peeled and diced parsnips or white sweet potatoes can be substituted for the potatoes for a similar creamy texture. If you have histamine sensitivities, substitute the onions with leeks for a milder, low-histamine alternative.

MAGICAL BENEFITS

Anthoxanthins ✦ Found in pale fruits and vegetables like white squash and potatoes, these colorless antioxidants neutralize free radicals and reduce inflammation.

Potassium and Magnesium ✦ Onions, potatoes, and squash are charged with potassium and magnesium, minerals essential for proper muscular, cardiovascular, and immune function.

Allicin and Onionin A ✦ These sulfur-containing compounds in white onions act as antioxidants.

Seaweed and Beet Salad
FOR OXYGENATION

Gluten-Free ✦ No Sugar Added ✦ Nut-Free

Algae, a category that includes seaweed, is estimated to produce the majority of Earth's oxygen. When eaten, seaweed can give you an oxygenating boost, too, thanks to its magical nutritive profile. This nourishing salad shows how deliciously seaweed blends with land greens and vegetables. Serve as a side with the heart-supporting Baked Purple Cauliflower and Potatoes with Rosemary Vinaigrette (page 214).

Serves 2 as a side

- 0.5 ounce (15 g) dried wakame or sugar kelp seaweed
- 4 small beets
- 2 tablespoons extra virgin olive oil
- 1 tablespoon balsamic vinegar
- 4 cups (120 g) loosely packed mixed baby greens
- 1 shallot, thinly sliced
- 2 teaspoons chia seeds

1 Add the wakame and 2 cups (480 ml) of cold water to a bowl and soak for 10 to 15 minutes, stirring occasionally to dislodge any additional salt. Drain well and squeeze out any excess water. Separate the seaweed strands and lay them on a clean dish towel to dry slightly. Using scissors, cut the rehydrated wakame into bite-size pieces.

2 While the wakame rehydrates, bring a medium saucepan of water to a boil over high heat. Boil the beets for about 15 minutes, or until tender, then blanch them in cold water before peeling and chopping. Set aside.

3 In a small bowl, whisk together the oil, vinegar, and a pinch of salt and pepper to make the dressing.

4 Combine the mixed baby greens, beets, shallot, and wakame in a large bowl, then drizzle the dressing over the salad, reserving some for serving. Gently toss to coat evenly.

5 Divide the salad between individual plates, top with the chia seeds, and finish with an extra drizzle of the dressing and a sprinkle of freshly ground black pepper. Serve immediately.

TIP: In addition to wakame, there are several other seaweeds that are great in salads. Nori (often used for sushi) can be toasted and crumbled over salads for added umami flavor and a flaky, crispy texture. Dulse adds a salty, savory punch and is delicious torn into pieces in salads or blended into dressings. Arame has a delicate, sweet flavor and a tender texture. Hijiki has a strong, earthy flavor and a slightly chewy texture and works well when lightly simmered and combined with grains or vegetables. Sea lettuce has a tender texture and a mild flavor and can be shredded and mixed into green salads or used as a garnish.

MAGICAL BENEFITS

Iron ✦ Seaweed and chia seeds are good sources of iron, a trace mineral essential for the production of hemoglobin, which carries oxygen in the blood and delivers it throughout the body.

Vitamin C ✦ Dark leafy greens and beets provide vitamin C, which enhances iron absorption from plant-based foods.

Natural Nitrates ✦ Unlike the harmful nitrates found in processed foods, the natural nitrates found in beets relax blood vessels to enhance oxygen delivery, regulate blood pressure, and support overall cardiovascular health.

Breaded Brussels Sprouts
FOR RECOVERY

Gluten-Free ♦ No Sugar Added ♦ Nut-Free

Brussels sprouts are powerhouses of protective and reparative potential thanks to their antioxidant actions. These restorative sprouts bring together indulgence and nourishment, making them the ultimate comfort food. Roasted until tender, the sprouts are complemented by the zesty lemon and a crispy, herbed bread crumb topping that provides a satisfying crunch. Serve as a side with the Comforting Potato and Corn Soup (page 147) or the Beet-Leek Quiche (page 155).

Serves 4 as a side

- 1 pound (450 g) brussels sprouts, stems trimmed and loose outer leaves removed, halved
- Juice of ½ lemon
- ¼ cup plus 2 tablespoons (90 ml) extra virgin olive oil
- ½ cup (60 g) dried gluten-free bread crumbs
- 1 teaspoon dried or 4 teaspoons fresh chopped oregano
- 1 teaspoon dried or 4 teaspoons fresh chopped basil

1. Preheat the oven to 400°F (200°C).

2. Bring a large saucepan of salted water to a boil over high heat. Add the brussels sprouts and boil for 15 to 20 minutes, until the sprouts can be easily pierced with a fork. Drain, then spread the sprouts in a single layer on a clean dish towel to dry slightly.

3. Divide the sprouts between small, single-serving oven-safe baking dishes or add them all to a single oven-safe pan or baking dish. Drizzle evenly with the lemon juice, followed by 3 tablespoons of the oil.

4. In a small bowl, mix together the bread crumbs, oregano, and basil, and season with salt and pepper. Sprinkle the herbed bread crumbs evenly over the sprouts, then drizzle with the remaining oil.

5. Roast for about 30 minutes, or until the bread crumb topping is golden brown. Serve right away with an extra sprinkle of freshly ground black pepper.

TIP: To boost the glucosinolate levels in the brussels sprouts, lightly freeze them for an hour before cooking. Frost not only activates glucosinolates but also softens fibers, making them easier to digest.

MAGICAL BENEFITS

Glucosinolates ♦ Chopping and chewing transforms these natural compounds found in cruciferous vegetables like brussels sprouts into antioxidants that support cardiovascular health, reduce cellular damage, and indirectly aid tissue repair.

Carvacrol and thymol ♦ These compounds found in oregano have antibacterial, antiviral, and anti-inflammatory effects.

Flavonoids ♦ Found in brussels sprouts, basil, and oregano, these antioxidant compounds protect cells from oxidative stress, reducing the risk of DNA mutations and supporting cellular health.

MAGICAL BENEFITS

Vitamin E ✦ Found in almonds and walnuts, this antioxidant vitamin shields brain cells from damaging free radicals while supporting memory, cognition, and overall neurological health.

Hericenones and Erinacines ✦ These active compounds in lion's mane mushrooms have been shown to protect the brain and support the production of brain cells.

Polyphenols ✦ Abundant in cinnamon, walnuts, and dates, these plant compounds support neurotransmitter activity and the formation of new neural connections.

Eve's Apple Torte
FOR COGNITION

Gluten-Free

When Eve gave into temptation by picking an apple from the tree of knowledge, perhaps she was tempted by their brain-supporting benefits. This golden apple torte layers caramelized apple slices with a spiced date caramel filling infused with the earthy, chocolate-like notes of medicinal mushrooms, all nestled in a crunchy nut crust. With its warm aromas of cinnamon, ginger, and roasted nuts, it is both an ode to Eve's pursuit of knowledge and a celebration of its ingredients' cognition-nourishing magic.

Serves 4 to 6

NUT CRUST

1½ cups (180 g) almond flour

¼ cup (60 g) cold-pressed virgin coconut oil, melted, plus 1 tablespoon for greasing

½ cup (60 g) walnuts, finely chopped

¼ cup (55 g) packed light brown sugar

DATE CARAMEL FILLING

1 cup (20 g) pitted dates, soaked in hot water for 10 minutes to soften

Half a 13.5-ounce (400 ml) can coconut milk

1 teaspoon lion's mane powder, optional

1 teaspoon vanilla extract or ½ teaspoon vanilla powder

CARAMELIZED APPLES

2 tablespoons cold-pressed virgin coconut oil

4 apples (Gala, Honeycrisp, McIntosh, or Pink Lady), peeled, cored, and thinly sliced

2 tablespoons packed light brown sugar

2 tablespoons ground ginger

1 tablespoon ground cinnamon

1 Preheat the oven to 350°F (180°C). Lightly grease a round 9-inch (23 cm) tart or cake pan with oil.

2 To make the nut crust, combine the almond flour, oil, walnuts, brown sugar, and a pinch of salt in a bowl. Mix until the mixture comes together into a rough, cohesive dough that holds its form, then press evenly into the bottom and ¾ inch (2 cm) up the sides of the prepared pan.

3 Bake for 12 to 15 minutes, until the crust is crisp and golden brown around the edges but soft and moist in the middle. Set aside to cool, leaving the oven on.

4 To make the date caramel filling, combine the dates, coconut milk, lion's mane powder, if using, vanilla, and a pinch of salt in a blender or the bowl of a food processor and blend until smooth and spreadable. Adjust the consistency, if desired, by adding more coconut milk to thin it out. Set aside.

5 To make the caramelized apples, add the oil to a large pan set over medium heat, then add the apples, brown sugar, ginger, and cinnamon. Sauté the apples for about 5 minutes, stirring gently so as not to break the slices, until slightly tender and caramelized. Remove from the heat and set aside.

6 Once the crust has cooled, spread the date caramel filling evenly over it, then arrange the caramelized apple slices on top in concentric circles.

7 Bake for an additional 30 minutes, or until the apples are soft and the edges of the crust are deep golden brown with the texture of a crisp cookie.

8 Remove from the oven and allow to cool completely. Serve at room temperature or chilled. Store in an airtight container for up to 2 days at room temperature, up to 5 days in the refrigerator, or up to 6 months in the freezer.

TIP: For an additional brain-nourishing boost, add 1 teaspoon ground turmeric (which has anti-inflammatory and neuron-protective properties) plus a pinch of freshly ground black pepper (to increase absorption) to the date caramel filling. The turmeric's flavor will be disguised by the sweetness of the apples and the warmth of the cinnamon and ginger.

Spiced Sweet Potato-Hibiscus Pie
FOR IMMUNITY

Gluten-Free

This pie contains multiple layers of protective root, flower, and nut magic. The almond-coconut crust, rich in healthy plant fats, offers a satisfying, buttery crunch. Beneath it lies the spiced sweet potato filling, its natural sweetness balanced by the tart hibiscus jelly on top. Bursting with color, flavor, and protective antioxidants, this pie is both nourishing and indulgent and makes for a perfect finale to an autumnal feast.

Serves 4 to 6

ALMOND CRUST

¾ cup plus 1 tablespoon (100 g) almond flour

½ cup (100 g) cane sugar

¼ cup (60 g) cold-pressed virgin coconut oil, melted, plus 1 tablespoon for greasing

2 tablespoons all-purpose gluten-free flour blend (see page 5)

½ teaspoon ground ginger or 1 teaspoon fresh grated ginger

SWEET POTATO FILLING

½ sweet potato, peeled and diced

1½ cups (300 g) cane sugar

Half a 13.5-ounce (400 ml) can coconut cream

3 tablespoons aquafaba (see page 5), chilled

1 tablespoon plus 1½ teaspoons all-purpose gluten-free flour blend (see page 5)

½ teaspoon salt

¼ teaspoon ground ginger

⅛ teaspoon ground nutmeg

HIBISCUS JELLY

2 cups (480 ml) filtered water

¼ cup (15 g) dried hibiscus flowers

1½ teaspoons agar-agar powder

1 Preheat the oven to 350°F (180°C). Grease a tart pan with a removable bottom with oil.

2 To make the almond crust, add the almond flour, sugar, oil, gluten-free flour, ginger, and a pinch of salt to a bowl and mix until the ingredients come together as a sticky dough. Press the dough evenly into the bottom and ¾ inch (2 cm) up the sides of the prepared tart pan.

3 Bake for about 15 minutes, or until the crust is crisp and golden brown around the edges but soft and moist in the middle. When you insert a toothpick into the center, it should come out clean or with just a few moist crumbs attached. Remove from the oven, leaving the oven on, and set aside to cool.

4 To make the sweet potato filling, bring a small saucepan of water to a boil over medium heat. Add the sweet potato and boil for 10 to 15 minutes, until tender enough to be pierced with a fork. Remove from the heat, drain, and transfer the sweet potato to a blender.

5 Add the sugar, coconut cream, aquafaba, gluten-free flour, salt, ginger, and nutmeg to the blender and blend until it reaches a smooth, batter-like consistency. Pour the filling over the cooled crust. Refrigerate the tart while you prepare the hibiscus jelly.

6 To make the hibiscus jelly, bring the filtered water to a boil in a small saucepan over high heat, then turn off the heat. Add the hibiscus flowers and let them steep for about 10 minutes to infuse the water with their flavor, then strain out the solids and discard.

7 Return the hibiscus tea to the saucepan and sprinkle over the agar-agar powder. Whisk to combine. Bring the mixture to a gentle boil over high heat, stirring constantly for 2 to 3 minutes, until the agar-agar is fully dissolved, then remove from the heat.

8 Allow the hibiscus mixture to cool for about 10 minutes, then carefully pour it over the sweet potato layer in the tart pan. Refrigerate the tart until the hibiscus jelly is set, at least 2 to 4 hours, before serving. Run a knife around the edges of the pie to loosen it before removing the sides of the springform pan. Store in an airtight container in the refrigerator for up to 4 days.

TIP: You can substitute any herb or tea you like, such as a chai tea blend or rooibos tea, for the hibiscus. Or substitute the hibiscus tea with fruit juice such as nutrient-packed cranberry juice.

MAGICAL BENEFITS

Beta-Carotene ✦ This carotenoid in plants like sweet potatoes and hibiscus acts as an antioxidant, neutralizing free radicals and supporting skin, vision, and immune health.

Magnesium ✦ This essential mineral, found in almond flour, sweet potatoes, and coconut cream, helps control inflammation and supports the production of enzymes that neutralize free radicals and remove environmental toxins.

Manganese ✦ This trace mineral found in sweet potatoes and almonds supports the body's natural defenses by neutralizing oxidative stress caused by harmful free radicals.

MAGICAL BENEFITS

Anethole ✦ In addition to its antioxidant actions, anethole, the primary medicinal component of star anise, is known for its vast anti-inflammatory benefits.

Omega-3 Fatty Acids ✦ Alpha-linolenic acid (ALA), a plant-based omega-3 abundant in nuts like walnuts and almonds, is converted by the body into compounds that calm inflammatory signals.

Cinnamaldehyde ✦ The key compound in cinnamon, cinnamaldehyde helps block molecules and enzymes that trigger inflammatory responses.

Fire-Cooling Cinnamon Rolls
FOR INFLAMMATION RELIEF

Gluten-Free

Tucked inside these golden cinnamon rolls are nutrients and medicinal compounds that help cool the fires of unchecked inflammation. A caramelized apple filling brings a buttery sweetness and soft, luscious texture. Topped with a maple–star anise glaze, they're a comforting treat for chilly days that soothes both body and soul. For extra comfort, serve with the Probiotic White Hot Chocolate (page 261).

Makes about 12 rolls

DOUGH

- 2 cups (480 ml) almond milk
- 4 star anise pods
- 2 cinnamon sticks or ½ teaspoon ground cinnamon, plus more for serving
- ½ cup (120 g) cold-pressed virgin coconut oil, melted, plus more for greasing
- ¼ cup (50 g) cane sugar
- 1½ teaspoons grated fresh ginger
- 1 teaspoon vanilla extract or ½ teaspoon vanilla powder
- 4 cups plus 3 tablespoons (500 g) all-purpose gluten-free flour blend (see page 5)
- 1 cup (120 g) arrowroot flour
- 1 packet active dry yeast

CARAMELIZED APPLE FILLING

- 3 apples (Gala, Honeycrisp, McIntosh, or Pink Lady), cored and diced
- ¾ cup plus 3 tablespoons (200 g) packed light brown sugar
- 1 tablespoon ground cinnamon, plus more for serving
- 1 cup (120 g) chopped walnuts

MAPLE–STAR ANISE GLAZE

- ¼ cup (60 ml) maple syrup
- 2 star anise pods
- ½ cup (60 g) powdered sugar
- ¼ teaspoon vanilla powder or ½ teaspoon vanilla extract

1. **To make the dough,** add the almond milk to a saucepan along with the star anise pods and cinnamon sticks and bring to a gentle simmer over low heat. Let the milk and spices infuse for about 10 minutes, lowering the heat as needed to prevent the milk from boiling. If you used whole spices, strain out the spices and discard.

2. Combine the infused almond milk, oil, sugar, ginger, and vanilla in a large bowl and let the mixture cool for about 5 minutes to avoid killing the yeast once it's added.

3. In a separate bowl, mix together the gluten-free flour, arrowroot flour, and yeast. Gradually add the dry ingredients to the wet ingredients, mixing until a sticky, malleable dough forms.

4. Knead the dough on a floured surface for 5 to 10 minutes, until smooth, then place it in a lightly oiled bowl, cover with a clean dish towel, and set in a warm location (near a heater, outside in the sun, or in an oven warmed to 80°F/30°C and then turned off). Let the dough rise for about 1 hour, until doubled in size.

5. **To make the caramelized apple filling,** while the dough rises, in a large pan over medium-high heat, cook the apples, brown sugar, cinnamon, and a pinch of salt, stirring occasionally, for 5 to 10 minutes, until the apples are tender and the sugar forms a caramelized glaze. Set aside.

6. Once the dough has risen, on a floured surface, roll it into a 10-by-15-inch (25 by 38 cm) rectangle about ¼ inch (6 mm) thick. Grease a rimmed baking sheet with oil.

7. Spread the apple mixture evenly over the dough, and then sprinkle the walnuts on top. Starting from the long edge, roll the dough into a tight cylinder, being careful not to press out the filling. Cut into slices about 1½ inches (4 cm) thick and transfer them to the prepared baking sheet.

8. Cover the rolls with a clean dish towel and let them rise for another 30 minutes at room temperature. While the rolls rise, preheat the oven to 350°F (180°C).

9. Bake for 30 to 35 minutes, until golden brown, then remove from the oven and let cool completely.

10. **To make the maple–star anise glaze,** add the maple syrup and star anise to a small saucepan and warm over low heat. Let the flavors infuse for 10 minutes, then turn off the heat and discard the star anise. Whisk the powdered sugar and vanilla into the infused syrup until you have a smooth, thick glaze.

11. Drizzle the glaze over the tops of the cooled rolls and decorate them with a dusting of cinnamon before serving. Store in an airtight container for up to 2 days at room temperature, up to 5 days in the fridge, or up to 3 months in the freezer.

TIP: Feel free to play around with the spices in this recipe. Other roots and seeds imbued with anti-inflammatory magic include turmeric, ground cloves, and cardamom.

Marzipan Muffins
FOR MOOD BALANCE

Gluten-Free

Baked into these ginger-spiced muffins is the mood-boosting plant magic that supports neurotransmitter function and emotional regulation. Their golden exteriors hide a surprise: In the middle of each is a creamy marzipan center that practically melts into the tender almond and buckwheat cake. Finished with a sprinkle of crunchy sliced almonds and sugar, these muffins are both indulgent and uplifting.

Makes 12 muffins

2 tablespoons cold-pressed virgin coconut oil, melted, for greasing

1 cup (200 g) buckwheat flour

¾ cup plus 3 tablespoons (200 g) packed dark brown sugar

Half a 13.5-ounce (400 ml) can coconut milk

1¼ cups (150 g) almond flour

¾ cup (150 g) cane sugar, plus more for sprinkling

3 tablespoons maple syrup

2 tablespoons grated fresh ginger

1½ teaspoons baking soda

1½ teaspoons ground cinnamon

½ teaspoon ground ginger

Grated zest and juice of ½ lemon

½ cup (120 ml) aquafaba (see page 5), chilled

¼ cup (60 g) vegan marzipan (see Tip)

¼ cup (30 g) sliced almonds

1 Preheat the oven to 350°F (180°C). Grease the wells of a muffin pan with oil or line them with paper liners.

2 Combine the buckwheat flour, brown sugar, coconut milk, almond flour, cane sugar, maple syrup, grated ginger, baking soda, cinnamon, ground ginger, lemon zest, and lemon juice in a large bowl. Mix until well combined, then gradually stir in the aquafaba until you achieve a smooth, thick batter. Spoon half of the batter into the wells of the muffin pan, filling each about one-third full.

3 Roll the marzipan into 12 small balls, each about the size of 1 teaspoon. Place 1 marzipan ball in the center of the batter in each cup. Divide the remaining batter among the muffin cups to completely cover the marzipan. Sprinkle with the sliced almonds and extra cane sugar.

4 Bake for 20 to 25 minutes, until a toothpick inserted off-center (so it doesn't hit the marzipan) comes out clean.

5 Allow the muffins to cool in the pan for a few minutes, then transfer them to a wire rack to cool completely before serving. Store in an airtight container for up to 3 days at room temperature, up to 1 week in the refrigerator, or up to 1 year in the freezer. If frozen, bring to room temperature and re-bake for about 15 minutes at 350°F (180°C) before serving.

TIP: If you can't find vegan marzipan (made with sugar that is not processed with bone char), you can make your own by processing almonds and sugar (2 parts almond flour to 1 part vegan powdered sugar or cane sugar, depending on whether you want a smoother or rougher texture) together in a food processor until they form a paste. You can also substitute any nuts you like for the almonds, such as walnuts, macadamia nuts, or pistachios.

MAGICAL BENEFITS

Magnesium ◆ This mineral found in almonds and buckwheat regulates neurotransmitters like serotonin. Stress depletes magnesium, so adequate levels may enhance resilience to chronic stress.

Gingerol ◆ This bioactive compound in ginger works to reduce inflammation by blocking processes that create harmful inflammatory substances that can interfere with neurotransmitter functions.

Monounsaturated Fats ◆ Almonds and certain nut oils provide healthy monounsaturated fats, which support the integrity of brain cell membranes and aid in the production and function of mood-regulating neurotransmitters.

Ginger-Spiced Hibiscus Pears
FOR DIGESTION

Gluten-Free ✦ Nut-Free

These blushing red hibiscus-poached pears are fragrant, sticky, tender, and filled with the kinds of fiber needed to balance the entire digestive system. The sweetness of the halved pears is offset by the tart hibiscus flowers in the poaching liquid. Served nestled on a bed of silky spiced coconut cream, this dinner-party perfect dessert is as beautiful as it is soothing for the digestive system.

Serves 4

STICKY PEARS

- 2 tablespoons dried hibiscus flowers
- ½ cup (100 g) cane sugar
- ¼ cup (60 ml) maple syrup or agave
- 1 teaspoon grated fresh ginger
- ½ teaspoon ground cinnamon
- 2 Bosc, Anjou, or Conference pears, halved and cored

GINGER-SPICED CREAM SAUCE

- One 13.5-ounce (400 ml) can coconut milk
- 2 tablespoons cane sugar
- ½ teaspoon ground cinnamon
- ½ teaspoon grated fresh ginger

1 **To make the sticky pears,** add the dried hibiscus flowers and 4¼ cups (1 L) of hot (not boiling) water to a large bowl and steep for 5 to 10 minutes, then strain into a saucepan large enough to hold the 2 halved pears comfortably. Add the sugar, maple syrup, ginger, and cinnamon.

2 Bring the liquid to a gentle simmer over high heat, stirring to dissolve the sugar. Once the sugar has completely dissolved, about 5 minutes, lower the heat to medium and gently place the pear halves into the poaching liquid.

3 Simmer for 20 to 25 minutes, until the pears have turned lightly pink and are tender, occasionally spooning the liquid over the pears for even flavor. They will float slightly, so gently turn them over halfway through to ensure even poaching and color.

4 **To make the ginger-spiced cream sauce,** heat the coconut milk with the sugar, cinnamon, and ginger in a small saucepan over low heat, whisking until well combined. Continue to simmer for 15 to 20 minutes, until the sauce thickens to a syrupy consistency.

5 Divide the sauce between shallow bowls or plates, then top each with one of the poached pear halves. Drizzle a generous amount of the syrup over the pears. Serve warm, or cooled to room temperature and then chilled in the refrigerator for 30 to 60 minutes.

TIP: The herbs and fruits in this recipe can be adapted for each season. Try poaching the pears in pine needle syrup in winter, poaching strawberries in Earl Grey tea in spring, or poaching peaches in rose syrup in summer.

MAGICAL BENEFITS

Tartaric Acid ✦ This weak acid, responsible for the sour flavor of hibiscus flowers, enhances the activity of digestive enzymes and fosters the growth of beneficial gut bacteria.

Gingerol ✦ The active ingredient in ginger, gingerol, stimulates digestive enzymes, reduces inflammation, calms the digestive system, and accelerates the emptying of the stomach to alleviate nausea.

Soluble and Insoluble Fiber ✦ Pears contain soluble fiber, like pectin, which forms a gel that softens bowel movements, as well as insoluble fiber, which adds bulk to help prevent constipation.

Adaptogenic Vinegar
FOR STRESS RELIEF

Gluten-Free ◆ No Sugar Added ◆ Nut-Free

With a blend of fruity, floral, nutty flavors and subtly bitter, spicy undertones, this vinegar is a versatile way to infuse adaptogenic medicine into salad dressings, sauces, sautés, and more. It takes several weeks of hands-off time to fully infuse the vinegar, but the wait is worth it! If you make it in advance, you'll be well stocked through the season.

Makes 4¼ cups (1 L)

¼ cup (15 g) dried ashwagandha root

¼ cup (15 g) dried holy basil (tulsi) leaves

¼ cup (15 g) dried eleuthero root (Siberian ginseng)

¼ cup (15 g) dried rhodiola root

4¼ cups (1 L) apple cider vinegar

1 Fill a clean 32-ounce (1 L) mason jar with all the dried plants. Pour in the vinegar and ensure the leaves are fully covered by weighing them down with a fermentation weight. If you don't have one, you can sterilize a rock that fits inside the jar's rim by boiling it for 10 minutes and use it to keep the plants submerged. This is essential, as any exposed plant matter can mold and spoil the tincture.

2 Seal the jar tightly to prevent evaporation and contamination and place it in a cool, dark location away from direct sunlight. Allow the mixture to steep for 2 weeks to 1 month, shaking the jar gently every few days to help circulate the vinegar around the plant matter and ensure that the plants' medicinal compounds are evenly extracted.

3 After the steeping period, strain the extraction through a fine-mesh strainer or cheesecloth, pressing down on the solids to extract as much liquid as possible, into clean, sterilized bottles or jars for storage, then discard the solids. Label the bottles with the contents and date, and store at room temperature away from direct sunlight for up to 6 months or refrigerate for up to 1 year.

TIP: The herbs in this vinegar can also be prepared as an alcohol-based tincture (see page 15) for an even more potent extraction that can be consumed like an alcoholic beverage or as a decoction-infusion (see page 15) to make an adaptogenic beverage.

MAGICAL BENEFITS

Withanolides ◆ Ashwagandha root, a plant used in Ayurvedic medicine, is renowned for its calming and rejuvenating effects. Withanolides, its active compounds, reduce cortisol levels, promote relaxation, and enhance stress resilience.

Ursolic Acid ◆ Holy basil (tulsi), revered for its ability to promote mental clarity and focus, contains ursolic acid, which lowers cortisol levels and supports stress resilience.

Eleutherosides ◆ These active compounds in the roots of the eleuthero plant, known for boosting energy and stamina, help regulate cortisol and adrenal activity and improve oxygen utilization.

Rosavins and Salidroside ◆ These compounds in rhodiola increase resistance to physical and mental stress by regulating adrenal activity, lowering cortisol, boosting serotonin and dopamine, and helping cells produce and use energy more efficiently.

Forest Tincture
FOR IMMUNITY

Gluten-Free ✦ *No Sugar Added* ✦ *Nut-Free*

This immune system-regulating tincture is infused with the essence of the forest in the form of medicinal berries, roots, and mushrooms. The woody, bitter aroma of reishi mushrooms, the potent fruity sweetness of elderberries, astragalus's licorice notes, and earthy eleuthero make this tincture the perfect base for an autumnal cocktail (or mocktail, if making the glycerine-based alcohol-free version!). It takes a few weeks of hands-off time to fully infuse the alcohol, but the wait is worth it! Consider making it in advance so you always have some on hand. To use, dilute approximately 1 teaspoon of the tincture into an 8-ounce (235 ml) glass of water or juice and take once or twice daily for immune support, or use as a spirit for cocktails.

Makes 4¼ cups (1 L)

¾ cup (50 g) dried reishi mushrooms

¼ cup (15 g) dried eleuthero root (Siberian ginseng)

⅓ cup (50 g) dried elderberries

¾ cup (50 g) dried astragalus root

4¼ cups (1 L) minimum 80-proof alcohol such as vodka, rum, or gin, or 3 cups (720 ml) vegetable glycerin plus 1½ cups (360 ml) distilled water

1 Place the reishi mushrooms, eleuthero root, elderberries, and astragalus root in a clean 32-ounce (1 L) glass jar and completely submerge in the alcohol.

2 Seal the jar tightly with the lid and store in a cool, dark place for at least 2 weeks or up to 6 weeks, shaking the jar gently every few days to help circulate the vinegar around the plant matter and ensure that the plants' medicinal compounds are evenly extracted.

3 The longer you let the ingredients infuse into the alcohol, the stronger the tincture will be.

4 After the steeping period, strain the tincture through a fine-mesh strainer or cheesecloth, pressing down on the solids to extract as much liquid as possible, into clean, sterilized bottles or jars for storage, then discard the solids. Label the bottles with the contents and date, and store away from direct sunlight for up to 3 years.

TIP: Consider mixing 1 part tincture with 4 parts tonic water or ginger ale (like the Turmeric Ginger Ale on page 138) for a delicious medicinal drink!

MAGICAL BENEFITS

Eleutherosides ✦ These active compounds in eleuthero root enhance the activity of immune cells and modulate inflammatory responses.

Beta-Glucans ✦ Reishi mushrooms are rich in bioactive compounds like beta-glucans, which help make the immune system more effective at fighting threats.

Anthocyanins ✦ These powerful antioxidant compounds in elderberries help reduce inflammation, protect cells from damage, and enhance immune response.

Polysaccharides ✦ Astragalus root is recognized for its immune-stimulating polysaccharides, which strengthen the immune system by boosting white blood cell production.

Floral Tea
FOR VIVID DREAMS

Gluten-Free ✦ No Sugar Added ✦ Nut-Free

Dreamland is still a relatively mystifying realm, but science has given us a few clues about what dreams are made of. This tea's bouquet of passionflower and blue lotus intertwines with the herbal earthiness of mugwort, creating an elixir that soothes the senses and stimulates dreams. The delicate floral notes are balanced by the grounding depth of lion's mane. With enough practice (and tea!), you might even achieve a lucid dream state.

Serves 1

1 tablespoon dried blue lotus flowers
1 tablespoon dried mugwort
1 tablespoon dried passionflower
1½ teaspoons lion's mane mushroom powder
1 cup (240 ml) filtered water

1 In a teapot or heat-safe container, combine the blue lotus flowers, mugwort, passionflower, and lion's mane mushroom powder.

2 Heat the filtered water to just below boiling, then pour the hot water over the dried plants. Let the mixture infuse for 5 to 10 minutes, depending on how strong you prefer your tea, then strain and discard the herbs.

3 Consume the tea immediately, ideally about 1 hour before sleep, to help stimulate dreams during the night!

TIP: To source medicinal herbs and mushrooms like those in this recipe, consider specialty suppliers, local farmers markets, or online herbal and mushroom suppliers.

MAGICAL BENEFITS

Apigenin ✦ This flavonoid found in passionflower binds to GABA receptors in the brain, promoting relaxation and creating conditions conducive to restful sleep and vivid dreaming.

Apomorphine and Nuciferine ✦ Present in blue lotus flowers, these compounds interact with serotonin and dopamine receptors, promoting relaxation, better mood, and vivid dreams.

Thujone ✦ Found in mugwort, this compound enhances dream recall and promotes lucid dreaming by increasing cerebral blood flow and influencing the neurotransmitters involved in REM sleep.

Hericenones and Erinacines ✦ These compounds in lion's mane mushrooms stimulate nerve growth factor, which helps the brain form new connections and consolidate memories during sleep, contributing to vivid and memorable dreams.

Flower Vinaigrette
FOR RADIANT SKIN

Gluten-Free ◆ Nut-Free

This versatile vinaigrette combines the vivid zing of hibiscus, the richness of a blend of skin-supporting flower oils, and the mild sweetness of minced shallots. The linseed, sunflower, and olive oils offer a variety of antioxidants that help connective tissue regenerate to keep your skin shining throughout the year. This dressing pairs great with any salad, especially the Citrus, Sugar Snap Pea, and Endive Salad (page 40), the Radish, Cucumber, and Hibiscus Salad (page 55), and the Peach and Flower Salad (page 113).

1 Combine the apple cider vinegar with the hibiscus flowers in a glass jar, seal tightly, and let infuse at room temperature, shaking occasionally to help extract the petals' essence, for 1 hour, or until the vinegar turns a vivid red color. Strain through a fine-mesh strainer, discarding the petals and reserving the vinegar.

2 In a bowl or jar, combine the hibiscus-infused vinegar, extra virgin olive oil, linseed oil, and sunflower oil. Add the shallots and agave, if using. Whisk or shake vigorously until the ingredients are emulsified. Season with salt and pepper and add more agave as desired.

3 Transfer the dressing to a clean, sterilized bottle or jar with a tight-fitting lid and refrigerate for up to 3 months. Shake well to re-emulsify before each use.

TIP: You can substitute any medicinal herbs or mushrooms you like for the hibiscus flowers to vary this dressing's medicinal benefits. Some suggestions: reishi mushrooms for immunity, dandelion root for kidney and liver support, or stinging nettle for anti-inflammatory healing. Or substitute 1 cup (240 ml) of the Hawthorn-Hibiscus Tonic (page 257) for the hibiscus flowers and vinegar if you have some on hand.

Makes 2 cups (480 ml)

1 cup (240 ml) apple cider vinegar
½ cup (25 g) dried hibiscus
¼ cup plus 2 tablespoons (90 ml) extra virgin olive oil
¼ cup (60 ml) linseed oil
¼ cup (60 ml) sunflower oil
2 shallots, minced
1½ to 4½ teaspoons agave, optional

MAGICAL BENEFITS

Anthocyanins ◆ Rich in anthocyanins, which account for its vivid color, hibiscus tea supports detoxification and connective tissue synthesis, and combats oxidative stress.

Omega-3 Fatty Acids ◆ Linseed oil, full of omega-3 fatty acids like ALA, offers anti-inflammatory benefits that help maintain the skin's moisture barrier.

Oleic Acid ◆ This monounsaturated fatty acid, abundant in olive oil and sunflower oil, is known to help maintain the skin's natural moisture barrier.

Guarana Latte
FOR ENERGY

Gluten-Free ✦ No Sugar Added ✦ Nut-Free

This energizing, caramel-hued mushroom, berry, and root-infused latte is for those moments when you need something even stronger than coffee (yes, truly!). Blended with the espresso are stimulating cordyceps mushrooms, which lend a subtle complexity, and lightly bitter powdered guarana beans. Creamy oat milk and agave (which is optional if you're avoiding sugar) balance the bitterness, resulting in a drink that delivers a long-lasting energy boost without the typical coffee crash.

Serves 2

2 cups (480 ml) oat milk

2 teaspoons instant espresso powder or 2 shots brewed espresso

1 tablespoon cordyceps powder

1 tablespoon maca powder

1 teaspoon guarana powder

1½ teaspoons agave, maple syrup, or cane sugar, optional

1 Heat the oat milk in a small saucepan over medium heat (or in a microwave) for 2 to 3 minutes, until small bubbles begin to form, being careful not to let it boil.

2 If using espresso powder, add it to ¼ cup (60 ml) of hot water and stir until fully dissolved.

3 Pour the milk into a blender or large bowl along with the espresso, cordyceps powder, maca powder, guarana powder, and agave, if using.

4 Blend the mixture on high speed for about 30 seconds (or whisk vigorously by hand) until well combined and frothy, then serve immediately.

TIP: If you have an espresso machine, instead of using espresso powder you can brew 2 tablespoons of ground espresso beans to yield 2 shots (¼ cup/60 ml) of espresso. For a summery version, let the latte cool to room temperature before serving over ice, or turn it into a granita by freezing it for 5 to 6 hours, until slushy, and then blending.

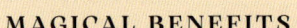

MAGICAL BENEFITS

Caffeine ✦ Guarana beans have twice as much caffeine as coffee, but it's released more slowly, so there's no sudden crash. The caffeine works by blocking a chemical in your brain that makes you tired, resulting in increased alertness and energy.

Cordycepin ✦ This active ingredient in cordyceps mushrooms helps the body produce more ATP (adenosine triphosphate), which fuels cells to improve stamina, endurance, and physical performance.

Macamides ✦ These unique compounds in maca root help balance hormones and support adrenal function, enhancing energy, reducing fatigue, and improving stress management.

Field and Forest Soup
FOR ENERGY

Gluten-Free ✦ Nut-Free

This soup combines resilient winter greens, grains, root vegetables, and hardy herbs, all of which thrive in the harsh conditions of winter. The name reflects the root vegetables' and grains' origins in the field and the mushrooms and bay leaves' origins in the forest, drawing their various nourishing nutrients from the earth. Their robustness translates into a comforting, protein-packed soup with fortifying and energizing benefits.

1   Add the broth to a pot and bring it to a gentle simmer over high heat, then add all the other ingredients. Season with salt and pepper.

2   Let the soup come back to a simmer, then reduce the heat to medium, cover, and gently simmer for about 20 minutes, or until the vegetables are tender enough to be pierced with a fork. Discard the bay leaves.

3   Season with salt and adjust the balance of acidity, richness, and sweetness with more wine and oil to taste. Allow to cool slightly before serving with extra freshly ground black pepper and a drizzle of olive oil.

TIP: Consider soaking the quinoa for a few hours, or up to a day, before cooking to help reduce its phytic acid, a defense compound that can inhibit the absorption of minerals like iron and zinc. Be sure to rinse it thoroughly before cooking.

Serves 4 to 6 as a main or 6 to 8 as a side

- 2 quarts (2 L) vegetable broth
- 2 sweet potatoes, peeled and diced
- 2 red onions, chopped
- 1 cup (200 g) quinoa
- 4 chard leaves, chopped
- ¼ cup plus 2 tablespoons (90 ml) extra virgin olive oil, plus more for drizzling
- ¼ cup (60 ml) white wine
- 1½ teaspoons agave
- 4 bay leaves
- 1 teaspoon fresh rosemary leaves or ¼ teaspoon dried rosemary, minced

MAGICAL BENEFITS

Manganese ✦ Sweet potatoes, quinoa, chard, and rosemary are rich in this trace mineral that helps the body efficiently produce and sustain energy.

Iron ✦ This trace mineral in sweet potatoes, quinoa, chard, bay leaves, shiitake mushrooms, and rosemary aids oxygen transport and energy metabolism.

Vitamin C ✦ The presence of this antioxidant vitamin in sweet potatoes and chard enhances the absorption of iron.

B Vitamins ✦ Sweet potatoes, chard, quinoa, and shiitake mushrooms provide essential B vitamins that support energy metabolism and vitality.

Caramelized Onion, Potato, and Bean Gratin
FOR STRENGTH

Gluten-Free ✦ No Sugar Added ✦ Nut-Free

Adequate protein intake is essential for strengthening our bodies. Beans are an excellent source of plant-based protein along with a range of muscle-supporting vitamins and minerals. This hearty gratin features layers of tender, rosemary-infused white beans, creamy mashed potatoes, and sweet caramelized onions peeking out from underneath a top layer of scalloped potatoes for a beautiful presentation.

Serves 4 to 6 as a main

MASHED POTATO LAYER

2 pounds (900 g) starchy potatoes (such as Russet or Idaho), peeled and chopped

3 tablespoons extra virgin olive oil

½ teaspoon garlic powder

CARAMELIZED ONION LAYER

2 tablespoons extra virgin olive oil

3 large onions, chopped

WHITE BEAN LAYER

One 29-ounce (820 g) can white beans

¼ cup (60 ml) extra virgin olive oil

3 tablespoons apple cider vinegar

2 teaspoons minced fresh rosemary leaves, or ¾ teaspoon minced dried rosemary

SCALLOPED POTATO LAYER

1.75 pounds (785 g) waxy, small potatoes, thinly sliced

2 tablespoons extra virgin olive oil

1 teaspoon fresh rosemary leaves, optional

1. Preheat the oven to 375°F (190°C).

2. **To make the mashed potato layer,** add the potatoes to a pot of cold, salted water and bring to a boil over high heat, then reduce the heat to medium and boil for about 20 minutes, or until tender enough to be pierced by a fork. Drain and mash the peeled potatoes in a large bowl with 2 tablespoons of the oil and the garlic powder, then season with salt and pepper. Grease a 9-by-13-inch (23 by 33 cm) baking dish with the remaining oil, then add the mashed potatoes and spread evenly.

3. **To make the caramelized onion layer,** add the oil to a pan over high heat and sauté the onions for 10 to 15 minutes, until caramelized, stirring frequently and adjusting the temperature as needed to prevent burning. Deglaze with a splash of water whenever they begin to stick and scrape the bottom of the pan to reincorporate any browned bits. Season with salt and pepper. While the onions caramelize, prepare the bean layer.

4. **To make the bean layer,** in another large bowl, combine the white beans, oil, vinegar, and rosemary, then season with salt and pepper. Spread the white beans over the mashed potato layer followed by the caramelized onions.

5. **To make the scalloped potato layer,** arrange the potato slices in slightly overlapping rows over the onion layer. You either can leave the center of the gratin exposed to show the layers beneath, or cover the top entirely with potato slices. Drizzle the oil evenly over the potato slices to help them crisp up in the oven.

6. Bake for 30 to 40 minutes, until the scalloped potatoes are golden brown and crispy. Just before serving, garnish with the rosemary, if using, and sprinkle with salt and pepper to taste.

TIP: This versatile dish can be made with any bean you like, such as lentils or black beans. You can also try mashed sweet potatoes in place of the mashed potatoes, and/or caramelized leek greens (which are lower in FODMAPs) in place of the onions.

MAGICAL BENEFITS

Vitamin B9 ✦ White beans, like other beans, are a good plant-based source of vitamin B9 (folate), which is used by the body to produce the red blood cells that deliver oxygen to muscles.

Trace Minerals ✦ Beans offer important trace minerals such as iron, magnesium, and potassium. Iron helps red blood cells transport oxygen and prevents fatigue, while magnesium and potassium aid muscle and nerve function.

Phytonutrients ✦ These antioxidant flavonoids and polyphenols in beans, onions, potatoes, and rosemary reduce oxidative stress and support blood vessel health, oxygen delivery, muscle function, and endurance.

Balsamic Parsnips with Citrus Cream
FOR EUPHORIA

Gluten-Free ✦ Nut-Free

Our moods often need a boost in winter, when many of us are exposed to less sunlight, time outdoors, and physical activity. These uplifting balsamic-glazed parsnips are tender on the inside yet crispy and caramelized on the outside, but the real star of the show is the tangy citrus-and-herb-infused cream sauce. To serve this a main, pair it with a protein-rich grain like amaranth, buckwheat, or quinoa.

1. Preheat the oven to 400°F (200°C).

2. Spread the parsnips in a single layer on a rimmed baking sheet and coat evenly with the oil, then season with salt and pepper. Once the oven is hot, roast the parsnips for about 30 minutes, flipping them halfway through for even cooking, until browned and tender enough to be pierced with a fork.

3. Remove them from the oven, drizzle with the balsamic vinegar, and then roast for about 15 minutes longer, or until coated with a caramelized glaze. Set aside to cool slightly.

4. Divide the citrus-dill sauce between individual plates, then top with the roasted parsnips, drizzle with extra oil, garnish with extra dill and freshly ground black pepper, and serve.

TIP: Other vegetables like asparagus, leeks, carrots, or mushrooms can be substituted for the parsnips. The sauce pairs well with almost any grain or vegetable!

Serves 4 as a main or 6 to 8 as a side

10 parsnips, peeled

3 tablespoons extra virgin olive oil, plus more for drizzling

1 tablespoon balsamic vinegar

1 recipe Creamy Citrus-Dill Sauce (page 258)

4 fresh dill sprigs, divided into fronds

MAGICAL BENEFITS

Complex Carbohydrates ✦ Parsnips are rich in complex carbohydrates, which help stabilize blood sugar levels, giving the brain a steady supply of glucose to support stable mood and cognitive function.

Vitamin B9 ✦ Parsnips are a good source of vitamin B9 (folate), which is vital for synthesizing mood-regulating neurotransmitters like serotonin, dopamine, and norepinephrine.

Anethole ✦ This active compound in dill interacts with neurotransmitters like GABA to provide anti-anxiety and sedative effects. Its antioxidant properties protect brain cells from oxidative stress and inflammation.

Cabbage and Potato Gratin
FOR COMFORT

Gluten-Free ✦ Nut-Free

Winter calls for comforting dishes that are both nourishing and easy to digest. This hearty yet striking gratin features tender cabbage leaves wrapped around a filling of caramelized onions and mashed sweet potatoes, all encased in a crispy scalloped purple potato crust. The colorful combination of mood-boosting winter vegetables, which shine their brightest in the darkest months, makes this a perfect centerpiece for a cozy winter meal.

Serves 4 to 6 as a main

¼ cup (60 ml) extra virgin olive oil

6 large red cabbage leaves

3 purple potatoes, peeled and cut into ⅛-inch (3 mm) slices

3 onions, chopped

2 sweet potatoes, peeled and chopped

2 tablespoons apple cider vinegar

1 teaspoon agave

MAGICAL BENEFITS

Anthocyanins ✦ These antioxidant pigments found in violet-hued foods like purple potatoes protect brain cells and reduce inflammation to support overall brain health.

Carotenoids ✦ Found in sweet potatoes, these antioxidant pigments are used by the body to make vitamin A, which reduces oxidative stress and inflammation in the brain and promotes neuron function to enhance mood.

Vitamin B6 ✦ This B vitamin present in cabbage and sweet potatoes helps make key neurotransmitters, like serotonin and dopamine, that affect mood and well-being.

1 Preheat the oven to 350°F (180°C). Grease the bottom and sides of a 9-inch (23 cm) springform pan with 1 tablespoon of the oil.

2 Bring a large saucepan of salted water to a boil over high heat. Cut away the hard stems at the base of each cabbage leaf. Add the leaves to the water and boil for about 30 minutes, or until tender, then remove from the water and pat dry. (This extended cooking time will fully soften the leaves for easier handling and better browning in the oven.) Set the saucepan of water aside, without draining it.

3 While the cabbage cooks, arrange the potato slices in two layers on the bottom and sides of the prepared pan to form a scalloped-potato crust. Begin by lining the sides of the pan with slightly overlapping slices, and then cover the base entirely with two layers of concentric circles.

4 After adding the potato slices, line the pan with the parboiled cabbage, letting the stem ends drape over the sides of the pan.

5 Cook the onions with the remaining oil in a large pan over high heat for 10 to 15 minutes, until tender and caramelized, stirring frequently. Deglaze with a splash of water whenever the onions begin to stick and scrape the bottom of the pan to reincorporate any browned bits.

6 Bring the water that was used to boil the cabbage back up to a boil over high heat, then reduce the heat to medium. Add the sweet potatoes and boil for about 15 minutes, or until tender.

7 Drain the sweet potatoes, then add them to the onions along with the vinegar and agave and mash with a spatula until mostly smooth. Season with salt and pepper. Scoop the filling into the springform pan on top of the cabbage leaves, then fold the ends of the leaves over the filling so that it is covered entirely. Using the remaining potato slices, either shingle them around the perimeter to create a border, leaving some of the cabbage leaves exposed (you may have some potato slices left over), or arrange them in concentric, slightly overlapping circles to cover the entire top.

8 Bake for 30 to 40 minutes, until the cabbage is crispy and slightly browned on top.

9 Let the gratin cool for about 15 minutes to allow the filling to set and the cabbage leaves to hold their form better. Run a knife along the edges of the gratin to loosen it before removing the sides of the springform pan. Using a serrated knife and spatula or large serving spoon, carefully cut and transfer slices to individual plates while still warm.

TIP: If you have leftovers, turn them into soup! Simply purée any leftovers with some vegetable broth to make a creamy sweet potato-cabbage soup.

Celery Root Steaks with Red Wine–Prune Sauce
FOR DIGESTION

Gluten-Free ✦ No Sugar Added ✦ Nut-Free

This dish elevates slices of unassuming celery root by marinating them in red wine, then pan-searing them to create hearty, steak-like centerpieces. Served with wine-infused lentils and a sauce of caramelized onions and sweet, fruity prunes, this main dish offers an indulgent flavor profile as well as gut- and digestion-supporting nutrients. The sauce and lentils can be prepared up to 2 days ahead, and the celery root can be marinated for up to 12 hours for an even deeper flavor.

1 **To make the celery root steaks,** add the celery root, red wine, and vinegar to a 9-by-13-inch (23 by 33 cm) baking dish and marinate for 1 hour, turning the steaks halfway through to ensure even coverage.

2 Heat the oil in a large pan over medium-high heat. Transfer the steaks to the pan, reserving the marinade. Sear until the steaks develop a golden-brown crust and are tender inside, about 10 minutes per side, adjusting the temperature as needed to prevent burning, then transfer to a plate and set aside.

3 **To make the lentils,** while the celery root steaks are searing, pour the marinade into a large saucepan over high heat, then add the coconut milk, lentils, broth, vinegar, and bay leaves. Bring to a gentle simmer, then lower the heat to medium and continually simmer uncovered, stirring to prevent the lentils from burning on the bottom, for about 15 minutes, until the lentils have absorbed all the liquid, become tender, and started to break down. Remove from the heat, discard the bay leaves, and cover to keep warm until you are ready to plate.

4 **To make the prune-wine sauce,** add the oil to the same pan used to cook the celery root steaks. Sauté the onions over high heat until they are soft and caramelized, 10 to 15 minutes, stirring frequently and adjusting the temperature as needed to prevent burning. Deglaze with a splash of water whenever they begin to stick and scrape the bottom of the pan to reincorporate any browned bits. Stir in the prunes and continue cooking for another 5 minutes, or until the prunes begin to break down.

5 Pour in the wine, reduce the heat to medium, and cook for about 5 minutes longer, or until the liquid is absorbed and the sauce has thickened and reduced by half. Season with salt and pepper.

6 Gently rewarm the lentils over low heat if needed, then divide the celery root steaks and lentils between individual plates, top the steaks with some of the sauce, and serve.

TIP: Any leftover celery root can be diced and used in a filling, such as for the Whole Roasted Pumpkin (page 143) or for the Adaptogenic Stuffed Zucchini (page 35).

Serves 2 to 4 as a main

CELERY ROOT STEAKS
½ celery root, peeled and cut into ½-inch (1.25 cm) slices
1½ cups (360 ml) red wine
2 tablespoons apple cider vinegar
2 tablespoons extra virgin olive oil

LENTILS
One 13.5-ounce (400 ml) can coconut milk
1½ cups (300 g) red lentils
1 cup (240 ml) vegetable broth or water
2 tablespoons apple cider vinegar
4 bay leaves

PRUNE-WINE SAUCE
2 tablespoons extra virgin olive oil
3 red onions, thinly sliced
8 prunes, pitted and chopped
½ cup (120 ml) red wine

MAGICAL BENEFITS

Sorbitol ✦ This sugar alcohol found in prunes draws water into the intestines, softening stool and promoting bowel movements.

Prebiotics ✦ Lentils, prunes, and onions contain soluble fibers, including prebiotic fibers, that ferment in the colon, producing short-chain fatty acids which nourish beneficial bacteria and support the gut lining.

Insoluble Fiber ✦ This kind of dietary fiber in lentils, prunes, and celery root adds bulk, preventing constipation while also promoting gut wall health.

Baked Purple Cauliflower and Potatoes with Rosemary Vinaigrette
FOR HEART SUPPORT

Gluten-Free ✦ No Sugar Added ✦ Nut-Free

The vibrant purple hues in this dish provide both striking visuals and heart-healthy benefits. The savory, herb-marinated cauliflower florets and thinly sliced potatoes are roasted until tender on the inside and crispy on the outside before being drizzled with a tangy-sweet rosemary-infused vinaigrette. To make this a heartier main, serve with lentils or a protein-rich grain like amaranth, buckwheat, or quinoa.

Serves 4 as a main or 6 to 8 as a side

- 1 purple cauliflower, cut into florets
- 1 pound (450 g) purple potatoes, peeled and thinly sliced
- 3 tablespoons extra virgin olive oil

ROSEMARY VINAIGRETTE

- ¼ cup (60 ml) extra virgin olive oil
- ¼ cup (60 ml) balsamic vinegar
- 1 teaspoon minced fresh rosemary leaves, plus a few fresh sprigs for serving

1. Preheat the oven to 425°F (220°C).

2. Combine the cauliflower and potatoes in a large bowl. Add the oil and toss to coat, then season with salt and pepper. Spread in a single layer on a rimmed baking sheet.

3. Once the oven is hot, roast for 30 to 35 minutes, stirring halfway through to ensure even cooking, until browned and crispy on the outside and tender on the inside. Remove from the oven and let cool for 5 minutes while you prepare the vinaigrette.

4. **To make the rosemary vinaigrette,** whisk together the oil, balsamic vinegar, and rosemary in a small bowl and season with salt and pepper.

5. Transfer the cauliflower and potatoes to a serving platter and drizzle evenly with the vinaigrette. Garnish with the fresh rosemary sprigs, and serve.

TIP: Turn leftovers into a creamy purple soup! Blend the roasted cauliflower and potatoes with vegetable broth, a splash of plant-based cream, and season to your liking.

MAGICAL BENEFITS

Anthocyanins ✦ This group of antioxidant pigments present in purple and blue-hued fruits and vegetables reduces inflammation, oxidative stress, and cholesterol and enhances the flexibility of blood vessel walls, thereby supporting the entire cardiovascular system.

Rosmarinic Acid ✦ This natural polyphenol and antioxidant in rosemary helps improve blood flow and combat inflammation and oxidative stress of the blood vessels.

Potassium ✦ The potassium in potatoes and cauliflower helps regulate blood pressure, reducing the risk of hypertension and supporting overall cardiovascular health.

MAGICAL BENEFITS

Quercetin ✦ This antioxidant flavonoid is abundant in onions and helps to neutralize harmful free radicals and support the liver's detoxification functions.

Glucosinolates ✦ When released through chewing or chopping, these natural compounds found in cauliflower and other cruciferous vegetables help the liver eliminate toxins more efficiently.

Allyl Sulfides ✦ These sulfur-containing compounds found in alliums like onions and garlic are known to protect the kidneys and help the liver break down toxins.

Dietary Fiber ✦ Red lentils are a good source of dietary fiber, which helps promote healthy digestion and regularity, indirectly supporting the elimination of waste and toxins.

Whole Roasted Cauliflower
FOR DETOX

Gluten-Free ✦ No Sugar Added ✦ Nut-Free

You wouldn't expect this sauce-covered centerpiece to be made with ingredients that help the body eliminate toxins, but it is! A whole cauliflower is marinated with an herbal vinaigrette before being roasted atop a bed of coconut-infused lentils and quinoa, the flavors of the marinade soaking into and melding the ingredients together. Before serving, the cauliflower is covered in a velvety thyme and pepper cream that renders this dish as indulgent as it is cleansing, making it a wonderful winter pick-me-up. Both the lentils and cream can be made up to 2 days ahead.

1 Preheat the oven to 375°F (190°C).

2 To make the coconut lentils and quinoa, combine all of the ingredients in a medium saucepan over medium heat. The quinoa and lentils should be covered by about ½ inch (1.25 cm) of liquid; add more broth if necessary. Stirring often, let the mixture simmer gently until the liquid is absorbed and the lentils and quinoa have become tender, about 15 minutes. Season with salt and pepper.

3 To make the whole roasted cauliflower, while the lentils and quinoa cook, bring a pot of salted water to a boil over high heat, then add the cauliflower. Reduce the heat to medium-high and boil for 15 to 20 minutes, until the stem is tender enough to be pierced with a fork. Drain and set aside in the empty pot.

4 Whisk together the vinegar, oil, and herbes de Provence in a small bowl and season with salt and pepper. Pour evenly over the cauliflower.

5 Transfer the lentil and quinoa mixture to an oven-safe pan or 9-inch (23 cm) square baking dish, then place the cauliflower on top in the center and pour the excess dressing over the lentils and quinoa. Roast for about 20 minutes, or until the cauliflower is browned and crispy on the outside.

6 For the thyme-pepper cream, while the cauliflower roasts, in a small saucepan set over medium heat, combine the coconut milk, thyme, arrowroot flour, and pepper, and season with salt. Gently simmer for 5 to 10 minutes, whisking continuously, until thickened.

7 Remove the cauliflower from the oven and pour the cream sauce evenly over it. Garnish with more thyme and a sprinkle of freshly ground black pepper, and serve warm.

TIP: You can purée any leftovers to make a soup! Add vegetable broth to thin it to your liking, as well as extra minced thyme, a little olive oil, and apple cider vinegar or white wine, and season with salt and pepper.

Serves 4 as a main

COCONUT LENTILS AND QUINOA

One 13.5-ounce (400 ml) can coconut milk

1 to 1½ cups (240 to 360 ml) vegetable broth or water

1 cup (200 g) red lentils

½ cup (100 g) quinoa

3 onions, chopped

¼ cup (60 ml) apple cider vinegar

2 tablespoons extra virgin olive oil

4 garlic cloves, thinly sliced

2 teaspoons minced fresh rosemary leaves

WHOLE ROASTED CAULIFLOWER

1 whole cauliflower

¼ cup plus 2 tablespoons (90 ml) apple cider vinegar

¼ cup (60 ml) extra virgin olive oil

1 tablespoon dried herbes de Provence

THYME-PEPPER CREAM

One 13.5-ounce (400 ml) can coconut milk

5 fresh thyme sprigs, leaves only, plus more for serving

1 tablespoon arrowroot flour or cornstarch

½ teaspoon pepper

Leek and Potato Dauphinoise
FOR SATIETY

Gluten-Free ✦ No Sugar Added ✦ Nut-Free

Based on the classic French dish of layered scalloped potatoes, this creamy gratin's magic resides in its healthy weight- and metabolism-supporting ingredients. The tender and crispy layers of scalloped potatoes, enrobed in a sauce of coconut cream and caramelized leeks, offer equal parts medicinal power and coziness. Serve as a side with the Whole Roasted Cauliflower (page 217) or the Citrusy Kale and Apple Salad (page 238).

Serves 6 to 8 as a side

CREAMY LEEK SAUCE

2 tablespoons extra virgin olive oil

2 leeks, thoroughly rinsed, minced

Two 13.5-ounce (400 ml) cans coconut milk

2 teaspoons Dijon mustard

POTATO LAYERS

2 tablespoons extra virgin olive oil

2 pounds (900 g) waxy potatoes (such as red or Yukon Gold), peeled and thinly sliced

3 garlic cloves, minced

Fresh thyme or oregano, optional

MAGICAL BENEFITS

Resistant Starch ✦ Leeks and potatoes contain slow-digesting resistant starch, which provides steady energy and promotes fullness, reducing the urge to eat soon after a meal.

MCTs ✦ Medium-chain triglycerides (MCTs), a type of fat found in coconut cream, are easily digestible and quickly converted into energy, contributing to feelings of satiety.

Fiber ✦ High-fiber, low-glycemic foods like leeks and potatoes help regulate the hormones ghrelin (produced in the stomach to stimulate hunger) and leptin (produced in fat cells to signal fullness) by promoting stable blood sugar levels.

1 Preheat the oven to 375°F (190°C).

2 **To make the creamy leek sauce,** add the oil to a saucepan over medium heat, add the leeks and season with salt and pepper, then sauté until tender, about 20 minutes. Increase the heat to high and continue cooking for about 10 minutes to brown the leeks, stirring frequently. Deglaze with a splash of water whenever they begin to stick and scrape the bottom of the pan to reincorporate any browned bits. Add the coconut milk and mustard and simmer until the milk has thickened and reduced by half, then set aside.

3 **To make the potato layers,** grease a 9-by-13-inch (23 by 33 cm) baking dish with the oil. Arrange about one-quarter of the potato slices in a single layer to cover the bottom of the dish, overlapping the edges slightly.

4 Pour about one-quarter of the leek sauce over the potato layer, spreading it evenly. Sprinkle about one-quarter of the garlic over the potato layer. Repeat layering the potatoes, sauce, and garlic until you've used all of both. You should have 4 layers of potato slices.

5 Cover the baking dish with foil and bake for 45 minutes, then uncover and bake for an additional 20 to 25 minutes, until the potatoes are golden brown. Remove from the oven and let rest for a few minutes to help the layers set a bit before serving. Garnish with the fresh thyme, if using, and serve.

TIP: To add even more satiety-boosting magic, top the dish with roasted pine nuts! Pine nuts contain pinolenic acid, which is believed to play a role in reducing appetite.

Sadness-Smashing Potatoes and Brussels Sprouts

FOR MOOD BALANCE

Gluten-Free ✦ No Sugar Added ✦ Nut-Free

Comforting recipes might not be able to cure depression, but they can offer relief during moments of sadness. These double-cooked smashed potatoes and brussels sprouts are boiled until tender, then squashed, drizzled with oil, and roasted with garlic and thyme until ultra-crispy. For a heartier midwinter meal, serve with a protein-rich grain such as amaranth, buckwheat, or quinoa and the Creamy Citrus-Dill Sauce (page 27) or Creamy Citrus Vinaigrette (page 258).

Serves 4 to 6 as a main or 6 to 8 as a side

¼ cup plus 2 tablespoons (90 ml) extra virgin olive oil, plus more for drizzling

1 pound (450 g) brussels sprouts, stems and loose outer leaves removed

1 pound (450 g) small rainbow potatoes

1 whole garlic head, cloves separated but unpeeled

¼ cup (60 ml) balsamic vinegar

5 to 8 fresh thyme sprigs

1 Preheat the oven to 400°F (200°C). Grease a rimmed baking sheet with 1 tablespoon of the oil.

2 Bring a large saucepan of well-salted water to a boil over high heat. Add the brussels sprouts and potatoes, then reduce the heat to medium and simmer for about 15 minutes, or until tender.

3 Drain, then spread the sprouts and potatoes evenly over the prepared baking sheet and flatten them using a spatula or potato masher. This will increase their surface area, maximizing crispiness.

4 Spread the garlic cloves around the sprouts and potatoes. Drizzle the balsamic vinegar over the vegetables, followed by the remaining oil. Season with salt and pepper. Remove some thyme leaves from the sprigs and scatter them over the vegetables, reserving a few whole sprigs for garnishing.

5 Roast for about 40 minutes, turning the vegetables halfway through, until crispy and well browned. Serve warm, garnishing with the thyme sprigs, an extra drizzle of oil, and a sprinkle of salt and freshly ground black pepper.

TIP: If you have leftovers, turn them into a vegetable "flatbread"! Spread the roasted potatoes and brussels sprouts over a rimmed baking sheet and flatten with a large spoon to form a ½-inch-thick (1.25 cm) disk. Bake at 375°F (190°C) for 20 to 30 minutes, or until browned and crispy on top. Remove from the oven, then top with tomato sauce and your favorite toppings, like mushrooms, shallots, or Cashew Cheese (page 229). Return to the oven briefly to heat the toppings, and enjoy!

MAGICAL BENEFITS

Vitamin K ✦ This vitamin bolsters brain health by reducing inflammation and supporting gut health, which influences mood via the gut-brain axis.

Vitamin B9 ✦ Found in brussels sprouts and potatoes, vitamin B9 (folate) aids serotonin production. Low folate levels are associated with depression and impaired mood regulation.

Polyphenols ✦ Rich in antioxidants, the polyphenols in thyme and balsamic vinegar protect cells, including neurons, from oxidative stress, reducing inflammation and supporting brain function and mood stability.

Crispy Kohlrabi Steaks
FOR DETOX

Gluten-Free ◆ Nut-Free

What if crispy, breaded comfort food could help support the body's natural detox processes? You don't have to wonder: These oven-baked, garlic-herb-crusted kohlrabi steaks are crispy on the outside, tender within, nutty-sweet, and filled with with liver-, kidney-, and digestive system–supporting magic. Serve as a main with a side of protein-rich grain such as amaranth, buckwheat, or quinoa, or with the Kale and Cabbage Coleslaw (page 171) for an extra detox boost!

Serves 2 as a main or 4 as a side

- 2 tablespoons extra virgin olive oil
- 2 to 3 kohlrabi bulbs, peeled and cut into ½-inch (1.25 cm) rounds
- ¼ cup (60 ml) oat or rice milk
- 1 cup (120 g) dried gluten-free bread crumbs
- 1 teaspoon dried herbes de Provence
- ½ teaspoon garlic powder
- ½ teaspoon salt
- ½ teaspoon pepper
- 1 cup Creamy Citrus-Dill Sauce (page 27)

1. Preheat the oven to 400°F (200°C). Grease a rimmed baking sheet with 1 tablespoon of the oil.

2. Bring a large saucepan of salted water to a boil over high heat, then add the kohlrabi. Reduce the heat to medium-high and boil for about 30 minutes, or until the slices can be easily pierced with a fork. Drain and pat dry with paper towels. Cut off any hard parts that did not soften during boiling. Set aside.

3. Pour the oat milk into a shallow bowl. In another shallow bowl, combine the bread crumbs with the herbes de Provence, garlic powder, salt, and pepper.

4. Working with one kohlrabi round at a time, dip it into the milk, then coat all sides in the bread crumb mixture. Place the breaded kohlrabi slices onto the prepared baking sheet in a single layer. Drizzle with the remaining oil.

5. Roast for about 30 minutes, turning the slices halfway through for even browning, until the kohlrabi steaks are golden brown and crispy. Remove from the oven and serve immediately with the Creamy Citrus-Dill Sauce on the side.

TIP: For an extra detox boost, instead of parboiling the kohlrabi in water, boil it in an infusion of liver-supporting plants like artichoke leaves or dandelion roots. Create a decoction by boiling 2 tablespoons of your preferred plant in 4¼ cups (1 L) of filtered water for 20 minutes, then covering, removing from the heat, and steeping for another 20 minutes. Strain and use the liquid to boil the kohlrabi.

MAGICAL BENEFITS

Glucosinolates ◆ These sulfur-containing compounds in kohlrabi protect liver cells and enhance the liver's natural detoxification processes.

Fiber ◆ Kohlrabi is rich in dietary fiber, which supports digestive health and promotes regular bowel movements, the body's way of removing waste and toxins.

High Water Content ◆ With its high water content, kohlrabi helps support the kidneys, which filter the blood to help flush out toxins.

Creamy Baked Portobellos
FOR MOOD BALANCE

Gluten-Free ◆ No Sugar Added ◆ Nut-Free

These tender portobello mushroom caps are stuffed with a velvety cream sauce of caramelized onions and leeks that infuses a hidden layer of quinoa with savory flavor. The dish is both irresistibly rich and packed with nutrients that support neurological functions and elevate mood. For an even heartier meal, pair it with rice, lentils, or an extra serving of a protein-rich grain such as amaranth, buckwheat, or extra quinoa.

1 Preheat the oven to 375°F (190°C). Lightly grease a baking dish or line it with parchment paper.

2 Add the quinoa to a saucepan with enough water to just barely cover it, about ½ cup (120 ml). Bring to a boil over high heat, then reduce the heat to medium, cover, and simmer for 15 minutes, or until fully cooked. Set aside.

3 While the quinoa simmers, begin preparing the sauce by removing the stems and scooping out the gills using a spoon to create space for the filling. Set the mushroom caps hollow side up in a single layer in the prepared baking dish. Chop the stems and gills.

4 Heat the oil in a large pan over medium-high heat. Add the chopped mushroom stems and gills, onion, and most of the leek, reserving a few slices for garnish. Sauté, stirring frequently and adjusting the temperature as needed to prevent burning, for 20 to 30 minutes. Deglaze with a splash of water whenever the vegetables begin to stick and scrape the bottom of the pan to reincorporate any browned bits, until the vegetables and mushroom pieces have reduced in size and caramelized.

5 Add the coconut cream and continue to sauté, stirring occasionally, for about 15 minutes, or until the mixture thickens and reduces by half. Season with salt and pepper.

6 Spoon about 2 tablespoons of cooked quinoa into each mushroom cap, spreading it into an even layer, leaving enough space for the cream filling on top.

7 Divide the filling between the mushroom caps. Top with the reserved leek slices. Bake for about 20 minutes, or until the mushrooms are slightly shrunken and browned. Garnish with the fresh chives and serve immediately.

TIP: Transform leftovers into a creamy mushroom pasta! Chop the stuffed mushrooms and stir them into cooked gluten-free pasta or spiralized zucchini noodles, and cover in any extra cream sauce, rehydrated with a splash of coconut cream if needed.

Serves 2 as a main or 4 as a side

¼ cup (50 g) quinoa

4 large portobello mushrooms or 8 to 10 cremini mushrooms

1 tablespoon extra virgin olive oil, plus more for greasing

1 large onion, thinly sliced

1 leek, thoroughly rinsed, thinly sliced

¾ cup plus 2 tablespoons (200 ml) coconut cream

1 teaspoon minced fresh chives, rosemary, or thyme

MAGICAL BENEFITS

Vitamin B6 ◆ Leeks, mushrooms, and onions are good sources of vitamin B6 (pyridoxine), which is essential for the synthesis of mood-modulating neurotransmitters like serotonin, dopamine, and GABA.

Vitamin B9 ◆ Found in leeks and mushrooms, vitamin B9 (folate) supports serotonin production, influencing mood and mental health.

Potassium ◆ This macro mineral found in leeks, mushrooms, and coconut cream supports mood by facilitating the use of neurotransmitters like serotonin, reducing stress hormones.

Slimming Seaweed and Mushroom Soup
FOR METABOLISM

Gluten-Free ✦ No Sugar Added ✦ Nut-Free

Seaweed is an eco-friendly nutritional powerhouse. In this soup, tender caramelized onions and mushrooms provide a savory base, wakame seaweed and creamy coconut milk add depth and umami richness, fresh ginger provides warmth, and a final sprinkle of dried wakame adds a salty crunch. To make this a heartier main, serve with a protein-rich grain like amaranth, buckwheat, or quinoa.

Serves 4 as a main or 6 to 8 as a side

- 2 tablespoons extra virgin olive oil
- 2 large yellow onions, diced
- 8 ounces (225 g) mushrooms such as white button mushrooms or shiitake, sliced
- 7 strips dried wakame seaweed
- 3 cups (720 ml) vegetable broth
- One 13.5-ounce (400 ml) can coconut milk
- 2 teaspoons apple cider vinegar
- 1 teaspoon grated fresh ginger

1 Heat the oil in a large saucepan over medium heat. Add the onions and cook for about 15 minutes. Deglaze with a splash of water whenever they begin to stick and scrape the bottom of the pan to reincorporate any browned bits, until caramelized.

2 Add the mushrooms and sauté until they shrink and begin to brown, about 20 minutes.

3 While the mushrooms cook, add 6 of the wakame strips to a bowl of cold water and soak until soft, about 10 minutes, then drain and rinse to remove the salt.

4 Add the broth, coconut milk, vinegar, ginger, and rinsed wakame to the onions and mushrooms and simmer gently for 10 to 15 minutes to meld the flavors. Season with salt and pepper.

5 Serve warm, crumbling the remaining wakame strip and sprinkling it over individual portions as a salty garnish.

TIP: Want to increase your iodine intake in general? Other than eating more seaweed, consider using iodized table salt instead of sea, kosher, or pink salt, which contain relatively less iodine.

MAGICAL BENEFITS

Protein ✦ Proteins like those found in mushrooms contribute to satiety by stimulating fullness hormones like GLP-1, slowing digestion, and promoting sustained energy release.

MCTs ✦ Primarily composed of medium-chain triglycerides (MCTs), the energy-dense fats in coconut milk slow digestion and trigger fullness hormones like cholecystokinin.

Iodine ✦ This essential mineral found in seaweed is needed to produce thyroid hormones, which regulate metabolism, energy production, and body temperature.

Persimmon and Spiced Walnut Salad
FOR GLOWING SKIN

Gluten-Free ✦ No Sugar Added

This salad is an enchantment for a sun-kissed complexion even in the dreary months of winter. The persimmons bring subtle sweetness with undertones of apricots, the spiced walnuts a warm, bitter kick, and the cashew cheese adds creamy, crumbly texture. Serve as a stunning appetizer to balance heartier dishes or with a side of quinoa for extra protein. Note that you will need to start the cheese at least 6 hours ahead of time, but most of that time is hands-off.

Serves 2 to 4 as a side

CASHEW CHEESE
- 1½ cups (180 g) raw, unsalted cashews
- ¾ cup (180 ml) filtered water
- 1 tablespoon apple cider vinegar
- 1 tablespoon lemon juice
- 1 tablespoon nutritional yeast
- ½ teaspoon garlic powder

SALAD
- 1 tablespoon extra virgin olive oil
- 1 tablespoon balsamic vinegar
- 3 persimmons, cut into ¼-inch (6 mm) slices
- 3 tablespoons unsweetened dried cranberries, plus more for serving

SPICED WALNUTS
- 1 cup (120 g) walnuts
- 1½ teaspoons extra virgin olive oil
- ⅛ teaspoon ground nutmeg
- ⅛ teaspoon ground ginger

1. **To make the cashew cheese,** soak the cashews in hot water for 4 to 6 hours to soften them or, for a faster method, fill a small saucepan with water and boil them for 15 minutes. Add the softened cashews, filtered water, vinegar, lemon juice, nutritional yeast, and garlic powder to a food processor or high-speed blender and blend until smooth. Season with salt and pepper.

2. To separate the liquid from what will become the crumbly cheese, line a fine-mesh strainer with a folded piece of cheesecloth and set it over a bowl. Pour the cheese mixture into the cheesecloth and wrap the cloth around the mixture, pressing to squeeze out as much of the liquid as possible. Use a rubber band to tie off the opening, then refrigerate for 6 to 12 hours to allow the excess liquid to drain into the bowl, leaving behind a crumbly plant-based cheese.

3. Once the cheese has drained, preheat the oven to 350°F (180°C).

4. **To make the salad,** add the oil and balsamic vinegar to a large bowl and whisk to combine. Season with salt and pepper. Add the persimmons and cranberries and toss gently to coat. Divide the salad between individual plates.

5. **To make the spiced walnuts,** spread the walnuts over a rimmed baking sheet and drizzle with the oil, nutmeg, and ginger, and toss gently to coat. Season with salt and pepper.

6. Roast for about 10 minutes, stirring often as they can burn easily, until the walnuts start to brown. Sprinkle the warm nuts over the salad, add a few chunks of the cashew cheese, garnish with extra dried cranberries, and serve.

TIP: You can use different nuts for vegan cheeses. Cashews offer a creamy base, while macadamia nuts give a rich, buttery flavor. Almonds introduce a texture more akin to traditional cheese, ideal for feta or ricotta styles. Brazil nuts have an earthy flavor suitable for sharper cheeses but are extremely high in selenium, an important nutrient but one that is possible to overdose, so it's best to limit servings of Brazil nut cheese to a couple tablespoons at a time.

MAGICAL BENEFITS

Vitamins A and C ✦ Rich in vitamins A and C, persimmons support connective tissue health. Vitamin A promotes the production of new skin cells, while vitamin C aids collagen synthesis. Deficiencies in these vitamins can cause dry skin, poor elasticity, and bruising.

Omega-3 Fatty Acids ✦ These healthy fats found in walnuts help keep skin soft, supple, and less prone to dryness by improving hydration and strengthening the skin's natural barrier.

Manganese and Phosphorus ✦ Essential for connective tissue health, manganese aids collagen, cartilage, and tendon formation, while phosphorus supports tissue repair and maintenance.

Parsnip, Leek, and Orange Soup
FOR SERENITY

Gluten-Free ✦ No Sugar Added ✦ Nut-Free

Nothing is cozier in winter than a warm soup, especially one made with a velvety blend of peppery, nutty parsnips, creamy potatoes, mellow leeks, and nutrient-packed kale, which all work in synergy to calm the nervous system. Although it's a sweet, citrusy ingredient for a savory root vegetable soup, the fortified orange juice adds a jolt of brightness and plenty of vitamin D. Serve as a light main with a side of gluten-free bread or protein-rich grain such as amaranth, buckwheat, or quinoa, or as a side for the Sadness-Smashing Potatoes and Brussels Sprouts (page 221) for extra mood-soothing magic.

Serves 4 to 6 as a main or 6 to 8 as a side

- 2 quarts (2 L) vegetable broth or water
- 3 to 4 parsnips (500 g), peeled and chopped
- 3 yellow onions, chopped
- 1 pound (450 g) waxy potatoes (such as red or Yukon Gold), peeled and chopped
- 2 leeks, thoroughly rinsed, chopped
- 4 garlic cloves, minced
- 2½ cups (600 ml) vitamin D–fortified unsweetened orange juice
- One 13.5-ounce (400 ml) can coconut milk
- ¼ cup plus 1 tablespoon (75 ml) apple cider vinegar
- ¼ cup plus 1 tablespoon (75 ml) extra virgin olive oil, plus more for drizzling
- 3 kale leaves, stems removed, torn into bite-size pieces

1 Add the broth, parsnips, onions, potatoes, leeks, and garlic to a large saucepan over high heat. Bring to a boil, then reduce the heat to medium and simmer, covered, for about 20 minutes, or until the vegetables are tender enough to be easily pierced with a fork.

2 Add the orange juice, coconut milk, vinegar, and oil, and season with salt and pepper. Carefully transfer the soup to a blender and purée until creamy and smooth. Season with salt and pepper and adjust the oil, vinegar, and orange juice to taste.

3 Garnish individual portions with the kale and an extra drizzle of olive oil just before serving.

TIP: For more protein and vitamin D and a meaty texture, consider sautéing some portobello mushrooms in extra virgin olive oil until crispy to use as an additional garnish.

MAGICAL BENEFITS

Potassium ✦ Foods like parsnips, leeks, onions, potatoes, and kale are rich in this macro mineral that helps relax muscles, lower blood pressure, and support nervous system function, indirectly reducing stress and anxiety.

Magnesium ✦ Found in parsnips, leeks, kale, and leafy greens, magnesium reduces stress by calming the nervous system, supporting GABA activity, and helping to balance sleep cycles.

Calcium ✦ Kale is a top plant-based source of calcium, which supports nerve function and may help maintain mood stability.

Balsamic-Caramelized Endives
FOR METABOLISM

Gluten-Free ◆ No Sugar Added

Feeling the need to balance out all those indulgent winter comfort dishes with a meal or two imbued with slimming magic? Consider these melt-in-your-mouth tender glazed endives, which support multiple digestive and metabolic functions. The apple slices, softened in the glaze, add a bright, fruity counterpoint, while the chopped pistachio garnish brings crunch. For extra metabolism-supporting benefits, serve as a side with the Creamy Mushroom Pasta (page 32).

1   Heat the oil in a pan over medium-high heat until it sizzles. Place the endives cut sides down in the pan and sear for about 5 minutes, pressing on them with a spatula to flatten for even cooking, or until golden brown on the bottoms.

2   Pour the balsamic vinegar over the endives, increase the heat to high, and continue cooking for about 5 minutes, or until the vinegar begins to reduce into a glaze, coating the endives. Reduce the heat to medium, cover, and continue cooking for another 10 minutes, or until tender.

3   Remove the lid, add the apple slices, and cook for another 5 minutes, turning the slices halfway through so that they are completely covered in the glaze. Season with salt and pepper.

4   Transfer the glazed endives and apples to a serving plate and garnish with the chopped pistachios. Serve immediately.

TIP: To revamp leftovers or turn this into a heartier meal, chop the glazed endives and apples into bite-size pieces, then toss them into some warm quinoa or amaranth to turn this into a grain salad.

Serves 4 as a side

2 tablespoons extra virgin olive oil
6 endives, halved
1 cup (240 ml) balsamic vinegar
2 apples, cored and sliced
½ cup (60 g) chopped pistachios

MAGICAL BENEFITS

Phytosterols ◆ These plant compounds found in pistachios compete with cholesterol for absorption in the intestines, helping to lower LDL (bad) cholesterol levels.

Inulin and Pectin ◆ These prebiotic dietary fibers found in endives and apples nourish beneficial gut bacteria, improve digestion, and promote feelings of fullness.

Acetic Acid ◆ Found in balsamic vinegar, acetic acid may support weight loss by enhancing satiety, improving insulin sensitivity, and boosting fat metabolism.

Smoky-Sweet Glazed Mushrooms
FOR IMMUNITY

Gluten-Free ✦ Nut-Free

Mushrooms have evolved over millennia to fight off viruses, bacteria, and other fungi to survive, making them powerhouses of immune-supporting magic that we can benefit from. Here, sweet and sour, tender but crispy seared portobello mushrooms are marinated in a glaze of balsamic vinegar, maple syrup, and smoky paprika for a satisfyingly chewy side with a barbecue-like flavor profile. Serve with a side of lentils, quinoa, rice, or tofu for extra protein, or with gluten-free toast or a salad.

Serves 2 to 3 as a side

- ¼ cup plus 1 tablespoon (75 ml) balsamic vinegar
- 3 tablespoons maple syrup
- 1 teaspoon Dijon mustard
- ¼ teaspoon smoked paprika
- 4 portobello mushrooms, cut into ½-inch (1.25 cm) slices, or 12 whole cremini or shiitake mushrooms
- 1 tablespoon extra virgin olive oil

1. Whisk together the balsamic vinegar, maple syrup, mustard, and smoked paprika in a bowl. Season with salt and pepper. Add the mushrooms and toss to coat, then let them marinate for 30 minutes. Strain, reserving the marinade.

2. Add the oil to a large pan over high heat. Once the oil is hot, add the mushrooms, and cook for about 5 minutes on each side, basting the mushrooms with a splash of the reserved marinade whenever they begin to stick to the bottom of the pan to help deglaze and form a sauce. Continue until the marinade creates a thick glaze and the mushrooms are browned, crispy, and reduced in size by half. Serve warm with a sprinkle of freshly ground black pepper.

TIP: To increase the mushrooms' vitamin D content, place them gill side up in a sunny spot for several hours before you cook them. The sunlight will trigger the synthesis of more vitamin D!

MAGICAL BENEFITS

Lectins ✦ Certain mushroom compounds, like lectins, help activate T-cells (a type of white blood cell), a critical step in mounting effective immune responses.

Beta-Glucans ✦ Found in mushroom cell walls, beta-glucans enhance immune function by stimulating immune cells to identify and destroy pathogens.

Ergosterol ✦ When exposed to sunlight, mushrooms convert this precursor into vitamin D, which supports defenses by regulating immune cells.

Blood Orange–Endive Salad
FOR ENERGY

Gluten-Free ✦ No Added Sugar ✦ Nut-Free

This vibrant salad combines the crisp, slightly bitter crunch of endives with a burst of berry-like sweetness from the blood oranges, which are richer in antioxidants and lower in acidity than other oranges (though other oranges or citrus fruits make fine substitutes). A sprinkle of nutty pumpkin seeds offer a boost of energy during the winter months when we need it most. Serve as a light starter for the Caramelized Onion, Potato, and Bean Gratin (page 206), or pair it with a protein-rich grain such as amaranth, buckwheat, or quinoa.

Serves 2 to 4 as a side

- 4 endives
- ¼ cup (60 ml) unsweetened plant-based yogurt
- Grated zest and juice from 1 blood orange or regular orange
- 2 tablespoons balsamic vinegar
- 1 tablespoon extra virgin olive oil
- 2 tablespoons raw pumpkin seeds

1 Trim the base of the endives to loosen the petal-like spears, then gently separate the large outer leaves, reserving the small inner leaves for another use. Divide the large outer leaves among individual plates or place in a large bowl for serving family style.

2 In a small bowl, add the yogurt, half of the blood orange zest, the blood orange juice, vinegar, and oil and whisk until smooth, then season with salt and pepper.

3 Drizzle the dressing over the endive spears and sprinkle with the pumpkin seeds and remaining blood orange zest. Serve immediately.

TIP: Try sautéing the leftover endive leaves with some extra virgin olive oil and balsamic vinegar until wilted and lightly browned and serve with rice, lentils, or tofu.

MAGICAL BENEFITS

Iron ✦ Pumpkin seeds are a potent source of iron, a trace mineral essential for oxygen transport. Low iron levels can cause fatigue, weakness, poor circulation, and other symptoms.

Vitamin K ✦ This vitamin in endive and pumpkin seeds is essential for blood clotting, bone mineralization, and preventing calcium buildup in blood vessels.

Vitamin E ✦ Found in pumpkin seeds and olive oil, vitamin E supports sustained energy by protecting mitochondria, aiding fat metabolism, and enhancing cellular efficiency.

Citrusy Kale and Apple Salad
FOR IMMUNITY

Gluten-Free ✦ Nut-Free

Winter can deplete energy levels and immune function, calling for meals that revive and fortify. This salad is filled with immunity-supporting, anti-inflammatory, and antioxidant-rich ingredients such as kale, sweet and crisp julienned apples, subtly sharp red onion, and tangy dried cranberries. A drizzle of Creamy Citrus Vinaigrette (page 258), infused with medicinal reishi and chaga mushrooms and lemon zest, ties the salad together.

Serves 2 to 4 as a side

6 to 8 kale leaves, stems removed, torn into bite-size pieces

2 apples (Winter Gem, Fuji, or Honeycrisp), cut into matchsticks

1 red onion, thinly sliced

½ cup (60 g) unsweetened dried cranberries

¼ to ½ cup (60 ml to 120 ml) Creamy Citrus Vinaigrette (page 258)

1. In a large salad bowl, combine the kale, apples, onion, and dried cranberries. Toss to mix.

2. Drizzle the dressing over the salad, tossing gently to coat, then serve.

TIP: Consider freezing kale for a few minutes before using it in salads or other dishes. This not only renders it easier to digest, but also brings out its natural sugars, making it taste sweeter! When grown in the winter, kale is traditionally harvested after a frost to enhance its flavor.

MAGICAL BENEFITS

Glucosinolates ✦ Found in kale and cruciferous vegetables, these natural compounds protect plants from pests and disease. When released through chewing or chopping, they have powerful antioxidant and anti-inflammatory actions in the body.

Vitamin C ✦ Found in cranberries, kale, and lemons (particularly the zest!), this antioxidant vitamin supports white blood cells, enhances antioxidant activity, and maintains immune function.

Vitamin A ✦ Abundant in kale as the precursor beta-carotene, this essential nutrient regulates immune cell activity and supports mucosal barriers, which protect against pathogens.

Pear, Fennel, and Grape Salad
FOR DETOX

Gluten-Free ◆ No Sugar Added ◆ Nut-Free

A refreshing antidote to the overindulgence that so often goes hand-in-hand with winter holidays, this light and invigorating winter salad combines the crisp sweetness of Asian pear, the licorice-like freshness of fennel, and the juicy burst of halved grapes. Brightened with Adaptogenic Vinegar (page 192), it's a perfect balance of vibrant flavors and kidney-, liver-, and gut health–supporting goodness. Serve as a palate-cleansing side, rejuvenating starter, or alongside whole grains or legumes for extra protein.

Serves 2 as a side

1 Asian pear or apple, thinly sliced

1 small fennel bulb, thinly sliced

1 cup (150 g) seedless grapes, halved

1 tablespoon chopped fresh dill, plus a few whole sprigs for serving

½ cup (120 ml) Adaptogenic Vinegar (page 192)

¼ cup (60 ml) extra virgin olive oil

1 In a large mixing bowl, combine the pear, fennel, grapes, and chopped dill. In a small bowl, whisk together the Adaptogenic Vinegar and oil and season with salt and pepper. Drizzle the vinaigrette over the salad and toss gently to combine.

2 Divide the salad among individual plates or serve family style. Just before serving, sprinkle with freshly ground black pepper, and garnish with the dill sprigs.

TIP: If you like, you can substitute ½ cup (120 ml) of the Creamy Citrus Vinaigrette (page 258) for the Adaptogenic Vinegar and oil. To amp up this salad with more pectin-rich produce, you can add citrus fruits such as peeled clementine or grapefruit slices.

MAGICAL BENEFITS

Pectin ◆ This soluble fiber found in Asian pears binds to toxins and heavy metals in the digestive tract, aiding in their elimination from the body. Pectin also helps to lower cholesterol levels and improve overall gut health due to its prebiotic, microbiota-nourishing effects.

Potassium ◆ Found in fennel and grapes, this essential mineral supports kidney function and electrolyte balance, which helps prevent the formation of kidney stones.

Resveratrol ◆ Grapes are rich in resveratrol, a powerful antioxidant that reduces oxidative stress and helps the liver produce detoxification enzymes.

Radicchio and Grapefruit Salad
FOR METABOLISM

Gluten-Free

The vibrant contrasting ingredients in this salad will brighten even the grayest winter days—crisp, bitter radicchio, sweet beets, and a juiciness and crunch from the grapefruit and pistachios. All are full of nutrients, working in harmony to support metabolic health, making this salad both delicious and revitalizing. It's perfect as a striking side or a light lunch when paired with a protein-packed grain like amaranth, buckwheat, or quinoa.

Serves 4 as a side

GRAPEFRUIT VINAIGRETTE
Grated zest of ½ grapefruit
½ cup (120 ml) grapefruit juice
¼ cup (60 ml) extra virgin olive oil
2 tablespoons vegan mayonnaise
1 tablespoon agave
1 tablespoon Dijon mustard

RADICCHIO SALAD
4 beets
1 grapefruit, peeled
2 radicchio heads
¼ cup (30 g) chopped pistachios

MAGICAL BENEFITS

Naringin ✦ This flavonoid found in citrus fruits is responsible for grapefruit's bitter taste. It supports fat metabolism, blood sugar regulation, and insulin sensitivity.

Protein ✦ The body burns more calories processing protein, like that found in pistachios, than any other macronutrient, using 20 to 30 percent of its total calories for digestion and absorption.

Pectin ✦ This type of soluble prebiotic fiber, abundant in grapefruit and beets, promotes fullness, regulates appetite hormones and blood sugar, and improves gut health.

1 **To make the grapefruit vinaigrette,** in a small bowl, whisk together the grapefruit zest, grapefruit juice, oil, mayonnaise, agave, and mustard. Season with salt and pepper.

2 **To make the radicchio salad,** bring a medium saucepan of salted water to a boil over high heat. Add the beets, reduce the heat to medium-high, and boil for 20 to 30 minutes, until tender enough to be pierced with a fork. Drain and set aside until cool enough to peel. Peel, then cut into quarters and set aside to cool completely.

3 Separate the grapefruit wedges and, using a paring knife, carefully cut away the thin, translucent membranes covering each wedge.

4 Separate the radicchio leaves and tear them into quarters, then add them to a large bowl along with the beets.

5 Add 2 tablespoons to ¼ cup (30 to 60 ml) of the vinaigrette, depending on how well dressed you like your salad, and toss to coat. Either divide the salad between individual plates or serve family style.

6 Top with the grapefruit slices and drizzle with more vinaigrette as desired. (Leftover vinaigrette can be refrigerated in an airtight container for up to 1 week.) Garnish with the pistachios and an extra sprinkle of salt and freshly ground black pepper and serve.

TIP: If you don't like or are avoiding grapefruit, you can substitute the Creamy Citrus Vinaigrette (page 258) for the grapefruit vinaigrette and replace the grapefruit slices with orange slices.

MAGICAL BENEFITS

Cordycepin ✦ The active compound in cordyceps mushrooms, cordycepin mimics adenosine (our cells' energy currency), helping cells produce energy more efficiently, improving oxygen use, and reducing fatigue.

Withanolides ✦ These naturally occurring compounds found in ashwagandha root have adaptogenic properties that help regulate cortisol levels, reduce stress, and support steady energy levels without overstimulation.

Eleutherosides ✦ These active compounds in eleuthero root enhance the body's stress response, boost energy levels, improve endurance, and support mental clarity without overstimulation.

Adaptogenic Apple Crumble
FOR STRESS RELIEF

Gluten-Free

This dessert is so good for you it can double as a comforting winter breakfast. The crumbly brown sugar, oat, and almond topping complements a spiced marzipan-and-apple filling, infused with stress-relieving magic of cordyceps, ashwagandha, and eleuthero powders. Baked until tender and gooey, this calming dish is ideal for cozy mornings or comforting nights, especially when paired with a dollop of whipped coconut cream or your favorite non-dairy ice cream.

1 Preheat the oven to 350°F (180°C).

2 **To make the crust,** combine the gluten-free flour, almond flour, sugar, cinnamon, and ginger in a bowl. Add the coconut cream and mix until a crumbly dough forms. Press the crust into the bottom of a 9-by-13-inch (23 by 33 cm) baking dish or large oven-safe pan, creating an even layer, and then push the dough up the sides to create a ½-inch (1.25 cm) high crust.

3 **To make the filling,** in a separate pan, heat the coconut oil over high heat. Add the apples and sauté for about 5 minutes, stirring so they don't burn, until slightly softened and browned.

4 Mix the almond flour, brown sugar, cinnamon, ginger, cordyceps mushroom powder, ashwagandha powder, and eleuthero powder together in a bowl, then add to the apples and toss to combine. Spread the apple mixture evenly over the crust.

5 **To make the topping,** in another bowl, combine the brown sugar, oats, almonds, and gluten-free flour. Sprinkle the crumble topping over the apple filling and then drizzle the coconut cream on top. Garnish with a sprinkle of brown sugar, cinnamon, and ginger for an extra-caramelized spice topping.

6 Bake for 30 to 40 minutes, until the topping is golden brown and the apples are completely tender. Let cool slightly, then serve.

TIP: This recipe can be adapted for any season with other fruits. For an autumnal version, try using sliced pears in place of the apples and adding ½ cup (85 g) of chopped dark chocolate to the topping. For a summery spin, try peaches, strawberries, or raspberries instead of the apples and chopped hazelnuts or pistachios in place of the slivered almonds. The sweet and slightly sour flavors of these fruits also pair well with the medicinal powders!

Serves 6 to 8

CRUST

1⅔ cups (200 g) all-purpose gluten-free flour blend (see page 5)

¾ cup plus 1 tablespoon (100 g) almond flour

¼ cup plus 2 tablespoons (75 g) cane sugar

3 tablespoons ground cinnamon

2 tablespoons ground ginger

¾ cup plus 2 tablespoons (200 ml) coconut cream

FILLING

1 tablespoon cold-pressed virgin coconut oil

5 apples (Gala, Honeycrisp, McIntosh, or Pink Lady), sliced

1⅔ cups (200 g) almond flour

¼ cup plus 3 tablespoons (100 g) packed light brown sugar

1 tablespoon ground cinnamon, plus 1 teaspoon for sprinkling

1 tablespoon ground ginger, plus 1 teaspoon for sprinkling

1 teaspoon cordyceps mushroom powder

½ teaspoon ashwagandha powder

½ teaspoon eleuthero powder

TOPPING

¾ cup plus 3 tablespoons (200 g) packed light brown sugar, plus more for sprinkling

1 cup (100 g) oats

½ cup (60 g) slivered almonds

¼ cup plus 3 tablespoons (50 g) all-purpose gluten-free flour blend (see page 5)

Half a 13.5-ounce (400 ml) can coconut cream

Candied Citrus Cream Pie

FOR IMMUNITY

Gluten-Free

This pie is stimulating, not just for our immune systems but our taste buds. It blends the bright, tangy flavors of lemon, orange, and candied kumquats with the nutty warmth of a reishi-and-ginger-infused almond crust and the rich cream filling subtly spiced with black pepper. Altogether, it's a spellbinding dessert, perfect for dinner parties, that helps fend off winter's chill with every immune-supporting slice! To make it even easier, you can prepare the crust and candied kumquats up to 2 days ahead.

Serves 4 to 6

REISHI-GINGER-ALMOND CRUST

1 ⅔ cups (200 g) almond flour

½ cup (60 g) all-purpose gluten-free flour blend (see page 5)

¼ cup plus 1 tablespoon (60 g) cane sugar

1½ teaspoons ground ginger

1 teaspoon reishi mushroom powder, plus more for sprinkling

½ cup (120 g) virgin coconut oil, melted, plus 1 teaspoon for greasing

3 tablespoons aquafaba (see page 5), chilled

CANDIED KUMQUATS

6 kumquats or 1 clementine, sliced

2 tablespoons agave

½ teaspoon ground ginger

CITRUS CREAM

One 13.5-ounce (400 ml) can coconut cream

½ cup (100 g) cane sugar

¼ cup plus 2 tablespoons (90 ml) aquafaba (see page 5), chilled

Grated zest and juice of 2 lemons

Grated zest and juice of 1 orange

3 tablespoons all-purpose gluten-free flour blend (see page 5)

½ teaspoon ground ginger

¼ teaspoon vanilla extract or ⅛ teaspoon vanilla powder

1   Preheat the oven to 350°F (180°C).

2   **To make the reishi-ginger-almond crust,** combine the almond flour, gluten-free flour, sugar, ginger, and reishi mushroom powder in a large bowl. Add the coconut oil and aquafaba and mix until well combined to form a sticky dough.

3   Press the mixture into the bottom and up the sides of a 9-inch (23 cm) pie dish to form a crust and poke a few holes into it with a fork to prevent air bubbles from forming while it bakes. Bake for 20 minutes, or until the crust is golden-brown and firm to the touch, like a crisp cookie, then set aside to cool on a wire rack. The unfilled crust can be wrapped in plastic and stored at room temperature for up to 2 days.

4   **To make the candied kumquats,** add the kumquats, agave, and ginger to a small saucepan along with just enough water to cover. Simmer over low heat for 15 to 20 minutes, until the syrup has thickened and clings to the kumquats. Set aside to cool. The kumquats can be transferred to an airtight container and stored in the refrigerator for up to 2 days.

5   **To make the citrus cream,** whisk together all the ingredients and a pinch of pepper in a bowl until smooth. Pour the cream filling into the cooled crust, then arrange the candied kumquats on top. Chill in the refrigerator for at least 4 hours, until set.

6   Serve chilled, garnished with a dusting of reishi powder, if desired.

TIP: You can transform this into a lemon cream pie by substituting more lemon juice and zest for the orange juice and zest and using candied lemon slices in place of the kumquats. Or you can substitute vitamin C-rich pomegranate juice for the citrus juice and sprinkle the pie with fresh pomegranate seeds right before serving.

MAGICAL BENEFITS

Beta-Glucans ✦ Reishi mushrooms boost the immune system with medicinal compounds like beta-glucans, triterpenes, and antioxidants, which enhance immune cell activity, support antibody responses, and regulate inflammation.

Vitamin C ✦ A powerful antioxidant, vitamin C enhances white blood cell function, supports T cell activity, aids antibody production, and protects immune cells from oxidative stress.

Gingerol ✦ The active compound in ginger, gingerol exhibits anti-inflammatory and antioxidant properties, regulating immune cells and inflammation levels.

Spiced Speculoos Cookies
FOR PAIN RELIEF

Gluten-Free

Inspired by the classic Dutch and Belgian biscuit, these chewy almond cookies have notes of molasses thanks to the brown sugar plus plenty of warming spice from the nutmeg, cloves, cinnamon, and ginger. These spices also imbue the cookies with analgesic magic. For extra soothing effects, enjoy with a cup of calming TranquiliTea (page 262) or Floral Tea (page 196).

1 Whisk together the gluten-free flour, almond flour, arrowroot flour, ginger, cinnamon, nutmeg, cloves, and a pinch of salt in a large bowl until well combined.

2 In another bowl, mix together the brown sugar, cane sugar, oil, and coconut cream.

3 Gradually add the wet ingredients to the dry, stirring continuously until it comes together into a cohesive dough that does not stick to your hands. If the dough is sticky, add a bit more gluten-free flour until it reaches a workable consistency. Wrap the dough in plastic wrap and refrigerate for at least 30 minutes for it to firm up.

4 While the dough chills, preheat the oven to 350°F (180°C) and line 2 cookie sheets with parchment paper.

5 Once chilled, scoop out 2-tablespoon portions of dough and roll them into balls. Place the balls on the prepared cookie sheets, leaving about 2 inches (5 cm) between each. Use the back of a fork or your hands to gently flatten each cookie.

6 Bake for 10 to 15 minutes, until the edges are golden brown. Allow the cookies to cool on the cookie sheets for a few minutes to firm up before transferring them to a wire rack to cool completely. Store in an airtight container at room temperature in a cool, dry place for up to 1 week, in the refrigerator for up to 2 weeks, or in the freezer for up to 6 months.

TIP: The powerful flavors of the spices used in these cookies make them a great vehicle for adding medicinal mushroom powders. Up the digestive benefits by adding 1 teaspoon chaga powder, or the stress-relieving properties by adding 1 teaspoon powdered adaptogenic mushrooms like reishi and cordyceps and plants like ashwagandha root, schisandra berries, holy basil (tulsi) leaves, or rhodiola root.

Makes 24 cookies

2 to 2¼ cups (240 to 270 g) all-purpose gluten-free flour blend (see page 5)

1¼ cups (150 g) almond flour

½ cup (60 g) arrowroot flour

3 tablespoons ground ginger

2 tablespoons ground cinnamon

1 tablespoon plus 1 teaspoon ground nutmeg

1 teaspoon ground cloves

¾ cup plus 3 tablespoons (200 g) packed light brown sugar

1 cup (200 g) cane sugar

½ cup (120 g) cold-pressed virgin coconut oil, melted

¾ cup plus 2 tablespoons (200 ml) coconut cream

MAGICAL BENEFITS

Myristicin ✦ Found in nutmeg, myristicin contributes to its aroma and offers anti-inflammatory and potentially pain-relieving effects by interacting with serotonin receptors and pain-sensing receptors in the central nervous system.

Gingerol ✦ The active compound in ginger, gingerol has anti-inflammatory actions and modulates pain perception through its effects on serotonin and dopamine receptors in the gut.

Eugenol ✦ Found in cloves, eugenol provides anti-inflammatory and pain-relieving benefits by regulating nerve-signaling receptors.

Spiced Pavlovas with Ginger-Coconut Cream
FOR DEFENSE

Gluten-Free ✦ Nut-Free

These plant-based pavlovas are airy and light yet indulgent, and brimming with cold season–combatting magic. They're made with an aquafaba-based meringue, infused with sweet citrus and licorice aromas of cardamom and star anise, and topped with whipped coconut cream scented with ginger. This recipe makes small, single-serving pavlovas, but you can make a single large one if you prefer; just increase the baking time to 3 hours. Cold medicine has its place, but a little sugar always helps the medicine go down!

Serves 4

SPICED PAVLOVAS

1 cup (240 ml) aquafaba (see page 5), chilled

4 cardamom pods, lightly crushed

4 star anise pods, plus more for serving

½ teaspoon cream of tartar

½ teaspoon lemon juice

1 cup (120 g) powdered sugar

1 teaspoon vanilla extract or ½ teaspoon vanilla powder

WHIPPED COCONUT-GINGER CREAM

One 13.5-ounce (400 ml) can coconut cream, chilled

¼ cup (30 g) powdered sugar, plus 2 tablespoons as garnish

1 tablespoon ground ginger

½ teaspoon vanilla extract or ¼ teaspoon vanilla powder

MAGICAL BENEFITS

Lauric Acid ✦ Coconut cream is one of the best sources of lauric acid, which is known for its antimicrobial properties and may contribute to the body's ability to fend off bacterial threats.

Shikimic Acid ✦ Star anise is a natural source of shikimic acid, a compound that is used in antiviral medications like Tamiflu. Shikimic acid interferes with the replication of certain viruses.

Anethole and Terpinene ✦ Anethole, a key compound in star anise, and terpinene, found in cardamom, both exhibit the ability to damage bacterial and fungal cell membranes.

1. Preheat the oven to 200°F (90°C) and line a cookie sheet with parchment paper.

2. **To make the spiced pavlovas,** add the aquafaba, cardamom, and star anise to a small saucepan over low heat. Bring to a simmer, and simmer for 10 minutes to infuse the spices and reduce the aquafaba by a couple of tablespoons. This will concentrate the proteins and starches, to help the meringue hold its form better after whipping. Strain into a large bowl, discard the spices, and set in the refrigerator or freezer until completely cool, 15 to 30 minutes.

3. Whip the aquafaba with a hand-held mixer on high speed for about 10 minutes, or until firm, white peaks form. Add the cream of tartar and lemon juice to help the meringues hold their form. Gradually add the sugar, 1 tablespoon at a time, while continuing to beat until the peaks become stiff and glossy, about 5 minutes. If the sugar is added too quickly, it can cause the meringue to collapse. Beat in the vanilla extract.

4. Spoon or pipe 3-inch (7.5 cm) diameter rounds of meringue, spaced 1 inch (2.5 cm) apart, onto the prepared cookie sheet. Use the back of a spoon to make a small dip in the center of each to hold the cream.

5. Bake for 2 hours, or until set and dry to the touch. Once done, allow the meringues to cool for about 1 hour inside the oven with the door slightly ajar. This allows the meringues to cool slowly and prevents humidity from building up, which can lead to chewiness. They will harden further as they cool.

6. **To make the whipped coconut-ginger cream,** scoop the solid part of the coconut cream into a fine-mesh strainer placed over a bowl, reserving the liquid for soups, smoothies, and other recipes. Make sure to separate as much of the liquid from the solid cream as possible because its high water content can interfere with the air bubbles that help keep the whipped cream fluffy. Put the strained coconut cream in a large bowl and add the powdered sugar, ginger, and vanilla. Whip with a hand-held mixer on high speed for 5 to 10 minutes, until dense but fluffy.

7. Right before serving, dollop or pipe the coconut cream into the center of each pavlova. Garnish with extra star anise pods for a festive effect (but don't eat them—the whole spices are for decoration only!). Sift over the remaining powdered sugar. Serve immediately for the best texture.

TIP: Make sure to keep the oven door closed while baking, as sudden temperature changes from opening the door can cause meringues to crack or collapse.

Rosemary-Clementine Cake
FOR COGNITION

Gluten-Free ✦ Nut-Free

The pine and olive notes of rosemary-infused olive oil meld with the brightness of clementines in this sweet sponge cake. Lightened with whipped aquafaba, it is baked to golden, airy perfection, and brimming with brain-boosting magic. This sticky glazed cake is a delightful tea-time treat or dessert and is even better paired with a Guarana Latte (page 200)!

1 Preheat the oven to 350°F (180°C). Grease a 9-inch (23 cm) cake pan or 9-by-13-inch (23 by 33 cm) baking pan with oil.

2 Fill a small saucepan with 2 to 3 inches (5 to 7.5 cm) of water and bring to a simmer over medium heat. Add the oil and rosemary to a heat-safe bowl and carefully set it over the saucepan. Keep the water at a low simmer and stir occasionally for 30 to 45 minutes to infuse the oil, then strain, let the oil cool, and store in a clean container until ready to use.

3 To a large bowl, add the aquafaba, clementine zest, clementine juice, and infused rosemary oil, then whip with a hand-held mixer on high speed for about 10 minutes, or until stiff, white peaks form. Add the cane sugar and continue whipping until the sugar dissolves and the peaks look glossy, about 5 minutes.

4 In a separate bowl, combine the gluten-free flour, arrowroot flour, baking soda, and a pinch of salt. Fold the dry ingredients into the wet and mix just until smooth.

5 Pour the batter into the prepared pan and bake for about 30 minutes, or until a toothpick inserted into the center comes out clean and the top is golden brown. Let the cake cool completely in the pan while preparing the glaze.

6 To make the orange glaze, in a small bowl, combine the powdered sugar, orange zest, and orange juice. Whisk until smooth and pourable but still thick enough to coat the back of a spoon. Add more orange juice, 1 teaspoon at a time, if the glaze is too thick, or more powdered sugar if too thin.

7 Drizzle or spread the glaze over the cooled cake and garnish with extra orange zest before serving.

TIP: When infusing herbs or plants into oils such as extra virgin olive oil, it is better to use dried herbs, as fresh herbs contain water which blocks the extraction of many medicinal compounds.

Serves 4 to 6

¼ cup (60 ml) extra virgin olive oil, plus more for greasing

2 teaspoons dried rosemary leaves, minced

1 cup (240 ml) aquafaba (see page 5), chilled

Grated zest and juice of 4 clementines or 2 oranges

1 cup (200 g) cane sugar

1¼ cups (150 g) all-purpose gluten-free flour blend (see page 5)

⅓ cup plus 1 tablespoon (50 g) arrowroot flour

½ teaspoon baking soda

ORANGE GLAZE

1 to 1¼ cups (120 to 150 g) powdered sugar

Grated zest and juice of ½ orange, plus more zest for serving

MAGICAL BENEFITS

Rosmarinic Acid ✦ Found in rosemary, rosmarinic acid neutralizes oxidative stress in the brain, supporting the growth, development, and survival of neurons critical for brain function.

Vitamin C ✦ This antioxidant in citrus protects brain cells from oxidative stress and supports neurotransmitter functions.

Monounsaturated Fats ✦ These healthy fats in olive oil support cognition by reducing brain inflammation, promoting healthy blood flow, and providing essential building blocks for cell membranes.

Antiviral Syrup
FOR IMMUNITY

Gluten-Free ✦ Nut-Free

Elderberries, astragalus root, echinacea, and reishi mushrooms combine their powerful antiviral and immune-modulating properties in this tart and herbal syrup. The elderberries add a rich, fruity tang, while astragalus root and echinacea contribute earthy, slightly bitter undertones that balance the syrup's sweetness. Reishi mushrooms deepen the flavor with their subtly chocolatey umami notes. To use, take 1 to 2 tablespoons daily during times of immune imbalance or as a preventative measure. You can consume the syrup straight, mix it into water or tea, or even drizzle it onto vegan yogurt or ice cream!

Makes 1 cup (240 ml)

1 cup (150 g) dried elderberries

3 cups (720 ml) filtered water

1 cup (240 ml) agave

2 tablespoons plus 1½ teaspoons dried astragalus root

2 tablespoons dried echinacea flowers

1 tablespoon dried reishi mushroom slices or 1 teaspoon reishi powder

MAGICAL BENEFITS

Flavonoids, Phenolic Acids, and Anthocyanins ✦ These compounds in elderberries interfere with viral replication and stop viruses from attaching to host cells. They may also boost immune cell production to fight infections.

Polysaccharides and Saponins ✦ Found in astragalus root, these antiviral compounds enhance the activity of immune cells, including macrophages, T cells, and natural killer cells.

Alkamides and Chicoric Acid ✦ These compounds in echinacea flowers stimulate immune cell production and anti-inflammatory markers, interfering with viral replication and stopping viruses from attaching to host cells.

Beta-Glucans and Triterpenes ✦ Reishi mushrooms contain compounds that enhance immune cell activity and may directly inhibit virus replication.

1. Combine the dried elderberries with 2 cups (480 ml) of the filtered water in a saucepan. Bring to a boil over high heat, then reduce the heat to medium and simmer for about 30 minutes, or until reduced by half. Remove from the heat and let cool slightly, then strain through a fine-mesh strainer, pressing on the berries to extract as much liquid as possible. Discard the solids.

2. In another saucepan, combine the remaining filtered water with the agave, astragalus root, echinacea flowers, and reishi mushroom slices. Heat the mixture over low heat for about 20 minutes, stirring occasionally, to extract the medicinal properties from the herbs and mushrooms, then remove from the heat. Strain, discarding the solids, and let cool.

3. Once both the elderberry juice and the medicinal infusion have cooled, combine them in a sterilized glass bottle or jar. Stir well to ensure that the mixture is thoroughly combined.

4. Seal tightly, label and date, and store in the refrigerator for up to 4 weeks. If you plan to keep the syrup longer, freeze it in smaller portions for up to a year for optimal flavor.

TIP: Transform this syrup into a tangy-sweet salad dressing by whisking 2 tablespoons of it with 1 tablespoon extra virgin olive oil, 1 tablespoon apple cider vinegar, and a touch of Dijon mustard.

Hawthorn-Hibiscus Tonic
FOR HEART SUPPORT

Gluten-Free ✦ No Sugar Added ✦ Nut-Free

The scarlet-red hawthorn berries and hibiscus flowers used in this vinegar extraction are particularly charged with heart-loving magic. The apple cider vinegar, infused with the floral aromas of tart hibiscus petals and the subtly sweet crabapple flavor of hawthorn berries, creates a versatile tonic that can be used in place of vinegar in salads, sauces, or sautés or diluted in water or juice. To use, consume the tonic as you would any vinegar, such as in salads, sauces, or soups. You can also dilute 1 to 2 teaspoons in water or juice and drink up to 3 times a day, or as recommended by a health care professional.

Makes 1¾ cups (420 ml)

½ cup (50 g) dried hawthorn berries
½ cup (25 g) dried hibiscus flowers
2 cups (480 ml) apple cider vinegar

1 Place the hawthorn berries and hibiscus flowers into a sterilized glass jar large enough to accommodate all the ingredients. Pour in the apple cider vinegar. Ensure the berries and flowers are fully covered by the vinegar by weighing them down with a fermentation weight. If you don't have one, you can sterilize a rock that fits inside the jar's rim by boiling it for 10 minutes and then use it to keep the plants submerged. This is essential, as any exposed plant matter can mold and spoil the tincture.

2 Seal the jar tightly to prevent evaporation and contamination and place it in a cool, dark place away from direct sunlight. Allow the mixture to infuse for 3 to 6 weeks, shaking the jar gently every few days to help circulate the vinegar around the plant matter and ensure that the plants' medicinal compounds are evenly extracted.

3 After the steeping period, strain the tincture through a fine-mesh strainer or cheesecloth, pressing down on the solids to extract as much liquid as possible, into clean, sterilized glass bottles or jars with airtight lids for storage, then discard the solids. Label the bottles with the contents and date, and store in a cool, dark place for up to 1 year.

TIP: This vinegar extraction can also be prepared as an alcohol or glycerine-based tincture by substituting 2 cups (480 ml) of high-proof (40 to 50 percent) alcohol or culinary-grade vegetable glycerine for the vinegar. The hawthorn berries and hibiscus can also be extracted through infusion and decoction (see pages 13 and 15).

MAGICAL BENEFITS

Quercetin and Rutin ✦ Antioxidant flavonoids like the quercetin and rutin in hawthorn berries increase blood flow, strengthen the heart muscle, and regulate heart rate and blood pressure.

Lycopene and Anthocyanins ✦ Hibiscus flowers contain antioxidants like lycopene and anthocyanins, which help reduce vascular inflammation, lower blood pressure, and decrease cholesterol levels.

Polyphenols ✦ Fermented apple juice (e.g., apple cider vinegar) contains polyphenols that reduce vascular inflammation, promote vasodilation, and improve blood flow, lowering stress on the heart.

Creamy Citrus Vinaigrette
FOR IMMUNITY

Gluten-Free ✦ Nut-Free

This vinaigrette delivers a burst of vitality for fighting off a winter chill, blending the zesty brightness of lemon, clementine, and amla berry powder with the richness of vegan mayonnaise and olive oil. Infused with immune-boosting mushroom powders like reishi and chaga, which add umami depth, it's perfect for salads, roasted vegetables, or drizzled over savory dishes.

Serves 4 to 6

¾ cup (180 ml) extra virgin olive oil

½ cup (120 ml) white balsamic vinegar or apple cider vinegar

Grated zest and juice (about ¼ cup/60 ml) of 2 clementines

Grated zest and juice (about ¼ cup/60 ml) of 2 lemons

¼ cup (60 ml) vegan mayonnaise

1 to 2 tablespoons agave

1 teaspoon Dijon mustard

1 teaspoon amla (Indian gooseberry) powder, optional

½ teaspoon reishi mushroom powder, optional

½ teaspoon chaga mushroom powder, optional

1 Combine the oil, vinegar, clementine zest and juice, lemon zest and juice, mayonnaise, 1 tablespoon of the agave, mustard, and amla, reishi, and chaga powders in a small bowl. Whisk until emulsified. Season with salt and pepper and adjust the sweetness with more agave to taste.

2 Transfer the vinaigrette to a mason jar or airtight container and refrigerate for up to 1 month or freeze for up to 3 months. Shake or stir well to re-emulsify before each use.

TIP: If you like, you can replace the amla powder with 1 teaspoon rose hip or acerola powder, which also contain considerable amounts of vitamin C.

MAGICAL BENEFITS

Vitamin C ✦ Citrus fruits and berries like Indian gooseberries (amla) are rich in vitamin C and antioxidants, which boost white blood cell production, neutralize free radicals, and reduce inflammation to support the body's overall defenses against infections.

Beta-Carotenoids ✦ Citrus fruits contain beta-carotene, a precursor to vitamin A, which supports immune function by protecting cells from free radical damage and enhancing the body's response to infections.

Probiotic White Hot Chocolate
FOR COGNITION AND DIGESTION

Gluten-Free ✦ Nut-Free

The winter months can take a toll on our immune systems and mood, both of which are closely tied to gut health. This velvety smooth drink is made with oat milk infused with gut and brain-nourishing probiotic powder. With its snowy-white hue, delicate sweetness, and subtle hints of spice, each sip offers comforting warmth that nourishes the body and lifts the spirits.

1 Bring the oat milk and sugar (adjusting the amount depending on how sweet you like your hot chocolate) to a simmer in a small saucepan over medium heat, being careful not to let it boil.

2 Once the milk begins to simmer, turn off the heat and add the white chocolate (using the greater amount if you prefer a richer drink) as well as the cinnamon and ginger. Stir continuously for about 5 minutes, or until the chocolate is completely melted and the mixture is smooth and creamy.

3 Remove from the heat and let cool for about 15 minutes, or until warm but not scalding, about 110°F (43°C), then add the probiotic powder and stir until fully dissolved. Pour into mugs and serve, garnished with shaved vegan white chocolate or powdered sugar for a snowy effect!

TIP: You can substitute dark chocolate for the white chocolate if you prefer. And you can give it an extra gut-loving boost by adding chaga powder, which supports gut health by promoting microbiota balance and reducing inflammation in the digestive tract.

Serves 2

2 cups (480 ml) oat milk or other plant milk

2 to 3 teaspoons cane sugar or agave

3 to 4 ounces (85 to 115 g) vegan white chocolate, chopped

Pinch of ground cinnamon

Pinch of ground ginger

1 teaspoon plant-based probiotic powder

Shaved vegan white chocolate or powdered sugar

MAGICAL BENEFITS

Probiotics ✦ These live microorganisms balance gut bacteria to improve digestion and nutrient absorption and ease gut inflammation. They also support brain health by influencing neurotransmitters via the gut-brain connection.

Gingerol ✦ Ginger's bioactive compound reduces inflammation, supports digestion by promoting gut motility, and helps regulate mood and cognition-influencing neurotransmitters.

Cinnamaldehyde ✦ The active compound in cinnamon improves blood flow and has neuroprotective and antioxidant effects. It also promotes gut health by fighting harmful gut bacteria and supporting beneficial microbes.

TranquiliTea
FOR DEEP SLEEP

Gluten-Free ◆ No Sugar Added ◆ Nut-Free

Restorative sleep is the foundation of vitality, yet nighttime anxiety can disrupt sleep cycles, affecting both mental and physical well-being. This calming tea blends the delicate herbal flavors and soothing power of St. John's wort flowers, valerian root, and chamomile flowers to quiet cycling thoughts and trigger relaxation for deep rest. Sip your way to serenity an hour before bed or whenever you need powerful calming magic.

Serves 1

1 cup (240 ml) filtered water
1 teaspoon dried chamomile flowers
1 teaspoon dried St. John's wort flowers
1 teaspoon dried valerian root pieces

MAGICAL BENEFITS

Hypericin and Hyperforin | These active compounds in St. John's Wort boost the neurotransmitters serotonin, dopamine, and GABA to enhance mood, relaxation, and sleep quality.

Valerenic Acid | Found in valerian root, valerenic acid interacts with GABA receptors to promote relaxation, reduce anxiety, and support deep, restorative sleep.

Apigenin | This flavonoid in chamomile flowers modulates GABA activity, promoting calmness, easing cycling thoughts, and enhancing deep, restorative sleep.

1   Heat the filtered water in a small saucepan or kettle until almost boiling, around 190°F to 200°F (88°C to 93°C).

2   Add the chamomile flowers, St. John's wort flowers, and valerian root to a teapot or tea infuser set directly over a mug, then pour the hot water over the plants. Cover the teapot or cup and let the tea steep for 5 to 10 minutes. The longer it steeps, the stronger the flavor and potential effects of the herbs.

3   Strain the tea or remove the tea infuser. Let it cool for about 5 minutes, then enjoy immediately to benefit from its most potent medicinal compounds and flavors, which begin to degrade over time.

TIP: Add a splash of nut-based milk like almond or coconut to increase the absorption of the fat-soluble medicinal compounds in St. John's wort, valerian root, and chamomile.

Glossary of Essential Vitamins and Minerals

VITAMINS

Vitamins are organic compounds that are required in small amounts to maintain various physiological functions in the body. They are essential for processes such as metabolism, immune function, and growth. Vitamins are typically obtained through diet, although some can be synthesized by the body or obtained through supplements. Vitamins are divided into two categories: **water-soluble vitamins**, which are processed via the kidneys (and excess vitamins are excreted through urine), and **fat-soluble vitamins**, which are deposited in the liver, fatty tissue, and muscles. It is possible to get too many fat-soluble vitamins, which are stored in the body more readily compared to water soluble.

WATER-SOLUBLE VITAMINS

Vitamin B1 (Thiamine): Essential for energy metabolism, like all B vitamins. Assists in converting carbohydrates into glucose, which is used as energy by the body's cells. Supports nerve function, muscle contraction, and nervous system function. Important for brain health, cognitive function, and neurotransmitter production. Good plant-based sources include sunflower seeds, peas, lentils, black beans, and soybeans.

Vitamin B2 (Riboflavin): Supports the conversion of carbohydrates, fats, and proteins into energy and helps in the production of coenzymes involved in energy metabolism. Supports normal growth and development. Supports healthy skin, eyes, and nerve function. Acts as an antioxidant, protecting cells from damage. Good plant-based sources include almonds, mushrooms, soybeans, spinach, chia seeds, lentils, and quinoa.

Vitamin B3 (Niacin): Takes part in the conversion of carbohydrates, fats, and proteins into usable energy. Supports DNA repair and skin health, and helps maintain the nervous system. Can help lower cholesterol levels and promote heart health. Good plant-based sources include sunflower seeds, peanuts, brown rice, barley, mushrooms, and lentils.

Vitamin B5 (Pantothenic Acid): Plays a key role in the synthesis of coenzyme A (CoA), which is involved in several metabolic pathways, including the breakdown of carbohydrates, fats, and proteins for energy. Supports hormone synthesis and adrenal function. Important for wound healing and skin health. Good plant-based sources include sunflower seeds, shiitake mushrooms, avocados, brown rice, sweet potatoes, chickpeas, lentils, corn, and parsnips.

Vitamin B6 (Pyridoxine): Necessary for the metabolism of carbohydrates, fats, and proteins. Helps convert amino acids into neurotransmitters. Supports the production of glucose from non-carbohydrate sources. Necessary for amino acid metabolism and neurotransmitter synthesis. Supports immune function and helps to balance hormones and regulate mood. Plays a role in hemoglobin synthesis and red blood cell production. Good plant-based sources include pistachios, sunflower seeds, sesame seeds, chickpeas, quinoa, spinach, sweet potatoes, mushrooms, cabbage, leeks, and onions.

Vitamin B7 (Biotin): Facilitates the breakdown of carbohydrates, fats, and proteins into energy by supporting enzymes involved in metabolism. Supports healthy skin, hair, and nails. Plays a role in gene regulation and cell signaling. Good plant-based sources include sunflower seeds, almonds, peanuts, walnuts, and spinach.

Vitamin B9 (Folate): Plays a role in amino acid metabolism and the synthesis of DNA and RNA and cell division. Contributes to the formation of red blood cells, which carry oxygen to body tissues for energy production. Crucial for preventing neural tube defects and for DNA synthesis/cell division during pregnancy, especially during periods of rapid fetal growth and development. Supports brain health and neurotransmitter function. Good plant-based sources include sunflower seeds, peanuts, spinach, lentils, chickpeas, soy, brussels sprouts, black beans, asparagus, endive, broccoli, avocado, peas, leeks, parsnips, and almonds.

Vitamin B12 (Cobalamin): Participates in the metabolism of fatty acids and amino acids. Aids in the formation of red blood cells, which are essential for oxygen transport and energy production. Necessary for DNA synthesis. Supports neurological functions, helps maintain nerve cells, and is important for energy metabolism. Good plant-based sources include fortified plant milks, fortified cereals, and nutritional yeast.
Note: Vitamin B12 naturally occurs only in animal products and certain algae and must be supplemented or consumed via fortified foods on a plant-based diet.

Vitamin C (Ascorbic Acid): Acts as an antioxidant, protecting cells from damage caused by free radicals. Supports immune function and enhances iron absorption. Necessary for collagen synthesis, promoting healthy skin, cartilage, and blood vessels. Good plant-based sources include bell peppers, guava, kiwi, brussels sprouts, papaya, strawberries, oranges, broccoli, kale, and spinach.

FAT-SOLUBLE VITAMINS

Vitamin A: Acts as an antioxidant, helping to neutralize harmful free radicals in the body that can cause oxidative damage to cells and tissues. Essential for vision, particularly in low-light conditions. Supports the immune system. Maintains the health of the skin and mucous membranes. Plays a role in cell growth and differentiation as well as reproduction and fetal development. Good plant-based sources include sweet potatoes, carrots, spinach, kale, chard, squash, and pumpkin.

Vitamin D2 (Ergocalciferol): Essential for calcium absorption and bone health. Supports immune function and helps regulate cell growth and differentiation. Plays a role in mood regulation and may reduce the risk of certain diseases. Good plant-based sources include mushrooms, fortified plant-based milks, fortified orange juice, fortified cereals, and fortified tofu.
Note: Vitamin D is primarily obtained through sunlight exposure, and very few plant-based foods naturally contain significant amounts of vitamin D. Therefore, fortification and supplementation are common strategies for vegans and individuals with limited sun exposure to ensure adequate vitamin D intake.

Vitamin E (Alpha-Tocopherol): Acts as an antioxidant, protecting cells and tissues from oxidative damage. Supports immune function, anti-inflammatory actions, and skin and eye health. Plays a role in cardiovascular health and may reduce the risk of heart disease. Good plant-based sources include sunflower seeds, almonds, hazelnuts, pine nuts, olive oil, flaxseeds, soy, and coconut.

Vitamin K1 (Phylloquinone): Essential for blood clotting and helping to prevent excessive bleeding. The plant-based form of vitamin K—vitamin K1, phylloquinone—plays a role in the synthesis of proteins involved in blood clotting, cellular growth, and regulating inflammation. In the body, some vitamin K1 can be converted into vitamin K2 (menaquinone), which supports bone and heart health by regulating calcium deposition and mineralization of bones and preventing calcification of soft tissues like arteries. Good plant-based sources include kale, collard greens, spinach, turnip greens, broccoli, brussels sprouts, cabbage, lettuce, and watercress.

MINERALS

Minerals are inorganic substances that are required in small amounts for various physiological functions in the body. They are essential for processes such as bone formation, hormone and enzyme synthesis, fluid balance, and muscle, brain, and nerve function. We cannot create minerals within our bodies, so they must be obtained through diet and/or mineral supplements. Minerals are divided into two categories: **major or macro minerals** (needed in larger amounts) and **trace or micro minerals** (needed in smaller amounts).

MAJOR (MACRO) MINERALS

Calcium: Essential for bone health and strength. Supports muscle function, nerve function and transmission, and hormone secretion. Plays a role in blood clotting and enzyme activation. Good plant-based sources include sesame seeds, chia seeds, tofu, almonds, collard greens, kale, spinach, pumpkin seeds, and endives.

Chloride: Works with sodium and potassium to maintain fluid balance. Helps regulate pH balance in the body. Supports proper digestion and the transport of nutrients. Found in high quantities in salts. Good plant-based sources include seaweed, olives, rye, celery, and lettuce.

Magnesium: Important for muscle function, including relaxation and contraction. Supports energy metabolism and the synthesis of proteins and DNA. Contributes to bone health and regulates blood pressure. Good plant-based sources include cacao powder, pumpkin seeds, buckwheat, cashews, almonds, peanuts, chard, kale, basil, sweet potatoes, squash, corn, coconut, and tomatoes.

Phosphorus: Works with calcium to build and maintain bone health. Supports energy metabolism by aiding in the production of ATP (adenosine triphosphate, which is the primary energy currency of cells, storing and transferring energy for various cellular processes). Necessary for the synthesis of DNA and RNA. Good plant-based sources include pumpkin seeds, almonds, sunflower seeds, soybeans, chickpeas, quinoa, and mushrooms.

Potassium: Regulates fluid balance, blood pressure, and muscle contractions. Supports nerve function and heart health. May help reduce the risk of kidney stones and bone loss. Good plant-based sources include apricots, beet greens, potatoes, white beans, soybeans, sweet potatoes, avocado, kidney beans, lentils, bananas, and tomatoes.

Sodium: Helps maintain fluid balance and regulate blood pressure. Necessary for nerve function and muscle contraction. Plays a role in nutrient absorption and transportation. Found primarily in table salt and also in trace amounts in plant-based sources, including celery, carrots, spinach, and broccoli.

TRACE (MICRO) MINERALS

Copper: Necessary for the formation of red blood cells and connective tissues. Supports energy metabolism and antioxidant defenses. Plays a role in iron metabolism and immune function. Good plant-based sources include sesame seeds, cashews, sunflower seeds, almonds, quinoa, and oats.

Fluoride: Promotes dental health by strengthening tooth enamel and preventing cavities. Supports overall oral health and hygiene. May have a role in bone mineralization and preventing osteoporosis. Fluoride content in plant-based foods is often minimal and varies by soil and water conditions, although some sources include black and green teas, spinach, kale, and asparagus. The best and most common source is fluoridated tap water.

Iodine: Essential for thyroid hormone production and regulation. Supports metabolic rate, growth, and development. Important for brain development during pregnancy and infancy. The best and most common source is iodized salt. Seaweeds are good plant-based sources.

Iron: Essential for the production of hemoglobin and oxygen transport. Supports energy metabolism and immune function. Important for cognitive function and overall growth and development. Good plant-based sources include spirulina, seaweed, pumpkin seeds, hemp seeds, cashews, almonds, lentils, chickpeas, quinoa, soy, and chard.
Note: Spinach is high in iron, but it contains oxalates, which inhibit iron absorption.

Manganese: Necessary for bone formation, collagen synthesis, and wound healing. Supports carbohydrate and lipid metabolism. Acts as an antioxidant and contributes to immune function. Good plant-based sources include pine nuts, hazelnuts, pecans, walnuts, oats, buckwheat flour, sesame seeds, chickpeas, soy, quinoa, almonds, chard, sweet potatoes, corn, and basil.

Selenium: Acts as an antioxidant, protecting cells from oxidative damage. Supports thyroid function and immune response. May reduce the risk of certain cancers and cardiovascular diseases. Good plant-based sources include Brazil nuts (1 to 2 nuts a day is enough; eating too many can risk selenium toxicity), sunflower seeds, chia seeds, flaxseeds, sesame seeds, mushrooms, and almonds.

Zinc: Plays a role in immune function and wound healing. Supports DNA synthesis, cell division, and growth. Contributes to taste perception, insulin regulation, and reproductive health. Good plant-based sources include hemp seeds, pumpkin seeds, cashews, chia seeds, almonds, oats, chickpeas, and walnuts.

Acknowledgments

This book would not have been possible without the guidance, support, and tireless efforts of so many magical individuals.

To the incredible publishing team at The Experiment: Matthew Lore, for believing in the magic of plants and this cookbook—thank you for bringing it to life. Sara Zatopek, my amazing editor, who worked tirelessly to make this cookbook the best it can be—your belief in this book, your guidance, and your vision made it possible! Beth Bugler, for your stunning design work and photography guidance. Jennifer Hergenroeder, for your brilliant marketing and publicity expertise. Ally Mitchell, for your incredible eye for detail and careful copy editing. Zach Pace, for meticulously reviewing every detail during the editing process. Pamela Schechter, for ensuring every logistical detail—from paper selection to printing deadlines—was seamlessly executed.

To Max Sinsheimer, my amazing agent, whose guidance, belief in my work, and dedication made this book possible. Your support has meant everything.

To the farmers who inspire me daily with their commitment to the earth and bringing its bounty to our kitchens, and for providing the ingredients for this cookbook. On Martha's Vineyard, where so many of these recipes were dreamt up: Morning Glory Farm, North Tabor Farm, Beetlebung Farm, MVM Mycology, Ghost Island Farm, Flaghole Farm, Whippoorwill Farm, North Tisbury Farm. As well as the farmers at the markets in Miami, Union Square Greenmarket in New York, the marchés of Paris, and the farms of the Normandy countryside—you've been my endless source of plant-based inspiration.

To the Café Select and Café Angelina in Paris, thank you for fueling my writing marathons with comforting tea and coffee and cheering me on.

To my herbalism teachers at l'École des Plantes de Paris, and all the administration, thank you for opening my eyes to the depths of plant magic.

To Dr. Brissot, Dr. Hamonet, Dr. Amoretti, Dr. Rottembourg, Dr. Le Ray, M. Bézire, Sandrine D'Agostino, Dr. Rossignol and his team at Hôpital Necker, and the Ehlers-Danlos Society, thank you for your unwavering dedication and support. Thanks especially to my doctors and healers for helping me find relief and write this cookbook in the face of health battles. To the inspiring Ehlers-Danlos community—thank you for your support and resilience.

To everyone who has supported me online and made my recipes—you're the reason I do this work. Thank you, endlessly.

To my family, who have tested so many of my recipes and supported me unconditionally—thank you for everything. To my dad, who taught me to write, always making time to help me with my writing in high school, and to my mom for being the best editor and photographer I could dream of. Carina and Daniel, for testing recipes and fueling farmers market splurges—I love you all!

Finally, to Ulysse, my constant companion and greatest source of magic—thank you for being by my side through it all.

Index

NOTE: Page references in *italics* refer to photographs.

A

Adaptogenic Apple Crumble, 244, *244*, 245
Adaptogenic Chocolate Mousse, 64, *65*
Adaptogenic Stuffed Zucchini, *34*, 35
Adaptogenic Vinegar, 192, *193*
alcohol tincture method, 15
almonds
    Almond-Cherry Clafoutis, *124*, 125
    Baked Asparagus with Almonds, *38*, 39
    Marzipan Muffins, 188, *189*
Anti-Allergy Vinegar, 68, *69*
Antioxidant Roots, Rainbow, 86, *87*
Antiviral Syrup, 254, *255*
apples
    Adaptogenic Apple Crumble, 244, *244*, 245
    Citrusy Kale and Apple Salad, 238, *239*
    Eve's Apple Torte, *182*, 183
    Stewed Cabbage with Apple-Mustard Cream, 156, *157*
Artichoke Pasta, Lemon-, 24, *25*
Artichoke-Potato Purée, Mushrooms with, 28, *29*
Artichoke Salad, Asparagus and, 48, *49*
asparagus
    Asparagus and Artichoke Salad, 48, *49*
    Asparagus and Pea Quiche, *30*, 31
    Baked Asparagus with Almonds, *38*, 39
    Cucumber and Asparagus Salad, *42*, 43
    Squash and Asparagus Sauté, 56, *57*

B

Baby Greens and Radish Salad, 110, *111*
Baked Asparagus with Almonds, *38*, 39
Baked Purple Cauliflower and Potatoes with Rosemary Vinaigrette, 214, *215*
Balancing Chia Lemonade, 130, *131*
balsamic vinegar
    Balsamic-Caramelized Endives, *232*, 233
    Balsamic Mushrooms and Radishes, 44, *45*
    Balsamic Parsnips with Citrus Cream, *208*, 209
    Balsamic-Roasted Onions, 172, *173*
basil
    Honeydew-Basil Salad, *100*, 101
    Magic Pesto, *136*, 137
    Pesto Avocado Salad, *96*, 97
    Sweet Potato Kale Salad with Magic Pesto, 160, *161*
Bean Gratin, Caramelized Onion, Potato, and, 206, 207, *207*
Bean Soup, White, *22*, 23
beets
    Beet-Leek Quiche, *154*, 155
    Blueberry-Beet Salad, 102, *103*
    Creamy Mushrooms and Beets, 152, *153*
    Potato-Beet Salad, *116*, 117
    Seaweed and Beet Salad, *178*, 179
    Tomato and Beet Soup, 118, *119*
berries
    Blueberry-Beet Salad, 102, *103*
    Blueberry Pizza, *84*, 85
    as herbal apothecary staple, 6
    Nectarine and Berry Galette, 122, *123*
    Strawberry Cream Cupcakes, 58, *58*, 59
    Strawberry-Lemon Squares, 62, *62*, 63
binding and thickening agents, 3
Blood Orange–Endive Salad, *236*, 237
Blueberry-Beet Salad, 102, *103*
Blueberry Pizza, *84*, 85
bones, 152
Breaded Brussels Sprouts, 180, *181*
Broccolini with Puréed Eggplant, *158*, 159
Brussels Sprouts, Breaded, 180, *181*
Brussels Sprouts, Sadness-Smashing Potatoes and, *220*, 221

Brussels Sprouts, Smoky-Sweet, *166*, 167
Buckwheat and Fungi Risotto, *150*, 151

C

cabbage
    Cabbage and Potato Gratin, 210, *211*
    Crispy Kohlrabi Steaks, 222, *223*
    Kale and Cabbage Coleslaw, *170*, 171
    Stewed Cabbage with Apple-Mustard Cream, 156, *157*
Cakes, Lion's Mane, 82, *83*
calm, 121
Candied Citrus Cream Pie, 246, 247, *247*
canned goods, 5
Caramelized Onion, Potato, and Bean Gratin, 206, 207, *207*
Caramelized Zucchini and Peas with Citrus-Dill Sauce, *26*, 27
Cauliflower, Golden, with Scallion-Ginger Cream, 144, *145*
Cauliflower, Whole Roasted, *216*, 217
Cauliflower and Potatoes with Rosemary Vinaigrette, Baked Purple, 214, *215*
Celery Root Steaks with Red Wine–Prune Sauce, *212*, 213
Cherry Clafoutis, Almond-, *124*, 125
Cherry Soup, Lychee-, *120*, 121
Chia Lemonade, Balancing, 130, *131*
Chilled Melon-Cucumber Soup, 114, *115*
Chocolate, Probiotic White Hot, *260*, 261
Chocolate Cake, *66*, 67
Chocolate Mousse, Adaptogenic, 64, *65*
Cinnamon Rolls, Fire-Cooling, *186*, *186*, 187
circulation, 160
citrus. *See also individual names of citrus fruits*
    Balsamic Parsnips with Citrus Cream, *208*, 209
    Candied Citrus Cream Pie, 246, 247, *247*
    Caramelized Zucchini and Peas with Citrus-Dill Sauce, *26*, 27
    Citrus, Sugar Snap Pea, and Endive Salad, 40, *41*
    Citrus-Scallion Sauce, 76, *77*
    Citrusy Kale and Apple Salad, 238, *239*
    Creamy Citrus Vinaigrette, 258, *259*
classic infusion method, 13
Clementine Cake, Rosemary-, *252*, 253
clinical herbalism, 2
Coconut Cream, Greens with, 148, *149*
Coconut Cream, Spiced Pavlovas with Ginger-, 250, *251*

cognition
    Blueberry-Beet Salad, 102, *103*
    Broccolini with Puréed Eggplant, *158*, 159
    Eve's Apple Torte, *182*, 183
    Lion's Mane Cakes, 82, *83*
    Probiotic White Hot Chocolate, *260*, 261
    Roasted Eggplant, 94, *95*
    Rosemary-Clementine Cake, *252*, 253
cold water infusion, 14
Coleslaw, Kale and Cabbage, *170*, 171
comfort, 210
Comforting Potato and Corn Soup, *146*, 147
corn
    Comforting Potato and Corn Soup, *146*, 147
    Corn Chowder, *88*, 89
    Raw Corn and Squash Salad, *108*, 109
    Shielding Succotash, 98, *99*
Creamy Baked Portobellos, *224*, 225
Creamy Citrus Vinaigrette, 258, *259*
Creamy Mushroom Pasta, 32, *33*
Creamy Mushrooms and Beets, 152, *153*
Crispy Kohlrabi Steaks, 222, *223*
cucumbers
    Chilled Melon-Cucumber Soup, 114, *115*
    Cucumber and Asparagus Salad, 42, *43*
    Cucumber-Fennel Salad, *104*, 105
    Radish, Cucumber, and Hibiscus Salad, *54*, 55

D

decoction method, 15
defense
    Beet-Leek Quiche, *154*, 155
    Ghostly Stuffed Squash, 176, *177*
    Smoky-Sweet Brussels Sprouts, *166*, 167
    Spiced Pavlovas with Ginger-Coconut Cream, 250, *251*
desserts
    Adaptogenic Apple Crumble, 244, *244*, 245
    Adaptogenic Chocolate Mousse, 64, *65*
    Almond-Cherry Clafoutis, *124*, 125
    Balancing Chia Lemonade, 130, *131*
    Candied Citrus Cream Pie, 246, 247, *247*
    Chocolate Cake, *66*, 67
    Eve's Apple Torte, *182*, 183
    Fire-Cooling Cinnamon Rolls, *186*, *186*, 187
    Ginger-Lychee Slushy, 126, *127*
    Ginger-Spiced Hibiscus Pears, *190*, 191
    Lilac Panna Cotta, 60, *61*

desserts (*continued*)
    Lychee-Cherry Soup, *120*, 121
    Marzipan Muffins, 188, *189*
    Nectarine and Berry Galette, 122, *123*
    Rose and Peach Cupcakes, *128*, 129
    Rosemary-Clementine Cake, *252*, 253
    Simple Dressing, *132*, 133
    Spiced Pavlovas with Ginger-Coconut Cream, 250, *251*
    Spiced Speculoos Cookies, *248*, 249
    Spiced Sweet Potato-Hibiscus Pie, 184, *185*, 185
    Strawberry Cream Cupcakes, 58, *58*, 59
    Strawberry-Lemon Squares, 62, *62*, 63
detox
    Crispy Kohlrabi Steaks, 222, *223*
    Kale and Cabbage Coleslaw, *170*, 171
    Lemon-Artichoke Pasta, 24, *25*
    Mushrooms with Artichoke-Potato Purée, 28, *29*
    Mustard-Caper Potatoes and Radishes, *50*, 51
    Pear, Fennel, and Grape Salad, *240*, 241
    Radish, Cucumber, and Hibiscus Salad, *54*, 55
    Squash and Parsnip Soup, 164, *165*
    Stewed Cabbage with Apple-Mustard Cream, 156, *157*
    Whole Roasted Cauliflower, *216*, 217
digestion
    Asparagus and Pea Quiche, *30*, 31
    Baby Greens and Radish Salad, 110, *111*
    Celery Root Steaks with Red Wine–Prune Sauce, *212*, 213
    Comforting Potato and Corn Soup, *146*, 147
    Cucumber-Fennel Salad, *104*, 105
    Ginger-Lychee Slushy, 126, *127*
    Ginger-Spiced Hibiscus Pears, *190*, 191
    Lemony Okra and Squash, 106, *107*
    Probiotic White Hot Chocolate, *260*, 261
    White Bean Soup, *22*, 23
Dill Sauce, Caramelized Zucchini and Peas with Citrus-, *26*, 27
dreams, lucid, 67
dreams, vivid, 196
Dressing, Simple, *132*, 133

E

Eggplant, Puréed, Broccolini with, *158*, 159
Eggplant, Roasted, 94, *95*
Ehlers-Danlos Syndrome, 1
endives
    Balsamic-Caramelized Endives, *232*, 233
    Blood Orange–Endive Salad, *236*, 237
    Citrus, Sugar Snap Pea, and Endive Salad, 40, *41*
    Endive and Leek Quiche, 20, *21*
energy
    Adaptogenic Chocolate Mousse, 64, *65*
    Blood Orange–Endive Salad, *236*, 237
    Field and Forest Soup, *204*, 205
    Guarana Latte, 200, *201*
    Lentil-Chard Plant Parcels, *18*, 19
    Nectarine and Berry Galette, 122, *123*
    Squash and Asparagus Sauté, 56, *57*
ethics, 11
euphoria
    Balsamic Parsnips with Citrus Cream, *208*, 209
    Greens with Coconut Cream, 148, *149*
    Iced Rose Latte, 134, *135*
    Lotus-Elderflower Liqueur, *74*, 75
    Strawberry-Lemon Squares, 62, *62*, 63
    Sunny Summer Pasta, *92*, 93
Eve's Apple Torte, *182*, 183

F

fat-soluble vitamins, glossary to, 265–66
fennel
    Cucumber-Fennel Salad, *104*, 105
    Pear, Fennel, and Grape Salad, *240*, 241
fermented foods, 8
fertility
    Baked Asparagus with Almonds, *38*, 39
    Endive and Leek Quiche, 20, *21*
    Herbal Vinegar, 72, *73*
    Mixed Greens Salad with Candied Pecans, 174, *174*, 175
    Strawberry Cream Cupcakes, 58, *58*, 59
Field and Forest Soup, *204*, 205
Fire-Cooling Cinnamon Rolls, 186, *186*, 187
flavor powerhouse ingredients, 5
flowers. *See also* hibiscus
    Floral Tea, 196, *197*
    Flower Syrup, *70*, 71
    Flower Vinaigrette, *198*, 199
    as herbal apothecary staple, 6
    Iced Rose Latte, 134, *135*
    Lilac Panna Cotta, 60, *61*
    Lotus-Elderflower Liqueur, *74*, 75
    Rose and Peach Cupcakes, *128*, 129
Forest Tincture, *194*, 195
Fruit Sauté, Savory, 90, *91*

G

Ghostly Stuffed Squash, 176, *177*
ginger
    Ginger-Lychee Slushy, 126, *127*
    Ginger-Spiced Hibiscus Pears, *190*, 191
    Golden Cauliflower with Scallion-Ginger Cream, 144, *145*
    Spiced Pavlovas with Ginger-Coconut Cream, 250, *251*
    Turmeric Ginger Ale, 138, *139*
glossary, 264–67
gluten-free foods, about, 3, 5
Golden Cauliflower with Scallion-Ginger Cream, 144, *145*
grains, gluten-free, 3
grains, sprouting, 8
Grapefruit Salad, Radicchio and, 242, *243*
Grape Salad, Pear, Fennel, and, *240*, 241
gratins
    Cabbage and Potato Gratin, 210, *211*
    Caramelized Onion, Potato, and Bean Gratin, 206, 207, *207*
    Leek and Potato Dauphinoise, 218, *219*
greens. *See also* cabbage; endives; *individual kale recipes*
    Baby Greens and Radish Salad, 110, *111*
    Field and Forest Soup, *204*, 205
    Greens with Coconut Cream, 148, *149*
    Lentil-Chard Plant Parcels, *18*, 19
    Mixed Greens Salad with Candied Pecans, 174, *174*, 175
    Radicchio and Grapefruit Salad, 242, *243*
Guarana Latte, 200, *201*

H

Hawthorn-Hibiscus Tonic, *256*, 257
heart support
    Asparagus and Artichoke Salad, 48, *49*
    Baked Purple Cauliflower and Potatoes with Rosemary Vinaigrette, 214, *215*
    Blueberry Pizza, *84*, 85
    Hawthorn-Hibiscus Tonic, *256*, 257
    Potato-Beet Salad, *116*, 117
herbalism
    about, 9
    clinical, learning about, 2
    herbal apothecary staples, 6
    magical benefits of (*see individual health conditions; individual names of recipes*)
    medicinal plants for, 10–11
    potion extraction methods, 13–15
    preparations and extractions, 10–11
    safety and interactions, 9–10
    sustainability and ethics, 11
    treatment and dosage, 11–12
Herbal Vinegar, 72, *73*
herbs in recipes. *See individual names of herbs*
hibiscus
    Ginger-Spiced Hibiscus Pears, *190*, 191
    Hawthorn-Hibiscus Tonic, *256*, 257
    Radish, Cucumber, and Hibiscus Salad, *54*, 55
    Spiced Sweet Potato-Hibiscus Pie, 184, *185*, *185*
Honeydew-Basil Salad, *100*, 101
hormone balance
    Pesto Avocado Salad, *96*, 97
    Zucchini Quiche, *80*, 81
hydration
    Honeydew-Basil Salad, *100*, 101
    Lemony Lettuce Wedges, *46*, 47

I

Iced Rose Latte, 134, *135*
Illumination Squash Soup, 168, *169*
immunity
    Anti-Allergy Vinegar, 68, *69*
    Antiviral Syrup, 254, *255*
    Balsamic-Roasted Onions, 172, *173*
    Candied Citrus Cream Pie, 246, *247*, *247*
    Citrusy Kale and Apple Salad, 238, *239*
    Creamy Citrus Vinaigrette, 258, *259*
    Forest Tincture, *194*, 195
    Maple-Roasted Roots, *162*, 163
    Rainbow Antioxidant Roots, 86, *87*
    Simple Dressing, *132*, 133
    Smoky-Sweet Glazed Mushrooms, 234, *235*
    Spiced Sweet Potato-Hibiscus Pie, 184, *185*, *185*
    Whole Roasted Pumpkin, 142, *142*, 143
inflammation relief
    Chilled Melon-Cucumber Soup, 114, *115*
    Cucumber and Asparagus Salad, 42, *43*
    Fire-Cooling Cinnamon Rolls, 186, *186*, 187
    Golden Cauliflower with Scallion-Ginger Cream, 144, *145*
    Turmeric Ginger Ale, 138, *139*
infusion methods, 13–15
ingredients
    herbal apothecary staples, 6
    pantry staples, 3–5
    shopping for, 3

Index

K

Kale and Apple Salad, Citrusy, 238, *239*
Kale and Cabbage Coleslaw, *170*, 171
Kale Salad with Magic Pesto, Sweet Potato, 160, *161*
Kohlrabi Steaks, Crispy, 222, *223*

L

leeks
    Beet-Leek Quiche, *154*, 155
    Endive and Leek Quiche, 20, *21*
    Leek and Potato Dauphinoise, 218, *219*
    Parsnip, Leek, and Orange Soup, 230, *231*
legumes, 3
lemons
    Balancing Chia Lemonade, 130, *131*
    Lemon-Artichoke Pasta, 24, *25*
    Lemony Lettuce Wedges, *46*, 47
    Lemony Okra and Squash, 106, *107*
    Strawberry-Lemon Squares, 62, *62*, 63
Lentil-Chard Plant Parcels, *18*, 19
Lettuce Wedges, Lemony, *46*, 47
libido, 71
Lilac Panna Cotta, 60, *61*
Lion's Mane Cakes, 82, *83*
Lotus-Elderflower Liqueur, *74*, 75
Lychee-Cherry Soup, *120*, 121

M

magic, as healing metaphor, 1–2
magical benefits of recipes. *See individual health conditions; individual names of recipes*
Magic Pesto, *136*, 137
Maple-Roasted Roots, *162*, 163
Marzipan Muffins, 188, *189*
medical conditions, chronic, 1–2
medicinal plants, about, 10–11. *See also* herbalism
melon
    Chilled Melon-Cucumber Soup, 114, *115*
    Honeydew-Basil Salad, *100*, 101
metabolism
    Balsamic-Caramelized Endives, *232*, 233
    Creamy Mushroom Pasta, 32, *33*
    Radicchio and Grapefruit Salad, *242*, 243
    Slimming Seaweed and Mushroom Soup, 226, *227*
minerals, glossary to, 266–67
minerals, plant-based diet tips for, 7–8
Mixed Greens Salad with Candied Pecans, 174, *174*, 175

mood balance
    Balsamic Mushrooms and Radishes, 44, *45*
    Creamy Baked Portobellos, *224*, 225
    Marzipan Muffins, 188, *189*
    Sadness-Smashing Potatoes and Brussels Sprouts, *220*, 221
mushrooms
    Balsamic Mushrooms and Radishes, 44, *45*
    Buckwheat and Fungi Risotto, *150*, 151
    Creamy Baked Portobellos, *224*, 225
    Creamy Mushroom Pasta, 32, *33*
    Creamy Mushrooms and Beets, 152, *153*
    as herbal apothecary staple, 6
    Lion's Mane Cakes, 82, *83*
    Mushroom Pizza, 36, *37*
    Mushrooms with Artichoke-Potato Purée, 28, *29*
    Slimming Seaweed and Mushroom Soup, 226, *227*
    Smoky-Sweet Glazed Mushrooms, 234, *235*
Mustard-Caper Potatoes and Radishes, *50*, 51
Mustard Cream, Stewed Cabbage with Apple-, 156, *157*

N

The Natural Witch's Cookbook (Wallance), 2
Nectarine and Berry Galette, 122, *123*
No Sugar Added labels, about, 2
Nut-Free labels, about, 2
nutrients, plant-based diet tips for, 7–8
nuts. *See also* almonds
    about, 3
    Persimmon and Spiced Walnut Salad, *228*, 229

O

oil extractions, 14
oils, as food ingredient, 5
Okra and Squash, Lemony, 106, *107*
onions. *See also* scallions; *individual leek recipes*
    Balsamic-Roasted Onions, 172, *173*
    Caramelized Onion, Potato, and Bean Gratin, 206, 207, *207*
oranges
    Blood Orange–Endive Salad, *236*, 237
    Parsnip, Leek, and Orange Soup, 230, *231*
oxygenation, 179

P

pain relief, 249
pantry staples, 3–5
Parcels, Lentil-Chard Plant, *18*, 19
Parsnip, Leek, and Orange Soup, 230, *231*
Parsnip Soup, Squash and, 164, *165*
Parsnips with Citrus Cream, Balsamic, *208*, 209
passion
    Lilac Panna Cotta, 60, *61*
    Mushroom Pizza, 36, *37*
pasta
    Creamy Mushroom Pasta, 32, *33*
    Lemon-Artichoke Pasta, 24, *25*
    Sunny Summer Pasta, *92*, 93
Peach and Flower Salad, *112*, 113
Peach Cupcakes, Rose and, *128*, 129
Pear, Fennel, and Grape Salad, *240*, 241
Pears, Ginger-Spiced Hibiscus, *190*, 191
peas
    Asparagus and Pea Quiche, *30*, 31
    Caramelized Zucchini and Peas with Citrus-Dill Sauce, *26*, 27
    Citrus, Sugar Snap Pea, and Endive Salad, 40, *41*
    Raw Zucchini and Sprouted Pea Salad, 52, *53*
Persimmon and Spiced Walnut Salad, *228*, 229
Pesto, Magic, *136*, 137
Pesto Avocado Salad, *96*, 97
Pizza, Blueberry, *84*, 85
Pizza, Mushroom, 36, *37*
plant-based diet, healing power of, 1–2
plant-based diet, tips for, 7–8
Postural Orthostatic Tachycardia Syndrome (POTS), 1
potassium, 26
potatoes
    Baked Purple Cauliflower and Potatoes with Rosemary Vinaigrette, 214, *215*
    Cabbage and Potato Gratin, 210, *211*
    Caramelized Onion, Potato, and Bean Gratin, 206, 207, *207*
    Comforting Potato and Corn Soup, *146*, 147
    Leek and Potato Dauphinoise, 218, *219*
    Mushrooms with Artichoke-Potato Purée, 28, *29*
    Mustard-Caper Potatoes and Radishes, *50*, 51
    Potato-Beet Salad, *116*, 117
    Sadness-Smashing Potatoes and Brussels Sprouts, *220*, 221
potion extraction methods
    decoction method, 15
    infusion methods, 13–15
    powder extractions, 15
    tinctures, 15
potions
    Adaptogenic Vinegar, 192, *193*
    Anti-Allergy Vinegar, 68, *69*
    Antiviral Syrup, 254, *255*
    Citrus-Scallion Sauce, 76, *77*
    Creamy Citrus Vinaigrette, 258, *259*
    Floral Tea, 196, *197*
    Flower Syrup, *70*, 71
    Flower Vinaigrette, *198*, 199
    Forest Tincture, *194*, 195
    Guarana Latte, 200, *201*
    Hawthorn-Hibiscus Tonic, *256*, 257
    Herbal Vinegar, 72, *73*
    Iced Rose Latte, 134, *135*
    Lotus-Elderflower Liqueur, *74*, 75
    Magic Pesto, *136*, 137
    Probiotic White Hot Chocolate, *260*, 261
    TranquiliTea, 262, *263*
    Turmeric Ginger Ale, 138, *139*
Probiotic White Hot Chocolate, *260*, 261
protection, 98
prunes, in Celery Root Steaks with Red Wine–Prune Sauce, *212*, 213
Pumpkin, Whole Roasted, 142, *142*, 143

Q

Quiche, Beet-Leek, *154*, 155
Quiche, Endive and Leek, 20, *21*
Quiche, Zucchini, *80*, 81

R

Radicchio and Grapefruit Salad, 242, *243*
radishes
    Baby Greens and Radish Salad, 110, *111*
    Balsamic Mushrooms and Radishes, 44, *45*
    Mustard-Caper Potatoes and Radishes, *50*, 51
    Radish, Cucumber, and Hibiscus Salad, *54*, 55
Rainbow Antioxidant Roots, 86, *87*
Raw Corn and Squash Salad, *108*, 109
Raw Zucchini and Sprouted Pea Salad, 52, *53*
recovery
    Almond-Cherry Clafoutis, *124*, 125
    Breaded Brussels Sprouts, 180, *181*
    Magic Pesto, *136*, 137
Red Wine–Prune Sauce, Celery Root Steaks with, *212*, 213

Risotto, Buckwheat and Fungi, *150*, 151
Roasted Eggplant, 94, *95*
roots, as herbal apothecary staple, 6
Roots, Maple-Roasted, *162*, 163
Roots, Rainbow Antioxidant, 86, *87*
Rose and Peach Cupcakes, *128*, 129
Rosemary-Clementine Cake, *252*, 253
Rosemary Vinaigrette, Baked Purple Cauliflower and Potatoes with, 214, *215*

S

Sadness-Smashing Potatoes and Brussels Sprouts, *220*, 221
safety and interactions, 9–10
salads
    Asparagus and Artichoke Salad, 48, *49*
    Baby Greens and Radish Salad, 110, *111*
    Blood Orange–Endive Salad, *236*, 237
    Blueberry-Beet Salad, 102, *103*
    Citrus, Sugar Snap Pea, and Endive Salad, 40, *41*
    Citrusy Kale and Apple Salad, 238, *239*
    Cucumber and Asparagus Salad, 42, *43*
    Cucumber-Fennel Salad, *104*, 105
    Honeydew-Basil Salad, *100*, 101
    Mixed Greens Salad with Candied Pecans, 174, *174*, 175
    Peach and Flower Salad, *112*, 113
    Pear, Fennel, and Grape Salad, *240*, 241
    Persimmon and Spiced Walnut Salad, *228*, 229
    Pesto Avocado Salad, *96*, 97
    Potato-Beet Salad, *116*, 117
    Radicchio and Grapefruit Salad, 242, *243*
    Radish, Cucumber, and Hibiscus Salad, 54, *55*
    Raw Corn and Squash Salad, *108*, 109
    Raw Zucchini and Sprouted Pea Salad, 52, *53*
    Seaweed and Beet Salad, *178*, 179
    Sweet Potato Kale Salad with Magic Pesto, 160, *161*
satiety
    Balancing Chia Lemonade, 130, *131*
    Buckwheat and Fungi Risotto, *150*, 151
    Citrus-Scallion Sauce, 76, *77*
    Corn Chowder, *88*, 89
    Leek and Potato Dauphinoise, 218, *219*
sauces and vinaigrette
    Baked Purple Cauliflower and Potatoes with Rosemary Vinaigrette, 214, *215*
    Caramelized Zucchini and Peas with Citrus-Dill Sauce, 26, *27*
    Celery Root Steaks with Red Wine–Prune Sauce, *212*, 213
    Golden Cauliflower with Scallion-Ginger Cream, 144, *145*
    Greens with Coconut Cream, 148, *149*
    Stewed Cabbage with Apple-Mustard Cream, 156, *157*
Sauté, Squash and Asparagus, 56, *57*
Savory Fruit Sauté, 90, *91*
Scallion-Ginger Cream, Golden Cauliflower with, 144, *145*
Scallion Sauce, Citrus-, 76, 77
Seaweed and Beet Salad, *178*, 179
Seaweed and Mushroom Soup, Slimming, *226*, 227
seeds, about, 3, 6
serenity, 230
Shielding Succotash, 98, *99*
shopping, for ingredients, 3
Simple Dressing, *132*, 133
skin (glowing)
    Citrus, Sugar Snap Pea, and Endive Salad, 40, *41*
    Illumination Squash Soup, 168, *169*
    Persimmon and Spiced Walnut Salad, *228*, 229
    Raw Corn and Squash Salad, *108*, 109
    Rose and Peach Cupcakes, *128*, 129
skin (radiant), Flower Vinaigrette for, *198*, 199
sleep, deep, 262
sleep, restful, 90
Slimming Seaweed and Mushroom Soup, *226*, 227
slow infusion method, 13
Smoky-Sweet Brussels Sprouts, *166*, 167
Smoky-Sweet Glazed Mushrooms, *234*, 235
soups
    Chilled Melon-Cucumber Soup, 114, *115*
    Comforting Potato and Corn Soup, *146*, 147
    Corn Chowder, *88*, 89
    Field and Forest Soup, *204*, 205
    Illumination Squash Soup, 168, *169*
    Lychee-Cherry Soup, *120*, 121
    Parsnip, Leek, and Orange Soup, 230, *231*
    Slimming Seaweed and Mushroom Soup, *226*, 227
    Squash and Parsnip Soup, 164, *165*
    Tomato and Beet Soup, 118, *119*
    White Bean Soup, 22, *23*
Spiced Pavlovas with Ginger-Coconut Cream, 250, *251*
Spiced Speculoos Cookies, *248*, 249
Spiced Sweet Potato-Hibiscus Pie, 184, *185*, 185
spices, whole, 5. *See also individual names of spices*
sprouting, 8
squash. *See also* zucchini

Ghostly Stuffed Squash, 176, *177*
Illumination Squash Soup, 168, *169*
Lemony Okra and Squash, 106, *107*
Raw Corn and Squash Salad, *108*, 109
Squash and Asparagus Sauté, 56, *57*
Squash and Parsnip Soup, 164, *165*
Whole Roasted Pumpkin, 142, *142*, 143
Stewed Cabbage with Apple-Mustard Cream, 156, *157*
Strawberry Cream Cupcakes, 58, *58*, 59
Strawberry-Lemon Squares, 62, *62*, 63
strength
    Caramelized Onion, Potato, and Bean Gratin, 206, 207, *207*
    Raw Zucchini and Sprouted Pea Salad, 52, *53*
    Tomato and Beet Soup, 118, *119*
stress relief
    Adaptogenic Apple Crumble, 244, *244*, 245
    Adaptogenic Stuffed Zucchini, *34*, 35
    Adaptogenic Vinegar, 192, *193*
Sunny Summer Pasta, *92*, 93
sun protection, 113
sustainability, 11
sweeteners, 5
Sweet Potato Kale Salad with Magic Pesto, 160, *161*

T

tinctures, 15
Tomato and Beet Soup, 118, *119*
TranquiliTea, 262, *263*
treatment and dosage, 11–12
Turmeric Ginger Ale, 138, *139*

V

Vinaigrette, Rosemary, Baked Purple Cauliflower and Potatoes with, 214, *215*
vinegars, 5
vision, 27
vitamins, glossary to, 264–66
vitamins, plant-based diet tips for, 7–8

W

Wallance, Lisanna, 2
Walnut Salad, Persimmon and, Spiced, *228*, 229
water-soluble vitamins, glossary to, 264–65
White Bean Soup, *22*, 23
Whole Roasted Cauliflower, *216*, 217

Whole Roasted Pumpkin, 142, *142*, 143
whole spices, 5. *See also individual names of spices*

Z

zucchini
    Adaptogenic Stuffed Zucchini, *34*, 35
    Caramelized Zucchini and Peas with Citrus-Dill Sauce, *26*, 27
    Raw Zucchini and Sprouted Pea Salad, 52, *53*
Zucchini Quiche, *80*, 81

About the Author

LISANNA WALLANCE is a chef, herbalist, and author of *The Natural Witch's Cookbook*, which has been published in four languages. She grew up in New York and attended Barnard College of Columbia University before moving to Paris, where she now lives. She was born with Ehlers-Danlos Syndrome, a connective tissue disorder that causes dysfunction throughout the body. When her symptoms suddenly worsened, she delved into cooking and plant medicine to help manage her symptoms. She has a degree in clinical herbalism from l'École des Plantes de Paris.

culinarywitch.com | culinary.witch

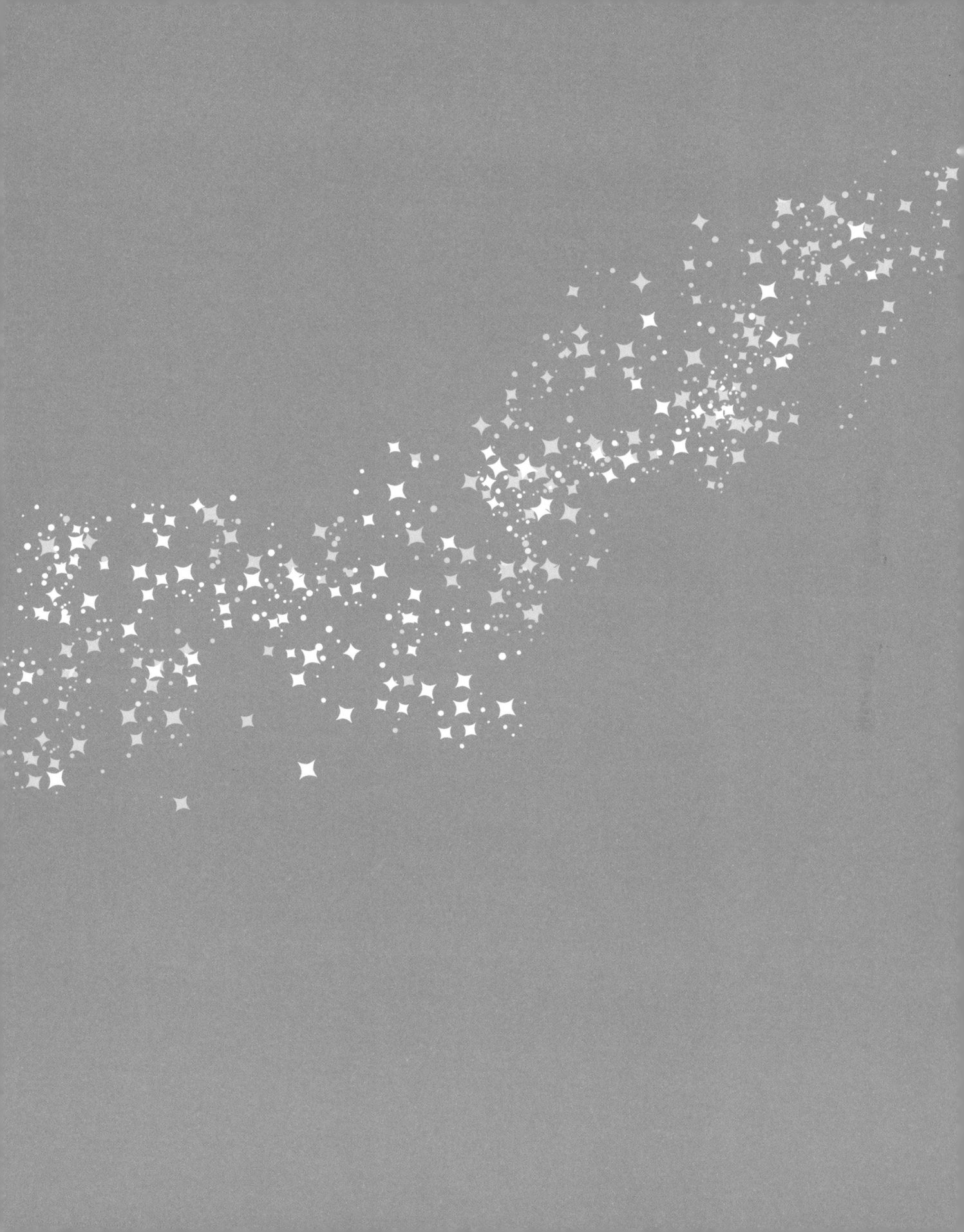